# Dick Sand
# A Captain at Fifteen

## Jules Verne

# PART I

## CHAPTER I.

## THE BRIG-SCHOONER "PILGRIM."

On February 2, 1876, the schooner "Pilgrim" was in latitude 43° 57' south, and in longitude 165° 19' west of the meridian of Greenwich.

This vessel, of four hundred tons, fitted out at San Francisco for whale-fishing in the southern seas, belonged to James W. Weldon, a rich Californian ship-owner, who had for several years intrusted the command of it to Captain Hull.

The "Pilgrim" was one of the smallest, but one of the best of that flotilla, which James W. Weldon sent each season, not only beyond Behring Strait, as far as the northern seas, but also in the quarters of Tasmania or of Cape Horn, as far as the Antarctic Ocean. She sailed in a superior manner. Her very easily managed rigging permitted her to venture, with a few men, in sight of the impenetrable fields of ice of the southern hemisphere. Captain Hull knew how to disentangle himself, as the sailors say, from among those icebergs, which, during the summer, drift by the way of New Zealand or the Cape of Good Hope, under a much lower latitude than that which they reach in the northern seas of the globe. It is true that only icebergs of small dimensions were found there; they were already worn by collisions, eaten away by the warm waters, and the greater number of them were going to melt in the Pacific or the Atlantic.

Under the command of Captain Hull, a good seaman, and also one of the most skilful harpooners of the flotilla, was a crew composed of five sailors and a novice. It was a small number for this whale-fishing, which requires a good many persons. Men are necessary as well for the management of the boats for the attack, as for the cutting up of the captured animals. But, following the example of certain ship-owners, James W. Weldon found it much more economical to embark at San Francisco only the number of sailors necessary for the management of the vessel. New Zealand did not lack harpooners, sailors of all nationalities, deserters or others, who sought to be hired for the season, and who followed skilfully the trade of fishermen. The busy period once over, they were paid, they were put on shore, and they waited till the whalers of the following year should come to claim their services again. There was obtained by this method better work from the disposable sailors, and a much larger profit derived by their co-operation.

They had worked in this way on board the "Pilgrim."

The schooner had just finished her season on the limit of the Antarctic Circle. But she had not her full number of barrels of oil, of coarse whalebones nor of fine. Even at that period, fishing was becoming difficult. The whales, pursued to excess, were becoming rare. The "right" whale, which bears the name of "North Caper," in the Northern Ocean, and that of "Sulphur Bottom," in the South Sea, was likely to disappear. The whalers had been obliged to fall back on the finback or jubarte, a gigantic mammifer, whose attacks are not without danger.

This is what Captain Hull had done during this cruise; but on his next voyage he calculated on reaching a higher latitude, and, if necessary, going in sight of Clarie and Adelie Lands, whose discovery, contested by the American Wilkes, certainly belongs to the illustrious commander of the "Astrolabe" and the Zelee, to the Frenchman, Dumont d'Urville.

In fact, the season had not been favorable for the "Pilgrim." In the beginning of January, that is to say, toward the middle of the Southern summer, and even when the time for the whalers to return had not yet arrived Captain Hull had been obliged to abandon the fishing places. His additional crew—a collection of pretty sad subjects—gave him an excuse, as they say, and he determined to separate from them.

The "Pilgrim" then steered to the northwest, for New Zealand, which she sighted on the 15th of January. She arrived at Waitemata, port of Auckland, situated at the lowest end of the Gulf of Chouraki, on the east coast of the northern island, and landed the fishermen who had been engaged for the season.

The crew was not satisfied. The cargo of the "Pilgrim" was at least two hundred barrels of oil short. There had never been worse fishing. Captain Hull felt the disappointment of a hunter who, for the first time, returns as he went away—or nearly so. His self-love, greatly excited, was at stake, and he did not pardon those scoundrels whose insubordination had compromised the results of his cruise.

It was in vain that he endeavored to recruit a new fishing crew at Auckland. All the disposable seamen were embarked on the other whaling vessels. He was thus obliged to give up the hope of completing the "Pilgrim's" cargo, and Captain Hull was preparing to leave Auckland definitely, when a request for a passage was made which he could not refuse.

Mrs. Weldon, wife of the "Pilgrim's" owner, was then at Auckland with her young son Jack, aged about five years, and one of her relatives, her Cousin Benedict. James W. Weldon, whom his business operations sometimes obliged to visit New Zealand, had brought the three there, and intended to bring them back to San Francisco.

But, just as the whole family was going to depart, little Jack became seriously ill, and his father, imperatively recalled by his business, was obliged to leave Auckland, leaving his wife, his son, and Cousin Benedict there.

Three months had passed away—three long months of separation, which were extremely painful to Mrs. Weldon. Meanwhile her young child was restored to health, and she was at liberty to depart, when she was informed of the arrival of the "Pilgrim."

Now, at that period, in order to return to San Francisco, Mrs. Weldon found herself under the necessity of going to Australia by one of the vessels of the Golden Age Trans-oceanic Company, which ply between Melbourne and the Isthmus of Panama by Papeiti. Then, once arrived at Panama, it would be necessary for her to await the departure of the American steamer, which establishes a regular communication between the Isthmus and California. Thence, delays, trans-shipments, always disagreeable for a woman and a child. It was just at this time that the "Pilgrim" came into port at Auckland. Mrs. Weldon did not hesitate, but asked Captain Hull to take her on board to bring her back to San Francisco—she, her son, Cousin Benedict, and Nan, an old negress who had served her since her infancy. Three thousand marine leagues to travel on a sailing vessel! But Captain Hull's ship was so well managed, and the season still so fine on both sides of the Equator! Captain Hull consented, and immediately put his own cabin at the disposal of his passenger. He wished that, during a voyage which might last forty or fifty days, Mrs. Weldon should be installed as well as possible on board the whaler.

There were then certain advantages for Mrs. Weldon in making the voyage under these conditions. The only disadvantage was that this voyage would be necessarily prolonged in consequence of this circumstance—the "Pilgrim" would go to Valparaiso, in Chili, to effect her unloading. That done, there would be nothing but to ascend the American coast, with land breezes, which make these parts very agreeable.

Besides, Mrs. Weldon was a courageous woman, whom the sea did not frighten. Then thirty years of age, she was of robust health, being accustomed to long voyages, for, having shared with her husband the fatigues of several passages, she did not fear the chances more or less contingent, of shipping on board a ship of moderate tonnage. She knew Captain Hull to be an excellent seaman, in whom James W. Weldon had every confidence. The "Pilgrim" was a strong vessel, capital sailer, well quoted in the flotilla of American whalers. The opportunity presented itself. It was necessary to profit by it. Mrs. Weldon did profit by it.

Cousin Benedict—it need not be said—would accompany her.

This cousin was a worthy man, about fifty years of age. But, notwithstanding his fifty years, it would not have been prudent to let him go out alone. Long, rather than tall, narrow, rather than thin, his figure bony, his skull enormous and very hairy, one recognized in his whole interminable person one of those worthy savants, with gold spectacles, good and inoffensive beings, destined to remain great children all their lives, and to finish very old, like centenaries who would die at nurse.

"Cousin Benedict"—he was called so invariably, even outside of the family, and, in truth, he was indeed one of those good men who seem to be the born cousins of all the world—Cousin Benedict, always impeded by his long arms and his long limbs, would be absolutely incapable of attending to matters alone, even in the most ordinary circumstances of life. He was not troublesome, oh! no, but rather embarrassing for others, and embarrassed for himself. Easily satisfied, besides being very accommodating, forgetting to eat or drink, if some one did not bring him something to eat or drink, insensible to the cold as to the heat, he seemed to belong less to the animal kingdom than to the vegetable kingdom. One must conceive a very useless tree, without fruit and almost without leaves, incapable of giving nourishment or shelter, but with a good heart.

Such was Cousin Benedict. He would very willingly render service to people if, as Mr. Prudhomme would say, he were capable of rendering it.

Finally, his friends loved him for his very feebleness. Mrs. Weldon regarded him as her child—a large elder brother of her little Jack.

It is proper to add here that Cousin Benedict was, meanwhile, neither idle nor unoccupied. On the contrary, he was a worker. His only passion—natural history—absorbed him entirely.

To say "Natural History" is to say a great deal.

We know that the different parts of which this science is composed are zoology, botany, mineralogy, and geology.

Now Cousin Benedict was, in no sense, a botanist, nor a mineralogist, nor a geologist.

Was he, then, a zoologist in the entire acceptation of the word, a kind of Cuvier of the New World, decomposing an animal by analysis, or putting it together again by synthesis, one of those profound connoisseurs, versed in the study of the four types to which modern science refers all animal existence, vertebrates, mollusks, articulates, and radiates? Of these four divisions, had the artless but studious savant observed the different classes, and sought the orders, the families, the tribes, the genera, the species, and the varieties which distinguish them?

No.

Had Cousin Benedict devoted himself to the study of the vertebrates, mammals, birds, reptiles, and fishes?

No.

Was it to the mollusks, from the cephalopodes to the bryozoans, that he had given his preference, and had malacology no more secrets for him?

Not at all.

Then it was on the radiates, echinoderms, acalephes, polypes, entozoons, sponges, and infusoria, that he had for such a long time burned the midnight oil?

It must, indeed, be confessed that it was not on the radiates.

Now, in zoology there only remains to be mentioned the division of the articulates, so it must be that it was on this division that Cousin Benedict's only passion was expended.

Yes, and still it is necessary to select.

This branch of the articulates counts six classes: insects, myriapodes, arachnides, crustaceans, cirrhopodes, and annelides.

Now, Cousin Benedict, scientifically speaking, would not know how to distinguish an earth-worm from a medicinal leech, a sand-fly from a glans-marinus, a common spider from a false scorpion, a shrimp from a frog, a gally-worm from a scolopendra.

But, then, what was Cousin Benedict? Simply an entomologist—nothing more.

To that, doubtless, it may be said that in its etymological acceptation, entomology is that part of the natural sciences which includes all the articulates. That is true, in a general way; but it is the custom to give this word a more restricted sense. It is then only applied, properly speaking, to the study of insects, that is to say: "All the articulate animals of which the body, composed of rings placed end to end, forms three distinct segments, and which possesses three pairs of legs, which have given them the name of hexapodes."

Now, as Cousin Benedict had confined himself to the study of the articulates of this class, he was only an entomologist.

But, let us not be mistaken about it. In this class of the insects are counted not less than ten orders:

1. Orthopterans as grasshoppers, crickets, etc. 2. Neuropters as ant-eaters, dragon-flies or libellula. 3. Hymenopters as bees, wasps, ants. 4. Lepidopters as butterflies, etc. 5. Hemipters as cicada, plant-lice, fleas, etc. 6. Coleopters as cockchafers, fire-flies, etc. 7. Dipters as gnats, musquitoes, flies. 8. Rhipipters as stylops. 9. Parasites as acara, etc. 10. Thysanurans as lepidotus, flying-lice, etc.

Now, in certain of these orders, the coleopters, for example, there are recognized thirty thousand species, and sixty thousand in the dipters; so subjects for study are not wanting, and it will be conceded that there is sufficient in this class alone to occupy a man!

Thus, Cousin Benedict's life was entirely and solely consecrated to entomology.

To this science he gave all his hours—all, without exception, even the hours of sleep, because he invariably dreamt "hexapodes." That he carried pins stuck in his sleeves and in the collar of his coat, in the bottom of his hat, and in the facings of his vest, need not be mentioned.

When Cousin Benedict returned from some scientific promenade his precious head-covering in particular was no more than a box of natural history, being bristling inside and outside with pierced insects.

And now all will be told about this original when it is stated, that it was on account of his passion for entomology that he had accompanied Mr. and Mrs. Weldon to New Zealand. There his collection was enriched by some rare subjects, and it will be readily understood that he was in haste to return to classify them in the cases of his cabinet in San Francisco.

So, as Mrs. Weldon and her child were returning to America by the "Pilgrim," nothing more natural than for Cousin Benedict to accompany them during that passage.

But it was not on him that Mrs. Weldon could rely, if she should ever find herself in any critical situation. Very fortunately, the prospect was only that of a voyage easily made during the fine season, and on board of a ship whose captain merited all her confidence.

During the three days that the "Pilgrim" was in port at Waitemata, Mrs. Weldon made her preparations in great haste, for she did not wish to delay the departure of the schooner. The native servants whom she employed in her dwelling in Auckland were dismissed, and, on the 22d January, she embarked on board the "Pilgrim," bringing only her son Jack, Cousin Benedict, and Nan, her old negress.

Cousin Benedict carried all his curious collection of insects in a special box. In this collection figured, among others, some specimens of those new staphylins, species of carnivorous coleopters, whose eyes are placed above the head, and which, till then, seemed to be peculiar to New Caledonia. A certain venomous spider, the "katipo," of the Maoris, whose bite is often fatal to the natives, had been very highly recommended to him. But a spider does not belong to the order of insects properly so called; it is placed in that of the arachnida, and, consequently, was valueless in Cousin Benedict's eyes. Thus he scorned it, and the most beautiful jewel of his collection was a remarkable staphylin from New Zealand.

It is needless to say that Cousin Benedict, by paying a heavy premium, had insured his cargo, which to him seemed much more precious than all the freight of oil and bones stowed away in the hold of the "Pilgrim."

Just as the "Pilgrim" was getting under sail, when Mrs. Weldon and her companion for the voyage found themselves on the deck of the schooner, Captain Hull approached his passenger:

"It is understood, Mrs. Weldon," he said to her, "that, if you take passage on board the 'Pilgrim,' it is on your own responsibility."

"Why do you make that observation to me, Mr. Hull?" asked Mrs. Weldon.

"Because I have not received an order from your husband in regard to it, and, all things considered, a schooner cannot offer you the guarantees of a good passage, like a packet-boat, specially intended to carry travelers."

"If my husband were here," replied Mrs. Weldon, "do you think, Mr. Hull, that he would hesitate to embark on the 'Pilgrim,' in company with his wife and child?"

"No, Mrs. Weldon, he would not hesitate," said Captain Hull; "no, indeed! no more than I should hesitate myself! The 'Pilgrim' is a good ship after all, even though she has made but a sad cruise, and I am sure of her, as much so as a seaman can be of the ship which he has commanded for several years. The reason I speak, Mrs. Weldon, is to get rid of personal responsibility, and to repeat that you will not find on board the comfort to which you have been accustomed."

"As it is only a question of comfort, Mr. Hull," replied Mrs. Weldon, "that should not stop me. I am not one of those troublesome passengers who complain incessantly of the narrowness of the cabins, and the insufficiency of the table."

Then, after looking for a few moments at her little Jack, whom she held by the hand, Mrs. Weldon said:

"Let us go, Mr. Hull!"

The orders were given to get under way at once, the sails were set, and the "Pilgrim," working to get out to sea in the shortest time possible, steered for the American coast.

But, three days after her departure, the schooner, thwarted by strong breezes from the east, was obliged to tack to larboard to make headway against the wind. So, at the date of February 2d, Captain Hull still found himself in a higher latitude than he would have wished, and in the situation of a sailor who wanted to double Cape Horn rather than reach the New Continent by the shortest course.

## CHAPTER II.
## DICK SAND.

Meanwhile the sea was favorable, and, except the delays, navigation would be accomplished under very supportable conditions.

Mrs. Weldon had been installed on board the "Pilgrim" as comfortably as possible.

Neither poop nor "roufle" was at the end of the deck. There was no stern cabin, then, to receive the passengers. She was obliged to be contented with Captain Hull's cabin, situated aft, which constituted his modest sea lodging. And still it had been necessary for the captain to insist, in order to make her accept it. There, in that narrow lodging, was installed Mrs. Weldon, with her child and old Nan. She took her meals there, in company with the captain and Cousin Benedict, for whom they had fitted up a kind of cabin on board.

As to the commander of the "Pilgrim," he had settled himself in a cabin belonging to the ship's crew—a cabin which would be occupied by the second officer, if there were a second one on board. But the brig-schooner was navigated, we know, under conditions which enabled her to dispense with the services of a second officer.

The men of the "Pilgrim," good and strong seamen, were very much united by common ideas and habits. This fishing season was the fourth which they had passed together. All Americans of the West, they were acquainted for a long period, and belonged to the same coast of the State of California.

These brave men showed themselves very thoughtful towards Mrs. Weldon, the wife of the owner of their ship, for whom they professed boundless devotion. It must be said that, largely interested in the profits of the ship, they had navigated till then with great gain. If, by reason of their small number, they did not spare themselves, it was because every labor increased their earnings in the settling of accounts at the end of each season. This time, it is true, the profit would be almost nothing, and that gave them just cause to curse and swear against those New Zealand scoundrels.

One man on board, alone among all, was not of American origin.

Portuguese by birth, but speaking English fluently, he was called

Negoro, and filled the humble position of cook on the schooner.

The "Pilgrim's" cook having deserted at Auckland, this Negoro, then out of employment, offered himself for the place. He was a taciturn man, not at all communicative, who kept to himself, but did his work satisfactorily. In engaging him, Captain Hull seemed to be rather fortunate, and since embarking, the master cook had merited no reproach.

Meanwhile, Captain Hull regretted not having had the time to inform himself sufficiently about Negoro's antecedents. His face, or rather his look, was only half in his favor, and when it is necessary to bring an unknown into the life on board, so confined, so intimate, his antecedents should be carefully inquired into.

Negoro might be forty years old. Thin, nervous, of medium height, with very brown hair, skin somewhat swarthy, he ought to be strong. Had he received any instruction? Yes; that appeared in certain observations which escaped him sometimes. Besides, he never spoke of his past life, he said not a word about his family. Whence he came, where he had lived, no one could tell. What would his future be? No one knew any more about that. He only announced his intention of going on shore at Valparaiso. He was certainly a singular man. At all events, he did not seem to be a sailor. He seemed to be even more strange to marine things than is usual with a master cook, part of whose existence is passed at sea.

Meanwhile, as to being incommoded by the rolling and pitching of the ship, like men who have never navigated, he was not in the least, and that is something for a cook on board a vessel.

Finally, he was little seen. During the day, he most generally remained confined in his narrow kitchen, before the stove for melting, which occupied the greater part of it. When night came and the fire in the stove was out, Negoro went to the cabin which was assigned to him at the end of the crew's quarters. Then he went to bed at once and went to sleep.

It has been already said that the "Pilgrim's" crew was composed of five sailors and a novice.

This young novice, aged fifteen, was the child of an unknown father and mother. This poor being, abandoned from his birth, had been received and brought up by public charity.

Dick Sand—that was his name—must have been originally from the State of New York, and doubtless from the capital of that State.

If the name of Dick—an abbreviation of Richard—had been given to the little orphan, it was because it was the name of the charitable passer-by who had picked him up two or three hours after his birth. As to the name of Sand, it was attributed to him in remembrance of the place where he had been found; that is to say, on that point of land called Sandy-Hook, which forms the entrance of the port of New York, at the mouth of the Hudson.

Dick Sand, when he should reach his full growth, would not exceed middle height, but he was well built. One could not doubt that he was of Anglo-Saxon origin. He was brown, however, with blue eyes, in which the crystalline sparkled with ardent fire. His seaman's craft had already prepared him well for the conflicts of life. His intelligent physiognomy breathed forth energy. It was not that of an audacious person, it was that of a darer. These three words from an unfinished verse of Virgil are often cited:

"Audaces fortuna juvat"....

but they are quoted incorrectly. The poet said:

"Audentes fortuna juvat"....

It is on the darers, not on the audacious, that Fortune almost always smiled. The audacious may be unguarded. The darer thinks first, acts afterwards. There is the difference!

Dick Sand was audens.

At fifteen he already knew how to take a part, and to carry out to the end whatever his resolute spirit had decided upon. His manner, at once spirited and serious, attracted attention. He did not squander himself in words and gestures, as boys of his age generally do. Early, at a period of life when they seldom discuss the problems of existence, he had looked his miserable condition in the face, and he had promised "to make" himself.

And he had made himself—being already almost a man at an age when others are still only children.

At the same time, very nimble, very skilful in all physical exercises, Dick Sand was one of those privileged beings, of whom it may be said that they were born with two left feet and two right hands. In that way, they do everything with the right hand, and always set out with the left foot.

Public charity, it has been said, had brought up the little orphan. He had been put first in one of those houses for children, where there is always, in America, a place for the little waifs. Then at four, Dick learned to read, write and count in one of those State of New York schools, which charitable subscriptions maintain so generously.

At eight, the taste for the sea, which Dick had from birth, caused him to embark as cabin-boy on a packet ship of the South Sea. There he learned the seaman's trade, and as one ought to learn it, from the earliest age. Little by little he instructed himself under the direction of officers who were interested in this little old man. So the cabin-boy soon became the novice, expecting something better, of course. The child who understands, from the beginning, that work is the law of life, the one who knows, from an early age, that he will gain his bread only by the sweat of his brow—a Bible precept which is the rule of humanity—that one is probably intended for great things; for some day he will have, with the will, the strength to accomplish them.

It was, when he was a cabin-boy on board a merchant vessel, that Dick Sand was remarked by Captain Hull. This honest seaman immediately formed a friendship with this honest young boy, and later he made him known to the ship-owner, James W. Weldon. The latter felt a lively interest in this orphan, whose education he completed at San Francisco, and he had him brought up in the Catholic religion, to which his family adhered.

During the course of his studies, Dick Sand showed a particular liking for geography, for voyages, while waiting till he was old enough to learn that branch of mathematics which relates to navigation. Then to this theoretical portion of his instruction, he did not neglect to join the practical. It was as novice that he was able to embark for the first time on the "Pilgrim." A good seaman ought to understand fishing as well as navigation. It is a good preparation for all the contingencies which the maritime career admits of. Besides, Dick Sand set out on a vessel of James W. Weldon's, his benefactor, commanded by his protector, Captain Hull. Thus he found himself in the most favorable circumstances.

To speak of the extent of his devotion to the Weldon family, to whom he owed everything, would be superfluous. Better let the facts speak for themselves. But it will be understood how happy the young novice was when he learned that Mrs. Weldon was going to take passage on board the "Pilgrim." Mrs. Weldon for several years had been a mother to him, and in Jack he saw a little brother, all the time keeping in remembrance his position in respect to the son of the rich ship-owner. But—his protectors knew it well—this good seed which they had sown had fallen on good soil. The orphan's heart was filled with gratitude, and some day, if it should be necessary to give his life for those who had taught him to instruct himself and to love God, the young novice would not hesitate to give it. Finally, to be only fifteen, but to act and think as if he were thirty, that was Dick Sand.

Mrs. Weldon knew what her protégé was worth. She could trust little Jack with him without any anxiety. Dick Sand cherished this child, who, feeling himself loved by this "large brother," sought his company. During those long leisure hours, which are frequent in a voyage, when the sea is smooth, when the well set up sails require no management, Dick and Jack were almost always together. The young novice showed the little boy everything in his craft which seemed amusing.

Without fear Mrs. Weldon saw Jack, in company with Dick Sand, spring out on the shrouds, climb to the top of the mizzen-mast, or to the booms of the mizzen-topmast, and come down again like an arrow the whole length of the backstays. Dick Sand went before or followed him, always ready to hold him up or keep him back, if his six-year-old arms grew feeble during those exercises. All that benefited little Jack, whom sickness had made somewhat pale; but his color soon came back on board the "Pilgrim," thanks to this gymnastic, and to the bracing sea-breezes.

So passed the time. Under these conditions the passage was being accomplished, and only the weather was not very favorable, neither the passengers nor the crew of the "Pilgrim" would have had cause to complain.

Meanwhile this continuance of east winds made Captain Hull anxious. He did not succeed in getting the vessel into the right course. Later, near the Tropic of Capricorn, he feared finding calms which would delay him again, without speaking of the equatorial current, which would irresistibly throw him back to the west. He was troubled then, above all, for Mrs. Weldon, by the delays for which, meanwhile, he was not responsible. So, if he should meet, on his course, some transatlantic steamer on the way toward America, he already thought of advising his passenger to embark on it. Unfortunately, he was detained in latitudes too high to cross a steamer running to Panama; and, besides, at that period communication across the Pacific, between Australia and the New World, was not as frequent as it has since become.

It then was necessary to leave everything to the grace of God, and it seemed as if nothing would trouble this monotonous passage, when the first incident occurred precisely on that day, February 2d, in the latitude and longitude indicated at the beginning of this history.

Dick Sand and Jack, toward nine o'clock in the morning, in very clear weather, were installed on the booms of the mizzen-topmast. Thence they looked down on the whole ship and a portion of the ocean in a largo circumference. Behind, the perimeter of the horizon was broken to their eyes, only by the mainmast, carrying brigantine and fore-staff. That beacon hid from them a part of the sea and the sky. In the front, they saw the bowsprit stretching over the waves, with its three jibs, which were hauled tightly, spread out like three great unequal wings. Underneath rounded the foremast, and above, the little top-sail and the little gallant-sail, whose bolt-rope quivered with the pranks of the breeze. The schooner was then running on the larboard tack, and hugging the wind as much as possible.

Dick Sand explained to Jack how the "Pilgrim," ballasted properly, well balanced in all her parts, could not capsize, even if she gave a pretty strong heel to starboard, when the little boy interrupted him.

"What do I see there?" said he.

"You see something, Jack?" demanded Dick Sand, who stood up straight on the booms.

"Yes—there!" replied little Jack, showing a point of the sea, left open by the interval between the stays of the standing-jib and the flying-jib.

Dick Sand looked at the point indicated attentively, and forthwith, with a loud voice, he cried;

"A wreck to windward, over against starboard!"

## CHAPTER III.
### THE WRECK.

Dick Sand's cry brought all the crew to their feet. The men who were not on watch came on deck. Captain Hull, leaving his cabin, went toward the bow.

Mrs. Weldon, Nan, even the indifferent Cousin Benedict himself, came to lean over the starboard rail, so as to see the wreck signaled by the young novice.

Negoro, alone, did not leave the cabin, which served him for a kitchen; and as usual, of all the crew, he was the only one whom the encounter with a wreck did not appear to interest.

Then all regarded attentively the floating object which the waves were rocking, three miles from the "Pilgrim."

"Ah! what can that be?" said a sailor.

"Some abandoned raft," replied another.

"Perhaps there are some unhappy shipwrecked ones on that raft," said Mrs. Weldon.

"We shall find out," replied Captain Hull. "But that wreck is not a raft. It is a hull thrown over on the side."

"Ah! is it not more likely to be some marine animal—some mammifer of great size?" observed Cousin Benedict.

"I do not think so," replied the novice.

"Then what is your idea, Dick?" asked Mrs. Weldon.

"An overturned hull, as the captain has said, Mrs. Weldon. It even seems to me that I see its copper keel glistening in the sun."

"Yes—indeed," replied Captain Hull. Then addressing the helmsman: "Steer to the windward, Bolton. Let her go a quarter, so as to come alongside the wreck."

"Yes, sir," replied the helmsman.

"But," continued Cousin Benedict, "I keep to what I have said.

Positively it is an animal."

"Then this would be a whale in copper," replied Captain Hull, "for, positively, also, I see it shine in the sun!"

"At all events, Cousin Benedict," added Mrs. Weldon, "you will agree with us that this whale must be dead, for it is certain that it does not make the least movement."

"Ah! Cousin Weldon," replied Cousin Benedict, who was obstinate, "this would not be the first time that one has met a whale sleeping on the surface of the waves."

"That is a fact," replied Captain Hull; "but to-day, the thing is not a whale, but a ship."

"We shall soon see," replied Cousin Benedict, who, after all, would give all the mammifers of the Arctic or Antarctic seas for an insect of a rare species.

"Steer, Bolton, steer!" cried Captain Hull again, "and do not board the wreck. Keep a cable's length. If we cannot do much harm to this hull, it might cause us some damage, and I do not care to hurt the sides of the 'Pilgrim' with it. Tack a little, Bolton, tack!"

The "Pilgrim's" prow, which had been directed toward the wreck, was turned aside by a slight movement of the helm.

The schooner was still a mile from the capsized hull. The sailors were eagerly looking at it. Perhaps it held a valuable cargo, which it would be possible to transfer to the "Pilgrim." We know that, in these salvages, the third of the value belongs to the rescuers, and, in this case, if the cargo was not damaged, the crew, as they say, would make "a good haul." This would be a fish of consolation for their incomplete fishing.

A quarter of an hour later the wreck was less than a mile from the "Pilgrim."

It was indeed a ship, which presented itself on its side, to the starboard. Capsized as far as the nettings, she heeled so much that it would be almost impossible to stand upon her deck. Nothing could be seen beyond her masts. From the port-shrouds were hanging only some ends of broken rope, and the chains broken by the cloaks of white-crested waves. On the starboard side opened a large hole between the timbers of the frame-work and the damaged planks.

"This ship has been run into," cried Dick Sand.

"There is no doubt of that," replied Captain Hull; "and it is a miracle that she did not sink immediately."

"If there has been a collision," observed Mrs. Weldon, "we must hope that the crew of this ship has been picked up by those who struck her."

"It is to be hoped so, Mrs. Weldon," replied Captain, Hull, "unless this crew sought refuge in their own boats after the collision, in case the colliding vessel should sail right on—which, alas! sometimes happens."

"Is it possible? That would be a proof of very great inhumanity, Mr. Hull."

"Yes, Mrs. Weldon. Yes! and instances are not wanting. As to the crew of this ship, what makes me believe that it is more likely they have left it, is that I do not see a single boat; and, unless the men on board have been picked up, I should be more inclined to think that they have tried to roach the land. But, at this distance from the American continent, or from the islands of Oceanica, it is to be feared that they have not succeeded."

"Perhaps," said Mrs. Weldon, "we shall never know the secret of this catastrophe. Meanwhile, it might be possible that some man of the crew is still on board."

"That is not probable, Mrs. Weldon," replied Captain Hull. "Our approach would be already known, and they would make some signals to us. But we shall make sure of it.—Luff a little, Bolton, luff," cried Captain Hull, while indicating with his hand what course to take.

The "Pilgrim" was now only three cables' length from the wreck, and they could no longer doubt that this hull had been completely abandoned by all its crew.

But, at that moment, Dick Sand made a gesture which imperiously demanded silence.

"Listen, listen!" said he.

Each listened.

"I hear something like a bark!" cried Dick Sand. In fact, a distant barking resounded from the interior of the hull. Certainly there was a living dog there, imprisoned perhaps, for it was possible that the hatches were hermetically closed. But they could not see it, the deck of the capsized vessel being still invisible.

"If there be only a dog there, Mr. Hull," said Mrs. "Weldon," we shall save it."

"Yes, yes!" cried little Jack, "we shall save it. I shall give it something to eat! It will love us well! Mama, I am going to bring it a piece of sugar!"

"Stay still, my child," replied Mrs. Weldon smiling. "I believe that the poor animal is dying of hunger, and it will prefer a good mess to your morsel of sugar."

"Well, then, let it have my soup," cried little Jack. "I can do without it very well."

At that moment the barking was more distinctly heard. Three hundred feet, at the most, separated the two ships. Almost immediately a dog of great height appeared on the starboard netting, and clung there, barking more despairingly than ever.

"Howik," said Captain Hull, turning toward the master of the

"Pilgrim's" crew, "heave to, and lower the small boat."

"Hold on, my dog, hold on!" cried little Jack to the animal, which seemed to answer him with a half-stifled bark.

The "Pilgrim's" sails were rapidly furled, so that the ship should remain almost motionless, less than half a cable's length from the wreck.

The boat was brought alongside. Captain Hull, Dick Sand and two sailors got into it at once.

The dog barked all the time. It tried to hold on to the netting, but every moment it fell back on the deck. One would say that its barks were no longer addressed to those who were coming to him. Were they then addressed to some sailors or passengers imprisoned in this ship?

"Is there, then, on board some shipwrecked one who has survived?" Mrs. Weldon asked herself.

A few strokes of the oars and the "Pilgrim's" boat would reach the capsized hull.

But, suddenly, the dog's manner changed. Furious barks succeeded its first barks inviting the rescuers to come. The most violent anger excited the singular animal.

"What can be the matter with that dog?" said Captain Hull, while the boat was turning the stern of the vessel, so as to come alongside of the part of the deck lying under the water.

What Captain Hull could not then observe, what could not be noticed even on board the "Pilgrim," was that the dog's fury manifested itself just at the moment when Negoro, leaving his kitchen, had just come toward the forecastle.

Did the dog then know and recognize the master cook? It was very improbable.

However that may be, after looking at the dog, without showing any surprise, Negoro, who, however, frowned for an instant, returned to the crew's quarters.

Meanwhile the boat had rounded the stern of the ship. Her aftboard carried this single name: "Waldeck."

"Waldeck," and no designation of the port attached. But, by the form of the hull, by certain details which a sailor seizes at the first glance, Captain Hull had, indeed, discovered that this ship was of American construction. Besides, her name confirmed it. And now, this hull, it was all that remained of a large brig of five hundred tons.

At the "Waldeck's" prow a large opening indicated the place where the collision had occurred. In consequence of the capsizing of the hull, this opening was then five or six feet above the water—which explained why the brig had not yet foundered.

On the deck, which Captain Hull saw in its whole extent, there was nobody.

The dog, having left the netting, had just let itself slip as far as the central hatch, which was open; and it barked partly toward the interior, partly toward the exterior.

"It is very certain that this animal is not alone on board!" observed

Dick Sand.

"No, in truth!" replied Captain Hull.

The boat then skirted the larboard netting, which was half under water.

A somewhat strong swell of the sea would certainly submerge the "Waldeck" in a few moments.

The brig's deck had been swept from one end to the other. There was nothing left except the stumps of the mainmast and of the mizzen-mast, both broken off two feet above the scuttles, and which had fallen in the collision, carrying away shrouds, back-stays, and rigging. Meanwhile, as far as the eye could see, no wreck was visible around the "Waldeck"—which seemed to indicate that the catastrophe was already several days old.

"If some unhappy creatures have survived the collision," said Captain Hull, "it is probable that either hunger or thirst has finished them, for the water must have gained the store-room. There are only dead bodies on board!"

"No," cried Dick Sand, "no! The dog would not bark that way. There are living beings on board!"

At that moment the animal, responding to the call of the novice, slid to the sea, and swam painfully toward the boat, for it seemed to be exhausted.

They took it in, and it rushed eagerly, not for a piece of bread that Dick Sand offered it first, but to a half-tub which contained a little fresh water.

"This poor animal is dying of thirst!" cried Dick Sand.

The boat then sought a favorable place to board the "Waldeck" more easily, and for that purpose it drew away a few strokes. The dog evidently thought that its rescuers did not wish to go on board, for he seized Dick Sand by his jacket, and his lamentable barks commenced again with new strength.

They understood it. Its pantomime and its language were as clear as a man's language could be. The boat was brought immediately as far as the larboard cat-head. There the two sailors moored it firmly, while Captain Hull and Dick Sand, setting foot on the deck at the same time as the dog, raised themselves, not without difficulty, to the hatch which opened between the stumps of the two masts.

By this hatch the two made their way into the hold.

The "Waldeck's" hold, half full of water, contained no goods. The brig sailed with ballast—a ballast of sand which had slid to larboard and which helped to keep the ship on her side. On that head, then, there was no salvage to effect.

"Nobody here," said Captain Hull.

"Nobody," replied the novice, after having gone to the foremost part of the hold.

But the dog, which was on the deck, kept on barking and seemed to call the captain's attention more imperatively.

"Let us go up again," said Captain Hull to the novice.

Both appeared again on the deck.

The dog, running to them, sought to draw them to the poop.

They followed it.

There, in the square, five bodies—undoubtedly five corpses—were lying on the floor.

By the daylight which entered in waves by the opening, Captain Hull discovered the bodies of five negroes.

Dick Sand, going from one to the other, thought he felt that the unfortunates were still breathing.

"On board! on board!" cried Captain Hull.

The two sailors who took care of the boat were called, and helped to carry the shipwrecked men out of the poop.

This was not without difficulty, but two minutes after, the five blacks were laid in the boat, without being at all conscious that any one was trying to save them. A few drops of cordial, then a little fresh water prudently administered, might, perhaps, recall them to life.

The "Pilgrim" remained a half cable's length from the wreck, and the boat would soon reach her.

A girt-line was let down from the main-yard, and each of the blacks drawn up separately reposed at last on the "Pilgrim's" deck.

The dog had accompanied them.

"The unhappy creatures!" cried Mrs. Weldon, on perceiving those poor men, who were only inert bodies.

"They are alive, Mrs. Weldon. We shall save them. Yes, we shall save them," cried Dick Sand.

"What has happened to them?" demanded Cousin Benedict.

"Wait till they can speak," replied Captain Hull, "and they will tell us their history. But first of all, let us make them drink a little water, in which we shall mix a few drops of rum." Then, turning round: "Negoro!" he called.

At that name the dog stood up as if it knew the sound, its hair bristling, its mouth open.

Meanwhile, the cook did not appear.

"Negoro!" repeated Captain Hull.

The dog again gave signs of extreme fury.

Negoro left the kitchen.

Hardly had he shown himself on the deck, than the dog sprang on him and wanted to jump at his throat.

With a blow from the poker with which he was armed, the cook drove away the animal, which some of the sailors succeeded in holding.

"Do you know this dog?" Captain Hull asked the master cook.

"I?" replied Negoro. "I have never seen it."

"That is singular," murmured Dick Sand.

## CHAPTER IV.
## THE SURVIVORS OF THE "WALDECK."

The slave trade was still carried on, on a large scale, in all equinoctial Africa. Notwithstanding the English and French cruisers, ships loaded with slaves leave the coasts of Angola and Mozambique every year to transport negroes to various parts of the world, and, it must be said, of the civilized world.

Captain Hull was not ignorant of it. Though these parts were not ordinarily frequented by slave-ships, he asked himself if these blacks, whose salvage he had just effected, were not the survivors of a cargo of slaves that the "Waldeck" was going to sell to some Pacific colony. At all events, if that was so, the blacks became free again by the sole act of setting foot on his deck, and he longed to tell it to them.

Meanwhile the most earnest care had been lavished on the shipwrecked men from the "Waldeck." Mrs. Weldon, aided by Nan and Dick Sand, had administered to them a little of that good fresh water of which they must have been deprived for several days, and that, with some nourishment, sufficed to restore them to life.

The eldest of these blacks—he might be about sixty years old—was soon able to speak, and he could answer in English the questions which were addressed to him.

"The ship which carried you was run into?" asked Captain Hull, first of all.

"Yes," replied the old black. "Ten days ago our ship was struck, during a very dark night. We were asleep——"

"But the men of the 'Waldeck'—what has become of them?"

"They were no longer there, sir, when my companions and I reached the deck."

"Then, was the crew able to jump on board the ship which struck the 'Waldeck'?" demanded Captain Hull.

"Perhaps, and we must indeed hope so for their sakes."

"And that ship, after the collision, did it not return to pick you up?"

"No."

"Did she then go down herself?"

"She did not founder," replied the old black, shaking his head, "for we could see her running away in the night."

This fact, which was attested by all the survivors of the "Waldeck," may appear incredible. It is only too true, however, that captains, after some terrible collision, due to their imprudence, have often taken flight without troubling themselves about the unfortunate ones whom they had put in danger, and without endeavoring to carry assistance to them.

That drivers do as much and leave to others, on the public way, the trouble of repairing the misfortune which they have caused, that is indeed to be condemned. Still, their victims are assured of finding immediate help. But, that men to men, abandon each other thus at sea, it is not to be believed, it is a shame!

Meanwhile, Captain Hull knew several examples of such inhumanity, and he was obliged to tell Mrs. Weldon that such facts, monstrous as they might be, were unhappily not rare.

Then, continuing:

"Whence came the 'Waldeck?'" he asked.

"From Melbourne."

"Then you are not slaves?"

"No, sir!" the old black answered quickly, as he stood up straight. "We are subjects of the State of Pennsylvania, and citizens of free America!"

"My friends," replied Captain Hull, "believe me that you have not compromised your liberty in coming on board of the American brig, the 'Pilgrim.'"

In fact, the five blacks which the "Waldeck" carried belonged to the State of Pennsylvania. The oldest, sold in Africa as a slave at the age of six years, then brought to the United States, had been freed already many years ago by the Emancipation Proclamation. As to his companions, much younger than he, sons of slaves liberated before their birth, they were born free; no white had ever had the right of property over them. They did not even speak that "negro" language, which does not use the article, and only knows the infinitive of the verbs—a language which has disappeared little by little, indeed, since the anti-slavery war. These blacks had, then, freely left the United States, and they were returning to it freely.

As they told Captain Hull, they were engaged as laborers at an

Englishman's who owned a vast mine near Melbourne, in Southern

Australia. There they had passed three years, with great profit to

themselves; their engagement ended, they had wished to return to

America.

They then had embarked on the "Waldeck," paying their passage like ordinary passengers. On the 5th of December they left Melbourne, and seventeen days after, during a very black night, the "Waldeck" had been struck by a large steamer.

The blacks were in bed. A few seconds after the collision, which was terrible, they rushed on the deck.

Already the ship's masts had fallen, and the "Waldeck" was lying on the side; but she would not sink, the water not having invaded the hold sufficiently to cause it.

As to the captain and crew of the "Waldeck," all had disappeared, whether some had been precipitated into the sea, whether others were caught on the rigging of the colliding ship, which, after the collision, had fled to return no more.

The five blacks were left alone on board, on a half-capsized hull, twelve hundred miles from any land.

Then oldest of the negroes was named Tom. His age, as well as his energetic character, and his experience, often put to the proof during a long life of labor, made him the natural head of the companions who were engaged with him.

The other blacks were young men from twenty-five to thirty years old, whose names were Bat (abbreviation of Bartholomew), son of old Tom, Austin, Acteon, and Hercules, all four well made and vigorous, and who would bring a high price in the markets of Central Africa. Even though they had suffered terribly, one could easily recognize in them magnificent specimens of that strong race, on which a liberal education, drawn from the numerous schools of North America, had already impressed its seal.

Tom and his companions then found themselves alone on the "Waldeck" after the collision, having no means of raising that inert hull, without even power to leave it, because the two boats on board had been shattered in the boarding. They were reduced to waiting for the passage of a ship, while the wreck drifted little by little under the action of the currents. This action explained why she had been encountered so far out of her course, for the "Waldeck," having left Melbourne, ought to be found in much lower latitude.

During the ten days which elapsed between the collision and the moment when the "Pilgrim" arrived in sight of the shipwrecked vessel the five blacks were sustained by some food which they had found in the office of the landing-place. But, not being able to penetrate into the steward's room, which the water entirely covered, they had had no spirits to quench their thirst, and they had suffered cruelly, the water casks fastened to the deck having been stove in by the collision. Since the night before, Tom and his companions, tortured by thirst, had become unconscious.

Such was the recital which Tom gave, in a few words, to Captain Hull. There was no reason to doubt the veracity of the old black. His companions confirmed all that he had said; besides, the facts pleaded for the poor men.

Another living being, saved on the wreck, would doubtless have spoken with the same sincerity if it had been gifted with speech.

It was that dog, that the sight of Negoro seemed to affect in such a disagreeable manner. There was in that some truly inexplicable antipathy.

Dingo—that was the name of the dog—belonged to that race of mastiffs which is peculiar to New Holland. It was not in Australia, however, that the captain of the "Waldeck" had found it. Two years before Dingo, wandering half dead of hunger, had been met on the western coast of Africa, near the mouth of the Congo. The captain of the "Waldeck" had picked up this fine animal, who, being not very sociable, seemed to be always regretting some old master, from whom he had been violently separated, and whom it would be impossible to find again in that desert country. S. V.—those two letters engraved on his collar—were all that linked this animal to a past, whose mystery one would seek in vain to solve.

Dingo, a magnificent and robust beast, larger than the dogs of the Pyrenees, was then a superb specimen of the New Holland variety of mastiffs. When it stood up, throwing its head back, it equaled the height of a man. Its agility—its muscular strength, would be sufficient for one of those animals which without hesitation attack jaguars and panthers, and do not fear to face a bear. Its long tail of thick hair, well stocked and stiff like a lion's tail, its general hue dark fawn-color, was only varied at the nose by some whitish streaks. This animal, under the influence of anger, might become formidable, and it will be understood that Negoro was not satisfied with the reception given him by this vigorous specimen of the canine race.

Meanwhile, Dingo, if it was not sociable, was not bad. It seemed rather to be sad. An observation which had been made by old Tom on board the "Waldeck" was that this dog did not seem to like blacks. It did not seek to harm them, but certainly it shunned them. May be, on that African coast where it wandered, it had suffered some bad treatment from the natives. So, though Tom and his companions were honest men, Dingo was never drawn toward them. During the ten days that the shipwrecked dog had passed on the "Waldeck," it had kept at a distance, feeding itself, they knew not how, but having also suffered cruelly from thirst.

Such, then, were the survivors of this wreck, which the first surge of the sea would submerge. No doubt it would have carried only dead bodies into the depths of the ocean if the unexpected arrival of the "Pilgrim," herself kept back by calms and contrary winds, had not permitted Captain Hull to do a work of humanity.

This work had only to be completed by bringing back to their country the shipwrecked men from the "Waldeck," who, in this shipwreck, had lost their savings of three years of labor. This is what was going to be done. The "Pilgrim," after having effected her unloading at Valparaiso, would ascend the American coast as far as California. There Tom and his companions would be well received by James W. Weldon—his generous wife assured them of it— and they would be provided with all that would be necessary for them to return to the State of Pennsylvania.

These honest men, reassured about the future, had only to thank Mrs. Weldon and Captain Hull. Certainly they owed them a great deal, and although they were only poor negroes, perhaps, they did not despair of some day paying this debt of gratitude.

# CHAPTER V.

## S. V.

Meanwhile, the "Pilgrim" had continued her course, making for the east as much as possible. This lamentable continuance of calms did not cease to trouble Captain Hull—not that he was uneasy about two or three weeks' delay in a passage from New Zealand to Valparaiso, but because of the extra fatigue which this delay might bring to his lady passenger.

Meanwhile, Mrs. Weldon did not complain, and philosophically took her misfortune in patience.

That same day, February 2d, toward evening, the wreck was lost sight of.

Captain Hull was troubled, in the first place, to accommodate Tom and his companions as conveniently as possible. The crew's quarters on the "Pilgrim," built on the deck in the form of a "roufle," would be too small to hold them. An arrangement was then made to lodge them under the forecastle. Besides, these honest men, accustomed to rude labors, could not be hard to please, and with fine weather, warm and salubrious, this sleeping-place ought to suffice for the whole passage.

The life on board, shaken for a moment from its monotony by this incident, then went on as usual.

Tom, Austin, Bat, Acteon, and Hercules would indeed wish to make themselves useful. But with these constant winds, the sails once set, there was nothing more to do. Meanwhile, when there was a veering about, the old black and his companions hastened to give a hand to the crew, and it must be confessed that when the colossal Hercules hauled some rope, they were aware of it. This vigorous negro, six feet high, brought in a tackle all by himself.

It was joy for little Jack to look at this giant. He was not afraid of him, and when Hercules hoisted him up in his arms, as if he were only a cork baby, there were cries of joy to go on.

"Lift me very high," said little Jack.

"There, Master Jack!" replied Hercules.

"Am I very heavy?"

"I do not even feel you."

"Well, higher still! To the end of your arm!" And Hercules, holding the child's two little feet in his large hand, walked him about like a gymnast in a circus. Jack saw himself, tall, taller, which amused him very much. He even tried to make himself heavy—which the colossus did not perceive at all.

Dick Sand and Hercules, they were two friends for little Jack. He was not slow in making himself a third—that was Dingo.

It has been said that Dingo was not a sociable dog. Doubtless that held good, because the society of the "Waldeck" did not suit it. On board the "Pilgrim" it was quite another thing. Jack probably knew how to touch the fine animal's heart. The latter soon took pleasure in playing with the little boy, whom this play pleased. It was soon discovered that Dingo was one of those dogs who have a particular taste for children. Besides, Jack did it no harm. His greatest pleasure was to transform Dingo into a swift steed, and it is safe to affirm that a horse of this kind is much superior to a pasteboard quadruped, even when it has wheels to its feet. So Jack galloped bare-back on the dog, which let him do it willingly, and, in truth, Jack was no heavier to it than the half of a jockey to a race-horse.

But what a break each day in the stock of sugar in the store-room!

Dingo soon became a favorite with the whole crew. Alone, Negoro continued to avoid any encounter with the animal, whose antipathy was always as strong as it was inexplicable.

Meanwhile, little Jack had not neglected Dick Sand, his friend of old, for Dingo. All the time that was unclaimed by his duties on board, the novice passed with the little boy.

Mrs. Weldon, it is needless to say, always regarded this intimacy with the most complete satisfaction.

One day, February 6th, she spoke of Dick to Captain Hull, and the captain praised the young novice in the highest terms.

"That boy," he said to Mrs. Weldon, "will be a good seaman some day, I'll guarantee. He has truly a passion for the sea, and by this passion he makes up for the theoretical parts of the calling which he has not yet learned. What he already knows is astonishing, when we think of the short time he has had to learn."

"It must be added," replied Mrs. Weldon, "that he is also an excellent person, a true boy, very superior to his age, and who has never merited any blame since we have known him."

"Yes, he is a good young man," continued the captain, "justly loved and appreciated by all."

"This cruise finished," said Mrs. Weldon, "I know that my husband's intention is to have him follow a course of navigation, so that, he may afterwards obtain a captain's commission."

"And Mr. Weldon is right," replied Captain Hull. "Dick Sand will one day do honor to the American marine."

"This poor orphan commenced life sadly," observed Mrs. Weldon. "He has been in a hard school!"

"Doubtless, Mrs. Weldon; but the lessons have not been lost on him. He has learned that he must make his own way in this world, and he is in a fair way to do it."

"Yes, the way of duty!"

"Look at him now, Mrs. Weldon," continued Captain Hull. "He is at the helm, his eye fixed on the point of the foresail. No distraction on the part of this young novice, as well as no lurch to the ship. Dick Sand has already the confidence of an old steersman. A good beginning for a seaman. Our craft, Mrs. Weldon, is one of those in which it is necessary to begin very young. He who has not been a cabin-boy will never arrive at being a perfect seaman, at least in the merchant marine. Everything must be learned, and, consequently, everything must be at the same time instinctive and rational with the sailor— the resolution to grasp, as well as the skill to execute."

"Meanwhile, Captain Hull," replied Mrs. Weldon, "good officers are not lacking in the navy."

"No," replied Captain Hull; "but, in my opinion, the best have almost all begun their career as children, and, without speaking of Nelson and a few others, the worst are not those who began by being cabin-boys."

At that moment they saw Cousin Benedict springing up from the rear companion-way. As usual he was absorbed, and as little conscious of this world as the Prophet Elias will be when he returns to the earth.

Cousin Benedict began to walk about on the deck like an uneasy spirit, examining closely the interstices of the netting, rummaging under the hen-cages, putting his hand between the seams of the deck, there, where the pitch had scaled off.

"Ah! Cousin Benedict," asked Mrs. Weldon, "do you keep well?"

"Yes—Cousin Weldon—I am well, certainly—but I am in a hurry to get on land."

"What are you looking for under that bench, Mr. Benedict?" asked Captain Hull.

"Insects, sir," returned Cousin Benedict. "What do you expect me to look for, if not insects?"

"Insects! Faith, I must agree with you; but it is not at sea that you will enrich your collection."

"And why not, sir? It is not impossible to find on board some specimen of ——"

"Cousin Benedict," said Mrs. Weldon, "do you then slander Captain Hull? His ship is so well kept, that you will return empty-handed from your hunt."

Captain Hull began to laugh.

"Mrs. Weldon exaggerates," replied he. "However, Mr. Benedict, I believe you will lose your time rummaging in our cabins."

"Ah! I know it well," cried Cousin Benedict, shrugging his shoulders.

"I have had a good search——"

"But, in the 'Pilgrim's' hold," continued Captain Hull, "perhaps you will find some cockroaches—subjects of little interest, however."

"Of little interest, those nocturnal orthopters which have incurred the maledictions of Virgil and Horace!" retorted Cousin Benedict, standing up straight. "Of little interest, those near relations of the 'periplaneta orientalis' and of the American kakerlac, which inhabit——"

"Which infest!" said Captain Hull.

"Which reign on board!" retorted Cousin Benedict, fiercely.

"Amiable sovereignty!"

"Ah! you are not an entomologist, sir?"

"Never at my own expense."

"Now, Cousin Benedict," said Mrs. Weldon, smiling, "do not wish us to be devoured for love of science."

"I wish, nothing, Cousin Weldon," replied, the fiery entomologist, "except to be able to add to my collection some rare subject which might do it honor."

"Are you not satisfied, then, with the conquests that you have made in New Zealand?"

"Yes, truly, Cousin Weldon. I have been rather fortunate in conquering one of those new staphylins which till now had only been found some hundreds of miles further, in New Caledonia."

At that moment Dingo, who was playing with Jack, approached Cousin Benedict, gamboling.

"Go away! go away!" said the latter, pushing off the animal.

"To love cockroaches and detest dogs!" cried Captain Hull. "Oh! Mr. Benedict!"

"A good dog, notwithstanding," said little Jack, taking Dingo's great head in his small hands.

"Yes. I do not say no," replied Cousin Benedict. "But what do you want? This devil of an animal has not realized the hopes I conceived on meeting it."

"Ah! my goodness!" cried Mrs. Weldon, "did you, then, hope to be able to classify it in the order of the dipters or the hymenopters?"

"No," replied Cousin Benedict, seriously. "But is it not true that this Dingo, though it be of the New Zealand race, was picked up on the western coast of Africa?"

"Nothing is more true," replied Mrs. Weldon, "and Tom had often heard the captain of the 'Waldeck' say so."

"Well, I had thought—I had hoped—that this dog would have brought away some specimens of hemipteras peculiar to the African fauna."

"Merciful heavens!" cried Mrs. Weldon.

"And that perhaps," added Cousin Benedict, "some penetrating or irritating flea—of a new species——"

"Do you understand, Dingo?" said Captain Hull. "Do you understand, my dog? You have failed in all your duties!"

"But I have examined it well," added the entomologist, with an accent of deep regret. "I have not been able to find a single insect."

"Which you would have immediately and mercilessly put to death, I hope!" cried Captain Hull.

"Sir," replied Cousin Benedict, dryly, "learn that Sir John Franklin made a scruple of killing the smallest insect, be it a mosquito, whose attacks are otherwise formidable as those of a flea; and meanwhile you will not hesitate to allow, that Sir John Franklin was a seaman who was as good as the next."

"Surely," said Captain Hull, bowing.

"And one day, after being frightfully devoured by a dipter, he blew and sent it away, saying to it, without even using thou or thee: 'Go! the world is large enough for you and for me!'"

"Ah!" ejaculated Captain Hull.

"Yes, sir."

"Well, Mr. Benedict," retorted Captain Hull, "another had said that long before Sir John Franklin."

"Another?"

"Yes; and that other was Uncle Toby."

"An entomologist?" asked Cousin Benedict, quickly.

"No! Sterne's Uncle Toby, and that worthy uncle pronounced precisely the same words, while setting free a mosquito that annoyed him, but which he thought himself at liberty to thee and thou: 'Go, poor devil,' he said to it, 'the world is large enough to contain us, thee and me!'"

"An honest man, that Uncle Toby!" replied Cousin Benedict. "Is he dead?"

"I believe so, indeed," retorted Captain Hull, gravely, "as he has never existed!"

And each began to laugh, looking at Cousin Benedict.

Thus, then, in these conversations, and many others, which invariably bore on some point of entomological science, whenever Cousin Benedict took part, passed away long hours of this navigation against contrary winds. The sea always fine, but winds which obliged the schooner to tack often. The "Pilgrim" made very little headway toward the east—the breeze was so feeble; and they longed to reach those parts where the prevailing winds would be more favorable.

It must be stated here that Cousin Benedict had endeavored to initiate the young novice into the mysteries of entomology. But Dick Sand had shown himself rather refractory to these advances. For want of better company the savant had fallen back on the negroes, who comprehended nothing about it. Tom, Acteon, Bat, and Austin had even finished by deserting the class, and the professor found himself reduced to Hercules alone, who seemed to him to have some natural disposition to distinguish a parasite from a thysanuran.

So the gigantic black lived in the world of coleopteras, carnivorous insects, hunters, gunners, ditchers, cicindelles, carabes, sylphides, moles, cockchafers, horn-beetles, tenebrions, mites, lady-birds, studying all Cousin Benedict's collection, not but the latter trembled on seeing his frail specimens in Hercules' great hands, which were hard and strong as a vise. But the colossal pupil listened so quietly to the professor's lessons that it was worth risking something to give them.

While Cousin Benedict worked in that manner, Mrs. Weldon did not leave little Jack entirely unoccupied; She taught him to read and to write. As to arithmetic, it was his friend Dick Sand who inculcated the first elements.

At the age of five, one is still only a little child, and is perhaps better instructed by practical games than by theoretical lessons necessarily a little arduous.

Jack learned to read, not in a primer, but by means of movable letters, printed in red on cubes of wood. He amused himself by arranging the blocks so as to form words. Sometimes Mrs. Weldon took these cubes and composed a word; then she disarranged them, and it was for Jack to replace them in the order required.

The little boy liked this manner of learning to read very much. Each day he passed some hours, sometimes in the cabin, sometimes on the deck, in arranging and disarranging the letters of his alphabet.

Now, one day this led to an incident so extraordinary, so unexpected, that it is necessary to relate with some detail.

It was on the morning of February 9th, Jack, half-lying on the deck, was amusing himself forming a word which old Tom was to put together again, after the letters had been mixed. Tom, with his hand over his eyes so as not to cheat, as he agreed, would see nothing, and did see nothing of the work of the little boy.

Of these different letters, about fifty in number, some were large, others small. Besides, some of these cubes carried a figure, which taught the child to form numbers as well as to form words.

These cubes were arranged on the deck, and little Jack was taking sometimes one, sometimes another, to make a word—a truly great labor.

Now, for same moments, Dingo was moving round the young child, when suddenly it stopped. Its eyes became fixed, its right paw was raised, its tail wagged convulsively. Then, suddenly throwing itself on one of the cubes, it seized it in its mouth and laid it on the deck a few steps from Jack.

This cube bore a large letter—the letter S.

"Dingo, well Dingo!" cried the little boy, who at first was afraid that his S was swallowed by the dog.

But Dingo had returned, and, beginning the same performance again, it seized another cube, and went to lay it near the first.

This second cube was a large V.

This time Jack gave a cry.

At this cry, Mrs. Weldon, Captain Hull, and the young novice, who were walking on the deck, assembled. Little Jack then told them what had just passed.

Dingo knew its letters; Dingo knew how to read! That was very certain, that! Jack had seen it!

Dick Sand wanted to go and take the two cubes, to restore them to his friend Jack, but Dingo showed him its teeth.

However, the novice succeeded in gaining possession of the two cubes, and he replaced them in the set.

Dingo advanced again, seized again the same two letters, and carried them to a distance. This time its two paws lay on them; it seemed decided to guard them at all hazards. As to the other letters of the alphabet, it did not seem as if it had any knowledge of them.

"That is a curious thing," said Mrs. Weldon.

"It is, in fact, very singular," replied Captain Hull, who was looking attentively at the two letters.

"S. V.," said Mrs. Weldon.

"S. V.," repeated Captain Hull. "But those are precisely the letters which are on Dingo's collar!"

Then, all at once, turning to the old black: "Tom," he asked, "have you not told me that this dog only belonged to the captain of the 'Waldeck' for a short time?"

"In fact, sir," replied Tom, "Dingo was only on board two years at the most."

"And have you not added that the captain of the 'Waldeck' had picked up this dog on the western coast of Africa?"

"Yes, sir, in the neighborhood of the mouth of the Congo. I have often heard the captain say so."

"So," asked Captain Hull, "it has never been known to whom this dog had belonged, nor whence it came?"

"Never, sir. A dog found is worse than a child! That has no papers, and, more, it cannot explain."

Captain Hull was silent, and reflected.

"Do those two letters, then, awake some remembrance?" Mrs. Weldon asked

Captain Hull, after leaving him to his reflections for some moments.

"Yes, Mrs. Weldon, a remembrance, or rather a coincidence at least singular."

What?"

"Those two letters might well have a meaning, and fix for us the fate of an intrepid traveler."

"What do you mean?" demanded Mrs. Weldon.

"Here is what I mean, Mrs. Weldon. In 1871—consequently two years ago—a French traveler set out, under the auspices of the Paris Geographical Society, with the intention of crossing Africa from the west to the east. His point of departure was precisely the mouth of the Congo. His point of arrival would be as near as possible to Cape Deldago, at the mouths of the Rovuma, whose course he would descend. Now, this French traveler was named Samuel Vernon."

"Samuel Vernon!" repeated Mrs. Weldon.

"Yes, Mrs. Weldon; and those two names begin precisely by those two letters which Dingo has chosen among all the others, and which are engraved on its collar."

"Exactly," replied Mrs. Weldon. "And that traveler——"

"That traveler set out," replied Captain Hull, "and has not been heard of since his departure."

"Never?" said the novice.

"Never," repeated Captain Hull.

"What do you conclude from it?" asked Mrs. Weldon.

"That, evidently, Samuel Vernon has not been able to reach the eastern coast of Africa, whether he may have been made prisoner by the natives, whether death may have struck him on the way."

"And then this dog?"

"This dog would have belonged to him; and, more fortunate than its master, if my hypothesis is true, it would have been able to return to the Congo coast, because it was there, at the time when these events must have taken place, that it was picked up by the captain of the 'Waldeck.'"

"But," observed Mrs. Weldon, "do you know if this French traveler was accompanied on his departure by a dog? Is it not a mere supposition on your part?"

"It is only a supposition, indeed, Mrs. Weldon," replied Captain Hull. "But what is certain is, that Dingo knows these two letters S and V, which are precisely the initials of the two names of the French traveler. Now, under what circumstances this animal would learn to distinguish them is what I cannot explain; but, I repeat it, it very certainly knows them; and look, it pushes them with its paw, and seems to invite us to read them with it."

In fact, they could not misunderstand Dingo's intention.

"Then was Samuel Vernon alone when he left the sea-coast of the Congo?" ask Dick Sand.

"That I know not," replied Captain Hull. "However, it is probable that he would take a native escort."

At that moment Negoro, leaving his post, showed himself on the deck. At first no one remarked his presence, and could not observe the singular look he cast on the dog when he perceived the two letters over which the animal seem to mount guard. But Dingo, having perceived the master-cook, began to show signs of the most extreme fury.

Negoro returned immediately to the crew's quarters, not without a menacing gesture at the dog's skill having escaped him.

"There is some mystery there," murmured Captain Hull, who had lost none of this little scene.

"But, sir," said the novice, "is it not very astonishing that a dog should know the letters of the alphabet?"

"No!" cried little Jack. "Mama has often told me the story of a dog which knew how to read and write, and even play dominoes, like a real schoolmaster!"

"My dear child," replied Mrs. Weldon, smiling, "that dog, whose name was Munito, was not a savant, as you suppose. If I may believe what has been told me about it, Munito would not have been able to distinguish the letters which served to compose the words. But its master, a clever American, having remarked what fine hearing Munito had, applied himself to cultivating that sense, and to draw from it some very curious effects."

"How did he set to work, Mrs. Weldon?" asked Dick Sand, whom the history interested almost as much as little Jack.

"In this way, my friend." When Munito was 'to appear' before the public, letters similar to these were displayed on a table. On that table the poodle walked about, waiting till a word was proposed, whether in a loud voice or in a low voice. Only, one essential condition was that its master should know the word."

"And, in the absence of its master—" said the novice.

"The dog could have done nothing," replied Mrs. Weldon, "and here is the reason. The letters spread out on the table, Munito walked about through this alphabet. When it arrived before the letter which it should choose to form the word required, it stopped; but if it stopped it was because it heard the noise—imperceptible to all others—of a toothpick that the American snapped in his pocket. That noise was the signal for Munito to take the letter and arrange it in suitable order."

"And that was all the secret?" cried Dick Sand.

"That was the whole secret," replied Mrs. Weldon. "It is very simple, like all that is done in the matter of prestidigitation. In case of the American's absence, Munito would be no longer Munito. I am, then, astonished, his master not being there—if, indeed, the traveler, Samuel Vernon, has ever been its master—that Dingo could have recognized those two letters."

"In fact," replied Captain Hull, "it is very astonishing. But, take notice, there are only two letters in question here, two particular letters, and not a word chosen by chance. After all, that dog which rang at the door of a convent to take possession of the plate intended for the poor passers-by, that other which commissioned at the same time with one of its kind, to turn the spit for two days each, and which refused to fill that office when its turn had not come, those two dogs, I say, advanced farther than Dingo into that domain of intelligence reserved for man. Besides, we are in the presence of an inscrutable fact. Of all the letters of that alphabet, Dingo has only chosen these two: S and V. The others it does not even seem to know. Therefore we must conclude that, for a reason which escapes us, its attention has been especially drawn to those two letters."

"Ah! Captain Hull," replied the young novice, "if Dingo could speak! Perhaps he would tell us what those two letters signify, and why it has kept a tooth ready for our head cook."

"And what a tooth!" replied Captain Hull, as Dingo, opening its mouth, showed its formidable fangs.

## CHAPTER VI.

### A WHALE IN SIGHT.

It will be remembered that this singular incident was made, more than once, the subject of conversation held in the stern of the "Pilgrim" between Mrs. Weldon, Captain Hull, and the young novice. The latter, more particularly, experienced an instinctive mistrust with regard to Negoro, whose conduct, meanwhile, merited no reproach.

In the prow they talked of it also, but they did not draw from it the same conclusions. There, among the ship's crew, Dingo passed merely for a dog that knew how to read, and perhaps even write, better than more than one sailor on board. As for talking, if he did not do it, it was probably for good reasons that he kept silent.

"But, one of these fine days," says the steersman, Bolton, "one fine day that dog will come and ask us how we are heading; if the wind is to the west-north-west-half-north, and we will have to answer him! There are animals that speak! Well, why should not a dog do as much if he took it into his head? It is more difficult to talk with a beak than with a mouth!"

"No doubt," replied the boatswain, Howik. "Only it has never been known."

It would have astonished these brave men to tell them that, on the contrary, it had been known, and that a certain Danish servant possessed a dog which pronounced distinctly twenty words. But whether this animal comprehended what he said was a mystery. Very evidently this dog, whose glottis was organized in a manner to enable him to emit regular sounds, attached no more sense to his words than do the paroquets, parrots, jackdaws, and magpies to theirs. A phrase with animals is nothing more than a kind of song or spoken cry, borrowed from a strange language of which they do not know the meaning.

However that might be, Dingo had become the hero of the deck, of which fact he took no proud advantage. Several times Captain Hull repeated the experiment. The wooden cubes of the alphabet were placed before Dingo, and invariably, without an error, without hesitation, the two letters, S and V, were chosen from among all by the singular animal, while the others never attracted his attention.

As for Cousin Benedict, this experiment was often renewed before him, without seeming to interest him.

"Meanwhile," he condescended to say one day, "we must not believe that the dogs alone have the privilege of being intelligent in this manner. Other animals equal them, simply in following their instinct. Look at the rats, who abandon the ship destined to founder at sea; the beavers, who know how to foresee the rising of the waters, and build their dams higher in consequence; those horses of Nicomedes, of Scanderberg, and of Oppien, whose grief was such that they died when their masters did; those asses, so remarkable for their memory, and many other beasts which have done honor to the animal kingdom. Have we not seen birds, marvelously erect, that correctly write words dictated by their professors; cockatoos that count, as well as a reckoner in the Longitude Office, the number of persons present in a parlor? Has there not existed a parrot, worth a hundred gold crowns, that recited the Apostle's Creed to the cardinal, his master, without missing a word? Finally, the legitimate pride of an entomologist should be raised to the highest point, when he sees simple insects give proofs of a superior intelligence, and affirm eloquently the axiom:

"'In minimis maximus Deus,'

those ants which, represent the inspectors of public works in the largest cities, those aquatic argyronetes which manufacture diving-bells, without having ever learned the mechanism; those fleas which draw carriages like veritable coachmen, which go through the exercise as well as riflemen, which fire off cannon better than the commissioned artillerymen of West Point? No! this Dingo does not merit so many eulogies, and if he is so strong on the alphabet, it is, without doubt, because he belongs to a species of mastiff, not yet classified in zoological science, the canis alphabeticus of New Zealand."

In spite of these discourses and others of the envious entomologist, Dingo lost nothing in the public estimation, and continued to be treated as a phenomenon in the conversations of the forecastle.

All this time, it is probable that Negoro did not share the enthusiasm of the ship in regard to the animal. Perhaps he found it too intelligent. However, the dog always showed the same animosity against the head cook, and, doubtless, would have brought upon itself some misfortune, if it had not been, for one thing, "a dog to defend itself," and for another, protected by the sympathy of the whole crew.

So Negoro avoided coming into Dingo's presence more than ever. But Dick Sand had observed that since the incident of the two letters, the reciprocal antipathy between the man and the dog was increased. That was truly inexplicable.

On February 10th, the wind from the northeast, which, till then, had always succeeded those long and overwhelming calms, during which the "Pilgrim" was stationary, began to abate perceptibly. Captain Hull then could hope that a change in the direction of the atmospheric currents was going to take place. Perhaps the schooner would finally sail with the wind. It was still only nineteen days since her departure from the port of Auckland. The delay was not yet of much account, and, with a favorable wind, the "Pilgrim," well rigged, would easily make up for lost time. But several days must still elapse before the breezes would blow right from the west.

This part of the Pacific was always deserted. No vessel showed itself in these parts. It was a latitude truly forsaken by navigators. The whalers of the southern seas were not yet prepared to go beyond the tropic. On the "Pilgrim," which peculiar circumstances had obliged to leave the fishing grounds before the end of the season, they must not expect to cross any ship bound for the same destination.

As to the trans-pacific packet-boats, it has been already said that they did not follow so high a parallel in their passages between Australia and the American continent.

However, even if the sea is deserted, one must not give up observing it to the extreme limits of the horizon. Monotonous as it may appear to heedless minds, it is none the less infinitely varied for him who knows how to comprehend it. Its slightest changes charm the imagination of one who feels the poetry of the ocean. A marine herb which floats up and down on the waves, a branch of sargasso whose light track zebras, the surface of the waters, and end of a board, whose history he would wish to guess, he would need nothing more. Facing this infinite, the mind is no longer stopped by anything. Imagination runs riot. Each of those molecules of water, that evaporation is continually changing from the sea to the sky, contains perhaps the secret of some catastrophe. So, those are to be envied, whose inner consciousness knows how to interrogate the mysteries of the ocean, those spirits who rise from its moving surface to the heights of heaven.

Besides, life always manifests itself above as well as below the seas. The "Pilgrim's" passengers could see flights of birds excited in the pursuit of the smallest fishes, birds which, before winter, fly from the cold climate of the poles. And more than once, Dick Sand, a scholar of Mrs. Weldon's in that branch as in others, gave proofs of marvelous skill with the gun and pistol, in bringing down some of those rapid-winged creatures.

There were white petrels here; there, other petrels, whose wings were embroidered with brown. Sometimes, also, companies of damiers passed, or some of those penquins whose gait on land is so heavy and so ridiculous. However, as Captain Hull remarked, these penquins, using their stumps like true fins, can challenge the most rapid fishes in swimming, to such an extent even, that sailors have often confounded them with bonitoes.

Higher, gigantic albatrosses beat the air with great strokes, displaying an extent of ten feet between the extremities of their wings, and then came to light on the surface of the waters, which they searched with their beaks to get their food.

All these scenes made a varied spectacle, that only souls closed to the charms of nature would have found monotonous.

That day Mrs. Weldon was walking aft on the "Pilgrim," when a rather curious phenomenon attracted her attention. The waters of the sea had become reddish quite suddenly. One might have believed that they had just been stained with blood; and this inexplicable tinge extended as far as the eye could reach.

Dick Sand. was then with little Jack near Mrs. Weldon.

"Dick," she said to the young novice, "Do you see that singular color of the waters of the Pacific? Is it due to the presence of a marine herb?"

"No, Mrs. Weldon," replied Dick Sand, "that tinge is produced by myriads of little crustaceans, which generally serve to nourish the great mammifers. Fishermen call that, not without reason, 'whales' food.'"

"Crustaceans!" said Mrs. Weldon. "But they are so small that we might almost call them sea insects. Perhaps Cousin Benedict would be very much enchanted to make a collection of them." Then calling: "Cousin Benedict!" cried she.

Cousin Benedict appeared out of the companion-way almost at the same time as Captain Hull.

"Cousin Benedict," said Mrs. Weldon, "see that immense reddish field which extends as far as we can see."

"Hold!" said Captain Hull. "That is whales' food. Mr. Benedict, a fine occasion to study this curious species of crustacea."

"Phew!" from the entomologist.

"How—phew!" cried the captain. "But you have no right to profess such indifference. These crustaceans form one of the six classes of the articulates, if I am not mistaken, and as such——"

"Phew!" said Cousin Benedict again, shaking his lead.

"For instance——I find you passably disdainful for an entomologist!"

"Entomologist, it may be," replied Cousin Benedict, "but more particularly hexapodist, Captain Hull, please remember."

"At all events," replied Captain Hull, "if these crustaceans do not interest you, it can't be helped; but it would be otherwise if you possessed a whale's stomach. Then what a regale! Do you see, Mrs. Weldon, when we whalers, during the fishing season, arrive in sight of a shoal of these crustaceans, we have only time to prepare our harpoons and our lines. We are certain that the game is not distant."

"Is it possible that such little beasts can feed such large ones?" cried Jack.

"Ah! my boy," replied Captain Hull, "little grains of vermicelli, of flour, of fecula powder, do they not make very good porridge? Yes; and nature has willed that it should be so. When a whale floats in the midst of these red waters, its soup is served; it has only to open its immense mouth. Myriads of crustaceans enter it. The numerous plates of those whalebones with which the animal's palate is furnished serve to strain like fishermen's nets; nothing can get out of them again, and the mass of crustaceans is ingulfed in the whale's vast stomach, as the soup of your dinner in yours."

"You think right, Jack," observed Dick Sand, "that Madam Whale does not lose time in picking these crustaceans one by one, as you pick shrimps."

"I may add," said Captain Hull, "that it is just when the enormous gourmand is occupied in this way, that it is easiest to approach it without exciting its suspicion. That is the favorable moment to harpoon it with some success."

At that instant, and as if to corroborate Captain Hull, a sailor's voice was heard from the front of the ship:

"A whale to larboard!"

Captain Hull strode up.

"A whale!" cried he.

And his fisherman's instinct urging him, he hastened to the "Pilgrim's" forecastle.

Mrs. Weldon, Jack, Dick Sand, Cousin Benedict himself, followed him at once.

In fact, four miles to windward a certain bubbling indicated that a huge marine mammifer was moving in the midst of the red waters. Whalers could not be mistaken in it. But the distance was still too considerable to make it possible to recognize the species to which this mammifer belonged. These species, in fact, are quite distinct.

Was it one of those "right" whales, which the fishermen of the Northern Ocean seek most particularly? Those cetaceans, which lack the dorsal fin, but whose skin covers a thick stratum of lard, may attain a length of eighty feet, though the average does not exceed sixty, and then a single one of those monsters furnishes as much as a hundred barrels of oil.

Was it, on the contrary, a "humpback," belonging to the species of baloenopters, a designation whose termination should at least gain it the entomologist's esteem? These possess dorsal fins, white in color, and as long as half the body, which resemble a pair of wings—something like a flying whale.

Had they not in view, more likely, a "finback" mammifer, as well known by the name "jubarte," which is provided with a dorsal fin, and whose length may equal that of the "right" whale?

Captain Hull and his crew could not yet decide, but they regarded the animal with more desire than admiration.

If it is true that a clockmaker cannot find himself in a room in the presence of a clock without experiencing the irresistible wish to wind it up, how much more must the whaler, before a whale, be seized with the imperative desire to take possession of it? The hunters of large game, they say, are more eager than the hunters of small game. Then, the larger the animal, the more it excites covetousness. Then, how should hunters of elephants and fishers of whalers feel? And then there was that disappointment, felt by all the "Pilgrim's" crew, of returning with an incomplete cargo.

Meanwhile, Captain Hull tried to distinguish the animal which had been signaled in the offing. It was not very visible from that distance. Nevertheless, the trained eye of a whaler could not be deceived in certain details easier to discern at a distance.

In fact, the water-spout, that is, that column of vapor and water which the whale throws back by its rents, would attract Captain Hull's attention, and fix it on the species to which this cetacean belonged.

"That is not a 'right' whale," cried he. "Its water-spout would be at once higher and of a smaller volume. On the other hand, if the noise made by that spout in escaping could be compared to the distant noise of a cannon, I should be led to believe that that whale belongs to the species of 'humpbacks;' but there is nothing of the kind, and, on listening, we are assured that this noise is of quite a different nature. What is your opinion on this subject, Dick?" asked Captain Hull, turning toward the novice.

"I am ready to believe, captain," replied Dick Sand, "that we have to do with a jubarte. See how his rents throw that column of liquid violently into the air. Does it not seem to you also—which would confirm my idea—that that spout contains more water than condensed vapor? And, if I am not mistaken, it is a special peculiarity of the jubarte."

"In fact, Dick," replied Captain Hull, "there is no longer any doubt possible! It is a jubarte which floats on the surface of these red waters."

"That's fine," cried little Jack.

"Yes, my boy! and when we think that the great beast is there, in process of breakfasting, and little suspecting that the whalers are watching it."

"I would dare to affirm that it is a jubarte of great size," observed Dick Sand.

"Truly," replied Captain Hull, who was gradually becoming more excited.

"I think it is at least seventy feet long!"

"Good!" added the boatswain. "Half a dozen whales of that size would suffice to fill a ship as large as ours!"

"Yes, that would be sufficient," replied Captain Hull, who mounted on the bowsprit to see better.

"And with this one," added the boatswain, "we should take on board in a few hours the half of the two hundred barrels of oil which we lack."

"Yes!—truly—yes!" murmured Captain Hull.

"That is true," continued Dick Sand; "but it is sometimes a hard matter to attack those enormous jubartes!"

"Very hard, very hard!" returned Captain Hull. "Those baloenopters have formidable tails, which must not be approached without distrust. The strongest pirogue would not resist a well-given blow. But, then, the profit is worth the trouble!"

"Bah!" said one of the sailors, "a fine jubarte is all the same a fine capture!"

"And profitable!" replied another.

"It would be a pity not to salute this one on the way!"

It was evident that these brave sailors were growing excited in looking at the whale. It was a whole cargo of barrels of oil that was floating within reach of their hands. To hear them, without doubt there was nothing more to be done, except to stow those barrels in the "Pilgrim's" hold to complete her lading. Some of the sailors, mounted on the ratlines of the fore-shrouds, uttered longing cries. Captain Hull, who no longer spoke, was in a dilemma. There was something there, like an irresistible magnet, which attracted the "Pilgrim" and all her crew.

"Mama, mama!" then cried little Jack, "I should like to have the whale, to see how it is made."

"Ah! you wish to have this whale, my boy? Ah! why not, my friends?" replied Captain Hull, finally yielding to his secret desire. "Our additional fishermen are lacking, it is true, but we alone——"

"Yes! yes!" cried the sailors, with a single voice.

"This will not be the first time that I have followed the trade of harpooner," added Captain Hull, "and you will see if I still know how to throw the harpoon!"

"Hurrah! hurrah! hurrah!" responded the crew.

## CHAPTER VII.
## PREPARATIONS.

It will be understood that the sight of this prodigious mammifer was necessary to produce such excitement on board the "Pilgrim."

The whale, which floated in the middle of the red waters, appeared enormous. To capture it, and thus complete the cargo, that was very tempting. Could fishermen let such an occasion escape them?

However, Mrs. Weldon believed she ought to ask Captain Hull if it was not dangerous for his men and for him to attack a whale under those circumstances.

"No, Mrs. Weldon," replied Captain Hull. "More than once it has been my lot to hunt the whale with a single boat, and I have always finished by taking possession of it. I repeat it, there is no danger for us, nor, consequently, for yourself."

Mrs. Weldon, reassured, did not persist.

Captain Hull at once made his preparations for capturing the jubarte. He knew by experience that the pursuit of that baloenopter was not free from difficulties, and he wished to parry all.

What rendered this capture less easy was that the schooner's crew could only work by means of a single boat, while the "Pilgrim" possessed a long-boat, placed on its stocks between the mainmast and the mizzen-mast, besides three whale-boats, of which two were suspended on the larboard and starboard pegs, and the third aft, outside the crown-work.

Generally these three whale-boats were employed simultaneously in the pursuit of cetaceans. But during the fishing season, we know, an additional crew, hired at the stations of New Zealand, came to the assistance of the "Pilgrim's" sailors.

Now, in the present circumstances, the "Pilgrim" could only furnish the five sailors on board—that is, enough to arm a single whale-boat. To utilize the group of Tom and his friends, who had offered themselves at once, was impossible. In fact, the working of a fishing pirogue requires very well trained seamen. A false move of the helm, or a false stroke of an oar, would be enough to compromise the safety of the whale-boat during an attack.

On the other hand, Captain Hull did not wish to leave his ship without leaving on board at least one man from the crew, in whom he had confidence. It was necessary to provide for all eventualities.

Now Captain Hull, obliged to choose strong seamen to man the whale-boat, was forced to put on Dick Sand the care of guarding the "Pilgrim."

"Dick," said he to him, "I shall charge you to remain on board during my absence, which I hope will be short."

"Well, sir," replied the young novice.

Dick Sand would have wished to take part in this fishing, which had a great attraction for him, but he understood that, for one reason, a man's arms were worth more than his for service in a whale-boat, and that for another, he alone could replace Captain Hull. So he was satisfied. The whale-boat's crew must be composed of the five men, including the master, Howik, which formed the whole crew of the "Pilgrim." The four sailors were going to take their places at the oars, and Howik would hold the stern oar, which serves to guide a boat of this kind. A simple rudder, in fact, would not have a prompt enough action, and in case the side oars should be disabled, the stern oar, well handled, could put the whale-boat beyond the reach of the monster's blows.

There was only Captain Hull besides. He had reserved to himself the post of harpooner, and, as he had said, this would not be his first attempt. It was he who must first throw the harpoon, then watch the unrolling of the long line fastened at its end; then, finally finish the animal with spears, when it should return to the surface of the ocean.

Whalers sometimes employ firearms for this kind of fishing. By means of a special instrument, a sort of small cannon, stationed either on board the ship or at the front of the boat, they throw either a harpoon, which draws with it the rope fastened to its end, or explosive balls, which produce great ravages in the body of the animal.

But the "Pilgrim" was not furnished with apparatus of this kind. This was, besides, an instrument of high price, rather difficult to manage, and fishermen, but little friendly to innovations, seem to prefer the employment of primitive weapons, which they use skilfully—that is to say,—the harpoon and spear.

It was then by the usual method, attacking the whale with the sword, that Captain Hull was going to attempt to capture the jubarte signaled five miles from his ship.

Besides, the weather would favor this expedition. The sea, being very calm, was propitious for the working of a whale-boat. The wind was going down, and the "Pilgrim" would only drift in an insensible manner while her crew were occupied in the offing.

So the starboard whale-boat was immediately lowered, and the four sailors went into it.

Howik passed them two of those long spears which serve as harpoons, then two long lances with sharp points. To those offensive arms he added five coils of those strong flexible ropes that the whalers call "lines," and which measure six hundred feet in length. Less would not do, for it sometimes happens that these cords, fastened end to end, are not enough for the "demand," the whale plunges down so deep.

Such were the different weapons which were carefully disposed in the front of the boat.

Howik and the four sailors only waited for the order to let go the rope.

A single place was vacant in the prow of the whale-boat—that which

Captain Hull would occupy.

It is needless to say that the "Pilgrim's" crew, before quitting her, had brought the ship's sails aback. In other words, the yards were braced in such a manner that the sails, counteracting their action, kept the vessel almost stationary.

Just as he was about to embark, Captain Hull gave a last glance at his ship. He was sure that all was in order, the halliards well turned, the sails suitably trimmed. As he was leaving the young novice on board during an absence which might last several hours, he wished, with a good reason, that unless for some urgent cause, Dick Sand would not have to execute a single maneuver.

At the moment of departing he gave the young man some last words of advice.

"Dick," said he, "I leave you alone. Watch over everything. If, as is possible, it should become necessary to get the ship under way, in case we should be led too far in pursuit of this jubarte, Tom and his companions could come to your aid perfectly well. After telling them clearly what they would have to do, I am assured that they would do it."

"Yes, Captain Hull," replied old Tom, "and Mr. Dick can count on us."

"Command! command!" cried Bat. "We have such a strong desire to make ourselves useful."

"On what must we pull?" asked Hercules, turning up the large sleeves of his jacket.

"On nothing just now," replied Dick Sand, smiling.

"At your service," continued the colossus.

"Dick," continued Captain Hull, "the weather is beautiful. The wind has gone down. There is no indication that it will freshen again. Above all, whatever may happen, do not put a boat to sea, and do not leave the ship."

"That is understood."

"If it should become necessary for the 'Pilgrim' to come to us, I shall make a signal to you, by hoisting a flag at the end of a boat-hook."

"Rest assured, captain, I shall not lose sight of the whale-boat," replied Dick Sand.

"Good, my boy," replied Captain Hull. "Courage and coolness. Behold yourself assistant captain. Do honor to your grade. No one has been such at your age!"

Dick Sand did not reply, but he blushed while smiling. Captain Hull understood that blush and that smile.

"The honest boy!" he said to himself; "modesty and good humor, in truth, it is just like him!"

Meanwhile, by these urgent recommendations, it was plain that, even though there would be no danger in doing it, Captain Hull did not leave his ship willingly, even for a few hours. But an irresistible fisherman's instinct, above all, the strong desire to complete his cargo of oil, and not fall short of the engagements made by James W. Weldon in Valparaiso, all that told him to attempt the adventure. Besides, that sea, so fine, was marvelously conducive to the pursuit of a cetacean. Neither his crew nor he could resist such a temptation. The fishing cruise would be finally complete, and this last consideration touched Captain Hull's heart above everything.

Captain Hull went toward the ladder.

"I wish you success," said Mrs. Weldon to him.

"Thank you, Mrs. Weldon."

"I beg you, do not do too much harm to the poor whale," cried little Jack.

"No, my boy," replied Captain Hull.

"Take it very gently, sir."

"Yes—with gloves, little Jack."

"Sometimes," observed Cousin Benedict, "we find rather curious insects on the back of these large mammals."

"Well, Mr. Benedict," replied Captain Hull, laughing, "you shall have the right to 'entomologize' when our jubarte will be alongside of the 'Pilgrim.'"

Then turning to Tom:

"Tom, I count on your companions and you," said he, "to assist us in cutting up the whale, when it is lashed to the ship's hull—which will not be long."

"At your disposal, sir," replied the old black.

"Good!" replied Captain Hull.

"Dick, these honest men will aid you in preparing the empty barrels. During our absence they will bring them on deck, and by this means the work will go fast on our return."

"That shall be done, captain."

For the benefit of those who do not know, it is necessary to say that the jubarte, once dead, must be towed as far as the "Pilgrim," and firmly lashed to her starboard side. Then the sailors, shod in boots, with cramp-hooks would take their places on the back of the enormous cetacean, and cut it up methodically in parallel bands marked off from the head to the tail. These bands would be then cut across in slices of a foot and a half, then divided into pieces, which, after being stowed in the barrels, would be sent to the bottom of the hold.

Generally the whaling ship, when the fishing is over, manages to land as soon as possible, so as to finish her manipulations. The crew lands, and then proceeds to melt the lard, which, under the action of the heat, gives up all its useful part—that is, the oil. In this operation, the whale's lard weighs about a third of its weight.

But, under present circumstances, Captain Hull could not dream of putting back to finish that operation. He only counted on melting this quantity of lard at Valparaiso. Besides, with winds which could not fail to hail from the west, he hoped to make the American coast before twenty days, and that lapse of time could not compromise the results of his fishing.

The moment for setting out had come. Before the "Pilgrim's" sails had been brought aback, she had drawn a little nearer to the place where the jubarte continued to signal its presence by jets of vapor and water.

The jubarte was all this time swimming in the middle of the vast red field of crustaceans, opening its large mouth automatically, and absorbing at each draught myriads of animalcules.

According to the experienced ones on board, there was no fear that the whale dreamt of escaping. It was, doubtless, what the whalers call a "fighting" whale.

Captain Hull strode over the netting, and, descending the rope ladder, he reached the prow of the whale-boat.

Mrs. Weldon, Jack, Cousin Benedict, Tom, and his companions, for a last time wished the captain success.

Dingo itself, rising on its paws and passing its head above the railing, seemed to wish to say good-by to the crew.

Then all returned to the prow, so as to lose none of the very attractive movements of such a fishing.

The whale-boat put off, and, under the impetus of its four oars, vigorously handled, it began to distance itself from the "Pilgrim."

"Watch well, Dick, watch well!" cried Captain Hull to the young novice for the last time.

"Count on me, sir."

"One eye for the ship, one eye for the whale-boat, my boy. Do not forget it."

"That shall be done, captain," replied Dick Sand, who went to take his place near the helm.

Already the light boat was several hundred feet from the ship. Captain Hull, standing at the prow, no longer able to make himself heard, renewed his injunctions by the most expressive gestures.

It was then that Dingo, its paws still resting on the railing, gave a sort of lamentable bark, which would have an unfavorable effect upon men somewhat given to superstition.

That bark even made Mrs. Weldon shudder.

"Dingo," said she, "Dingo, is that the way you encourage your friends?

Come, now, a fine bark, very clear, very sonorous, very joyful."

But the dog barked no more, and, letting itself fall back on its paws, it came slowly to Mrs. Weldon, whose hand it licked affectionately.

"It does not wag its tail," murmured Tom in a low tone. "Bad sign—bad sign."

But almost at once Dingo stood up, and a howl of anger escaped it.

Mrs. Weldon turned round.

Negoro had just left his quarters, and was going toward the forecastle, with the intention, no doubt, of looking for himself at the movements of the whale-boat.

Dingo rushed at the head cook, a prey to the strongest as well as to the most inexplicable fury.

Negoro seized a hand-spike and took an attitude of defense.

The dog was going to spring at his throat.

"Here, Dingo, here!" cried Dick Sand, who, leaving his post of observation for an instant, ran to the prow of the ship.

Mrs. Weldon on her side, sought to calm the dog.

Dingo obeyed, not without repugnance, and returned to the young novice, growling secretly.

Negoro had not pronounced a single word, but his face had grown pale for a moment. Letting go of his hand-spike, he regained his cabin.

"Hercules," then said Dick Sand, "I charge you especially to watch over that man."

"I shall watch," simply replied Hercules, clenching his two enormous fists in sign of assent.

Mrs. Weldon and Dick Sand then turned their eyes again on the whale-boat, which the four oarsmen bore rapidly away.

It was nothing but a speck on the sea.

## CHAPTER VIII.

### THE JUBARTE.

Captain Hull, an experienced whaler, would leave nothing to chance. The capture of a jubarte is a difficult thing. No precaution ought to be neglected. None was in this case.

And, first of all, Captain Hull sailed so as to come up to the whale on the leeward, so that no noise might disclose the boat's approach.

Howik then steered the whale-boat, following the rather elongated curve of that reddish shoal, in the midst of which floated the jubarte. They would thus turn the curve.

The boatswain, set over this work, was a seaman of great coolness, who inspired Captain Hull with every confidence. He had not to fear either hesitation or distraction from Howik.

"Attention to the steering, Howik," said Captain Hull. "We are going to try to surprise the jubarte. We will only show ourselves when we are near enough to harpoon it."

"That is understood, sir," replied the boatswain.

"I am going to follow the contour of these reddish waters, so as to keep to the leeward."

"Good!" said Captain Hull. "Boys, as little noise as possible in rowing."

The oars, carefully muffled with straw, worked silently. The boat, skilfully steered by the boatswain, had reached the large shoal of crustaceans. The starboard oars still sank in the green and limpid water, while those to larboard, raising the reddish liquid, seemed to rain drops of blood.

"Wine and water!" said one of the sailors.

"Yes," replied Captain Hull, "but water that we cannot drink, and wine that we cannot swallow. Come, boys, let us not speak any more, and heave closer!"

The whale-boat, steered by the boatswain, glided noiselessly on the surface of those half-greased waters, as if it were floating on a bed of oil.

The jubarte did not budge, and did not seem to have yet perceived the boat, which described a circle around it.

Captain Hull, in making the circuit, necessarily went farther than the "Pilgrim," which gradually grew smaller in the distance. This rapidity with which objects diminish at sea has always an odd effect. It seems as if we look at them shortened through the large end of a telescope. This optical illusion evidently takes place because there are no points of comparison on these large spaces. It was thus with the "Pilgrim," which decreased to the eye and seemed already much more distant than she really was.

Half an hour after leaving her, Captain Hull and his companions found themselves exactly to the leeward of the whale, so that the latter occupied an intermediate point between the ship and the boat.

So the moment had come to approach, while making as little noise as possible. It was not impossible for them to get beside the animal and harpoon it at good range, before its attention would be attracted.

"Row more slowly, boys," said Captain Hull, in a low voice.

"It seems to me," replied Howik, "that the gudgeon suspects something.

It breathes less violently than it did just now!"

"Silence! silence!" repeated Captain Hull.

Five minutes later the whale-boat was at a cable's length from the jubarte. A cable's length, a measure peculiar to the sea, comprises a length of one hundred and twenty fathoms, that is to say, two hundred meters.

The boatswain, standing aft, steered in such a manner as to approach the left side of the mammal, but avoiding, with the greatest care, passing within reach of the formidable tail, a single blow of which would be enough to crush the boat.

At the prow Captain Hull, his legs a little apart to maintain his equilibrium, held the weapon with which he was going to give the first blow. They could count on his skill to fix that harpoon in the thick mass which emerged from the waters.

Near the captain, in a pail, was coiled the first of the five lines, firmly fastened to the harpoon, and to which they would successively join the other four if the whale plunged to great depths.

"Are we ready, boys?" murmured Captain Hull.

"Yes," replied Howik, grasping his oar firmly in his large hands.

"Alongside! alongside!"

The boatswain obeyed the order, and the whale-boat came within less than ten feet of the animal.

The latter no longer moved, and seemed asleep.

Whales thus surprised while asleep offer an easier prize, and it often happens that the first blow which is given wounds them mortally.

"This immovableness is quite astonishing!" thought Captain Hull. "The rascal ought not to be asleep, and nevertheless——there is something there!"

The boatswain thought the same, and he tried to see the opposite side of the animal.

But it was not the moment to reflect, but to attack.

Captain Hull, holding his harpoon by the middle of the handle, balanced it several times, to make sure of good aim, while he examined the jubarte's side. Then he threw it with all the strength of his arm.

"Back, back!" cried he at once.

And the sailors, pulling together, made the boat recoil rapidly, with the intention of prudently putting it in safety from the blows of the cetacean's tail.

But at that moment a cry from the boatswain made them understand why the whale was so extraordinarily motionless for so long a time on the surface of the sea.

"A young whale!" said he.

In fact, the jubarte, after having been struck by the harpoon, was almost entirely overturned on the side, thus discovering a young whale, which she was in process of suckling.

This circumstance, as Captain Hull well knew, would render the capture of the jubarte much more difficult. The mother was evidently going to defend herself with greater fury, as much for herself as to protect her "little one "—if, indeed, we can apply that epithet to an animal which did not measure less than twenty feet.

Meanwhile, the jubarte did not rush at the boat, as there was reason to fear, and there was no necessity, before taking flight, to quickly cut the line which connected the boat with the harpoon. On the contrary, and as generally happens, the whale, followed by the young one, dived, at first in a very oblique line; then rising again with an immense bound, she commenced to cleave the waters with extreme rapidity.

But before she had made her first plunge, Captain Hull and the boatswain, both standing, had had time to see her, and consequently to estimate her at her true value.

This jubarte was, in reality, a whale of the largest size. From the head to the tail, she measured at least eighty feet. Her skin, of a yellowish brown, was much varied with numerous spots of a darker brown.

It would indeed be a pity, after an attack so happily begun, to be under the necessity of abandoning so rich a prey.

The pursuit, or rather the towing, had commenced. The whale-boat, whose oars had been raised, darted like an arrow while swinging on the tops of the waves.

Howik kept it steady, notwithstanding those rapid and frightful oscillations. Captain Hull, his eye on his prey, did not cease making his eternal refrain:

"Be watchful, Howik, be watchful!"

And they could be sure that the boatswain's vigilance would not be at fault for an instant.

Meanwhile, as the whale-boat did not fly nearly as fast as the whale, the line of the harpoon spun out with such rapidity that it was to be feared that it would take fire in rubbing against the edge of the whale-boat. So Captain Hull took care to keep it damp, by filling with water the pail at the bottom of which the line was coiled.

All this time the jubarte did not seem inclined to stop her flight, nor willing to moderate it. The second line was then lashed to the end of the first, and it was not long before it was played out with the same velocity.

At the end of five minutes it was necessary to join on the third line, which ran off under the water.

The jubarte did not stop. The harpoon had evidently not penetrated into any vital part of the body. They could even observe, by the increased obliquity of the line, that the animal, instead of returning to the surface, was sinking into lower depths.

"The devil!" cried Captain Hull, "but that rascal will use up our five lines!"

"And lead us to a good distance from the 'Pilgrim,'" replied the boatswain.

"Nevertheless, she must return to the surface to breathe," replied Captain Hull. "She is not a fish, and she must have the provision of air like a common individual."

"She has held her breath to run better," said one of the sailors, laughing.

In fact, the line was unrolling all the time with equal rapidity.

To the third line, it was soon necessary to join the fourth, and that was not done without making the sailors somewhat anxious touching their future part of the prize.

"The devil! the devil!" murmured Captain Hull. "I have never seen anything like that! Devilish jubarte!"

Finally the fifth line had to be let out, and it was already half unrolled when it seemed to slacken.

"Good! good!" cried Captain Hull. "The line is less stiff. The jubarte is getting tired."

At that moment, the "Pilgrim" was more than five miles to the leeward of the whale-boat. Captain Hull, hoisting a flag at the end of a boat-hook, gave the signal to come nearer.

And almost at once, he could see that Dick Sand, aided by Tom and his companions, commenced to brace the yards in such a manner as to trim them close to the wind.

But the breeze was feeble and irregular. It only came in short puffs. Most certainly, the "Pilgrim" would have some trouble in joining the whale-boat, if indeed she could reach it. Meanwhile, as they had foreseen, the jubarte had returned to the surface of the water to breathe, with the harpoon fixed in her side all the time. She then remained almost motionless, seeming to wait for her young whale, which this furious course must have left behind.

Captain Hull made use of the oars so as to join her again, and soon he was only a short distance from her.

Two oars were laid down and two sailors armed themselves, as the captain had done, with long lances, intended to strike the enemy.

Howik worked skilfully then, and held himself ready to make the boat turn rapidly, in case the whale should turn suddenly on it.

"Attention!" cried Captain Hull. "Do not lose a blow! Aim well, boys!

Are we ready, Howik?"

"I am prepared, sir," replied the boatswain, "but one thing troubles me. It is that the beast, after having fled so rapidly, is very quiet now."

"In fact, Howik, that seems to me suspicious. Let us be careful!"

"Yes, but let us go forward."

Captain Hull grew more and more animated.

The boat drew still nearer. The jubarte only turned in her place. Her young one was no longer near her; perhaps she was trying to find it again.

Suddenly she made a movement with her tail, which took her thirty feet away.

Was she then going to take flight again, and must they take up this interminable pursuit again on the surface of the waters?

"Attention!" cried Captain Hull. "The beast is going to take a spring and throw herself on us. Steer, Howik, steer!"

The jubarte, in fact, had turned in such a manner as to present herself in front of the whale-boat. Then, beating the sea violently with her enormous fins, she rushed forward.

The boatswain, who expected this direct blow, turned in such a fashion that the jubarte passed by the boat, but without reaching it.

Captain Hull and the two sailors gave her three vigorous thrusts on the passage, seeking to strike some vital organ.

The jubarte stopped, and, throwing to a great height two columns of water mingled with blood, she turned anew on the boat, bounding, so to say, in a manner frightful to witness.

These seamen must have been expert fishermen, not to lose their presence of mind on this occasion.

Howik again skilfully avoided the jubarte's attack, by darting the boat aside.

Three new blows, well aimed, again gave the animal three new wounds. But, in passing, she struck the water so roughly with her formidable tail, that an enormous wave arose, as if the sea were suddenly opened.

The whale-boat almost capsized, and, the water rushing in over the side, it was half filled.

"The bucket, the bucket!" cried Captain Hull.

The two sailors, letting go their oars, began to bale out the boat rapidly, while the captain cut the line, now become useless.

No! the animal, rendered furious by grief, no longer dreamt of flight.

It was her turn to attack, and her agony threatened to be terrible.

A third time she turned round, "head to head," a seaman would say, and threw herself anew on the boat.

But the whale-boat, half full of water, could no longer move with the same facility. In this condition, how could it avoid the shock which threatened it? If it could be no longer steered, there was still less power to escape.

And besides, no matter how quickly the boat might be propelled, the swift jubarte would have always overtaken it with a few bounds. It was no longer a question of attack, but of defense.

Captain Hull understood it all.

The third attack of the animal could not be entirely kept off. In passing she grazed the whale-boat with her enormous dorsal fin, but with so much force that Howik was thrown down from his bench.

The three lances, unfortunately affected by the oscillation, this time missed their aim.

"Howik! Howik!" cried Captain Hull, who himself had been hardly able to keep his place.

"Present!" replied the boatswain, as he got up. But he then perceived that in his fall his stern oar had broken in the middle.

"Another oar!" said Captain Hull.

"I have one," replied Howik.

At that moment, a bubbling took place under the waters only a few fathoms from the boat.

The young whale had just reappeared. The jubarte saw it, and rushed towards it.

This circumstance could only give a more terrible character to the contest. The whale was going to fight for two.

Captain Hull looked toward the "Pilgrim." His hand shook the boat-hook, which bore the flag, frantically.

What could Dick Sand do that had not been already done at the first signal from the captain? The "Pilgrim's" sails were trimmed, and the wind commenced to fill them. Unhappily the schooner did not possess a helix, by which the action could be increased to sail faster.

To lower one of the boats, and, with the aid of the blacks, row to the assistance of the captain, would be a considerable loss of time; besides, the novice had orders not to quit the ship, no matter what happened. However, he had the stern-boat lowered from its pegs, and towed it along, so that the captain and his companions might take refuge in it, in case of need.

At that moment the jubarte, covering the young whale with her body, had returned to the charge. This time she turned in such a manner as to reach the boat exactly.

"Attention, Howik!" cried Captain Hull, for the last time.

But the boatswain was, so to speak, disarmed. Instead of a lever, whose length gave force, he only held in his hand an oar relatively short. He tried to put about; it was impossible.

The sailors knew that they were lost. All rose, giving a terrible cry, which was perhaps heard on the "Pilgrim."

A terrible blow from the monster's tail had just struck the whale-boat underneath. The boat, thrown into the air with irresistible violence, fell back, broken in three pieces, in the midst of waves furiously lashed by the whale's bounds.

The unfortunate sailors, although grievously wounded, would have had, perhaps, the strength to keep up still, either by swimming or by hanging on to some of the floating wreck. That is what Captain Hull did, for he was seen for a moment hoisting the boatswain on a wreck.

But the jubarte, in the last degree of fury, turned round, sprang up, perhaps in the last pangs of a terrible agony, and with her tail she beat the troubled waters frightfully, where the unfortunate sailors were still swimming.

For some minutes one saw nothing but a liquid water-spout scattering itself in sheafs on all sides.

A quarter of an hour after, when Dick Sand, who, followed by the blacks, had rushed into the boat, had reached the scene of the catastrophe, every living creature had disappeared. There was nothing left but some pieces of the whale-boat on the surface of the waters, red with blood.

## CHAPTER IX.
## CAPTAIN SAND.

The first impression felt by the passengers of the "Pilgrim" in presence of this terrible catastrophe was a combination of pity and horror. They only thought of this frightful death of Captain Hull and the five sailors. This fearful scene had just taken place almost under their eyes, while they could do nothing to save the poor men. They had not even been able to arrive in time to pick up the whale-boat's crew, their unfortunate companions, wounded, but still living, and to oppose the "Pilgrim's" hull to the jubarte's formidable blows. Captain Hull and his men had forever disappeared.

When the schooner arrived at the fatal place, Mrs. Weldon fell on her knees, her hands raised toward Heaven.

"Let us pray!" said the pious woman.

She was joined by her little Jack, who threw himself on his knees, weeping, near his mother. The poor child understood it all. Dick Sand, Nan, Tom, and the other blacks remained standing, their heads bowed. All repeated the prayer that Mrs. Weldon addressed to God, recommending to His infinite goodness those who had just appeared before Him.

Then Mrs. Weldon, turning to her companions, "And now, my friends," said she, "let us ask Heaven for strength and courage for ourselves."

Yes! They could not too earnestly implore the aid of Him who can do all things, for their situation was one of the gravest!

This ship which carried them had no longer a captain to command her, no longer a crew to work her. She was in the middle of that immense Pacific Ocean, hundreds of miles from any land, at the mercy of the winds and waves.

What fatality then had brought that whale in the "Pilgrim's" course? What still greater fatality had urged the unfortunate Captain Hull, generally so wise, to risk everything in order to complete his cargo? And what a catastrophe to count among the rarest of the annals of whale-fishing was this one, which did not allow of the saving of one of the whale-boat's sailors!

Yes, it was a terrible fatality! In fact, there was no longer a seaman on board the "Pilgrim." Yes, one—Dick Sand—and he was only a beginner, a young man of fifteen. Captain, boatswain, sailors, it may be said that the whole crew was now concentrated in him.

On board there was one lady passenger, a mother and her son, whose presence would render the situation much more difficult. Then there were also some blacks, honest men, courageous and zealous without a doubt, ready to obey whoever should undertake to command them, but ignorant of the simplest notions of the sailor's craft.

Dick Sand stood motionless, his arms crossed, looking at the place where Captain Hull had just been swallowed up—Captain Hull, his protector, for whom he felt a filial affection. Then his eyes searched the horizon, seeking to discover some ship, from which he would demand aid and assistance, to which he might be able at least to confide Mrs. Weldon. He would not abandon the "Pilgrim," no, indeed, without having tried his best to bring her into port. But Mrs. Weldon and her little boy would be in safety. He would have had nothing more to fear for those two beings, to whom he was devoted body and soul.

The ocean was deserted. Since the disappearance of the jubarte, not a speck came to alter the surface. All was sky and water around the "Pilgrim." The young novice knew only too well that he was beyond the routes followed by the ships of commerce, and that the other whalers were cruising still farther away at the fishing-grounds.

However, the question was, to look the situation in the face, to see things as they were. That is what Dick Sand did, asking God, from the depths of his heart, for aid and succor. What resolution was he going to take?

At that moment Negoro appeared on the deck, which he had left after the catastrophe. What had been felt in the presence of this irreparable misfortune by a being so enigmatical, no one could tell. He had contemplated the disaster without making a gesture, without departing from his speechlessness. His eye had evidently seized all the details of it. But if at such a moment one could think of observing him, he would be astonished at least, because not a muscle of his impassible face had moved. At any rate, and as if he had not heard it, he had not responded to the pious appeal of Mrs. Weldon, praying for the engulfed crew. Negoro walked aft, there even where Dick Sand was standing motionless. He stopped three steps from the novice.

"You wish to speak to me?" asked Dick Sand.

"I wish to speak to Captain Hull," replied Negoro, coolly, "or, in his absence, to boatswain Howik."

"You know well that both have perished!" cried the novice.

"Then who commands on board now?" asked Negoro, very insolently.

"I," replied Dick Sand, without hesitation.

"You!" said Negoro, shrugging his shoulders. "A captain of fifteen years?"

"A captain of fifteen years!" replied the novice, advancing toward the cook.

The latter drew back.

"Do not forget it," then said Mrs. Weldon. "There is but one captain here—Captain Sand, and it is well for all to remember that he will know how to make himself obeyed."

Negoro bowed, murmuring in an ironical tone a few words that they could not understand, and he returned to his post.

We see, Dick's resolution was taken.

Meanwhile the schooner, under the action of the breeze, which commenced to freshen, had already passed beyond the vast shoal of crustaceans.

Dick Sand examined the condition of the sails; then his eyes were cast on the deck. He had then this sentiment, that, if a frightful responsibility fell upon him in the future, it was for him to have the strength to accept it. He dared to look at the survivors of the "Pilgrim," whose eyes were now fixed on him. And, reading in their faces that he could count on them, he said to them in two words, that they could in their turn count on him.

Dick Sand had, in all sincerity, examined his conscience.

If he was capable of taking in or setting the sails of the schooner, according to circumstances, by employing the arms of Tom and his companions, he evidently did not yet possess all the knowledge necessary to determine his position by calculation.

In four or five years more, Dick Sand would know thoroughly that beautiful and difficult sailor's craft. He would know how to use the sextant—that instrument which Captain Hull's hand had held every day, and which gave him the height of the stars. He would read on the chronometer the hour of the meridian of Greenwich, and from it would be able to deduce the longitude by the hour angle. The sun would be made his counselor each day. The moon—the planets would say to him, "There, on that point of the ocean, is thy ship!" That firmament, on which the stars move like the hands of a perfect clock, which nothing shakes nor can derange, and whose accuracy is absolute—that firmament would tell him the hours and the distances. By astronomical observations he would know, as his captain had known every day, nearly to a mile, the place occupied by the "Pilgrim," and the course followed as well as the course to follow.

And now, by reckoning, that is by the progress measured on the log, pointed out by the compass, and corrected by the drift, he must alone ask his way.

However, he did not falter.

Mrs. Weldon understood all that was passing in the young novice's resolute heart.

"Thank you, Dick," she said to him, in a voice which did not tremble. "Captain Hull is no more. All his crew have perished with him. The fate of the ship is in your hands! Dick, you will save the ship and those on board!"

"Yes, Mrs. Weldon," replied Dick Sand, "yes! I shall attempt it, with the aid of God!"

"Tom and his companions are honest men on whom you can depend entirely."

"I know it, and I shall make sailors of them, and we shall work together. With fine weather that will be easy. With bad weather—well, with bad weather, we shall strive, and we shall save you yet, Mrs. Weldon—you and your little Jack, both! Yes, I feel that I shall do it."

And he repeated:

"With the aid of God!"

"Now, Dick, can you tell where the 'Pilgrim' is?" asked Mrs. Weldon.

"Easily," replied the novice. "I have only to consult the chart on board, on which her position was marked yesterday by Captain Hull."

"And will you be able to put the ship in the right direction?"

"Yes, I shall be able to put her prow to the east, nearly at the point of the American coast that we must reach."

"But, Dick," returned Mrs. Weldon, "you well understand, do you not, that this catastrophe may, and indeed must, modify our first projects? It is no longer a question of taking the 'Pilgrim' to Valparaiso. The nearest port of the American coast is now her port of destination."

"Certainly, Mrs. Weldon," replied the novice. "So fear nothing! We cannot fail to reach that American coast which stretches so far to the south."

"Where is it situated?" asked Mrs. Weldon.

"There, in that direction," replied Dick Sand, pointing to the east, which he knew by means of the compass.

"Well, Dick, we may reach Valparaiso, or any other part of the coast. What matter? What we want is to land."

"And we shall do it, Mrs. Weldon, and I shall land you on a good place," replied the young man, in a firm voice. "Besides, in standing in for the land, I do not renounce the hope of encountering some of those vessels which do the coasting trade on that shore. Ah! Mrs. Weldon, the wind begins to blow steadily from the northwest! God grant that it may keep on; we shall make progress, and good progress. We shall drive in the offing with all our sails set, from the brigantine to the flying-jib!"

Dick Sand had spoken with the confidence of the seaman, who feels that he stands on a good ship, a ship of whose every movement he is master. He was going to take the helm and call his companions to set the sails properly, when Mrs. Weldon reminded him that he ought first to know the "Pilgrim's" position.

It was, indeed, the first thing to do. Dick Sand went into the captain's cabin for the chart on which the position of the day before was indicated. He could then show Mrs. Weldon that the schooner was in latitude 43° 35', and in longitude 164° 13', for, in the last twenty-four hours, she had not, so to say, made any progress.

Mrs. Weldon leaned over this chart. She looked at the brown color which represented the land on the right of the ocean. It was the coast of South America, an immense barrier thrown between the Pacific and the Atlantic from Cape Horn to the shores of Columbia. To consider it in that way, that chart, which, was then spread out under her eyes, on which was drawn a whole ocean, gave the impression that it would be easy to restore the "Pilgrim's" passengers to their country. It is an illusion which is invariably produced on one who is not familiar with the scale on which marine charts are drawn. And, in fact, it seemed to Mrs. Weldon that the land ought to be in sight, as it was on that piece of paper!

And, meanwhile, on that white page, the "Pilgrim" drawn on an exact scale, would be smaller than the most microscopic of infusoria! That mathematical point, without appreciable dimensions, would appear lost, as it was in reality in the immensity of the Pacific!

Dick Sand himself had not experienced the same impression as Mrs. Weldon. He knew how far off the land was, and that many hundreds of miles would not suffice to measure the distance from it. But he had taken his part; he had become a man under the responsibility which had fallen upon him.

The moment to act had come. He must profit by this northwest breeze which was blowing up. Contrary winds had given place to favorable winds, and some clouds scattered in the zenith under the cirrous form, indicated that they would blow steadily for at least a certain time.

Dick called Tom and his companions.

"My friends," he said to them, "our ship has no longer any crew but you. I cannot work without your aid. You are not sailors, but you have good arms. Place them, then, at the 'Pilgrim's' service and we can steer her. Every one's salvation depends on the good work of every one on board."

"Mr. Dick," replied Tom, "my companions and I, we are your sailors. Our good will shall not be wanting. All that men can do, commanded by you, we shall do it."

"Well spoken, old Tom," said Mrs. Weldon.

"Yes, well spoken," continued Dick Sand; "but we must be prudent, and I shall not carry too much canvas, so as not to run any risk. Circumstances require a little less speed, but more security. I will show you, my friends, what each will have to do in the work. As to me, I shall remain at the helm, as long as fatigue does not oblige me to leave it. From time to time a few hours' sleep will be sufficient to restore me. But, during those few hours, it will be very necessary for one of you to take my place. Tom, I shall show you how we steer by means of the mariner's compass. It is not difficult, and, with a little attention, you will soon learn to keep the ship's head in the right direction."

"Whenever you like, Mr. Dick," replied the old black.

"Well," replied the novice, "stay near me at the helm till the end of the day, and if fatigue overcomes me, you will then be able to replace me for a few hours."

"And I," said little Jack, "will I not be able to help my friend, Dick, a little?"

"Yes, dear child," replied Mrs. Weldon, clasping Jack in her arms, "you shall learn to steer, and I am sure that while you are at the helm we shall have good winds."

"Very sure—very sure. Mother, I promise it to you," replied the little boy, clapping his hands.

"Yes," said the young novice, smiling, "good cabin-boys know how to maintain good winds. That is well known by old sailors." Then, addressing Tom, and the other blacks: "My friends," he said to them, "we are going to put the 'Pilgrim' under full sail. You will only have to do what I shall tell you."

"At your orders," replied Tom, "at your orders, Captain Sand."

## CHAPTER X.

## THE FOUR DAYS WHICH FOLLOW.

Dick Sand was then captain of the "Pilgrim," and, without losing an instant, he took the necessary measures for putting the ship under full sail.

It was well understood that the passengers could have only one hope—that of reaching some part of the American coast, if not Valparaiso. What Dick Sand counted on doing was to ascertain the direction and speed of the "Pilgrim," so as to get an average. For that, it was sufficient to make each day on the chart the way made, as it has been said, by the log and the compass. There was then on board one of those "patent logs," with an index and helix, which give the speed very exactly for a fixed time. This useful instrument, very easily handled, could render the most useful services, and the blacks were perfectly adapted to work it.

A single cause of error would interfere—the currents. To combat it, reckoning would be insufficient; astronomical observations alone would enable one to render an exact calculation from it. Now, those observations the young novice was still unable to make.

For an instant Dick Sand had thought of bringing the "Pilgrim" back to New Zealand. The passage would be shorter, and he would certainly have done it if the wind, which, till then, had been contrary, had not become favorable. Better worth while then to steer for America.

In fact, the wind had changed almost to the contrary direction, and now it blew from the northwest with a tendency to freshen. It was then necessary to profit by it and make all the headway possible.

So Dick Sand prepared to put the "Pilgrim" under full sail.

In a schooner brig-rigged, the foremast carries four square sails; the foresail, on the lower mast; above, the top-sail, on the topmast; then, on the top-gallant mast, a top-sail and a royal.

The mainmast, on the contrary, has fewer sails. It only carries a brigantine below, and a fore-staffsail above. Between these two masts, on the stays which support them at the prow, a triple row of triangular sails may be set.

Finally, at the prow, on the bowsprit, and its extreme end, were hauled the three jibs.

The jibs, the brigantine, the fore-staff, and the stay-sails are easily managed. They can be hoisted from the deck without the necessity of climbing the masts, because they are not fastened on the yards by means of rope-bands, which must be previously loosened.

On the contrary, the working of the foremast sails demands much greater proficiency in seamanship. In fact, when it is necessary to set them, the sailors must climb by the rigging—it may be in the foretop, it may be on the spars of the top-gallant mast, it may be to the top of the said mast—and that, as well in letting them fly as in drawing them in to diminish their surface in reefing them. Thence the necessity of running out on foot-ropes—movable ropes stretched below the yards—of working with one hand while holding on by the other—perilous work for any one who is not used to it. The oscillation from the rolling and pitching of the ship, very much increased by the length of the lever, the flapping of the sails under a stiff breeze, have often sent a man overboard. It was then a truly dangerous operation for Tom and his companions.

Very fortunately, the wind was moderate. The sea had not yet had time to become rough. The rolling and pitching kept within bounds.

When Dick Sand, at Captain Hull's signal, had steered toward the scene of the catastrophe, the "Pilgrim" only carried her jibs, her brigantine, her foresail, and her top-sail. To get the ship under way as quickly as possible, the novice had only to make use of, that is, to counter-brace, the foresail. The blacks had easily helped him in that maneuver.

The question now was to get under full sail, and, to complete the sails, to hoist the top-sails, the royal, the fore-staff, and the stay-sails.

"My friends," said the novice to the five blacks, "do as I tell you, and all will go right."

Dick Sand was standing at the wheel of the helm.

"Go!" cried he. "Tom, let go that rope quickly!"

"Let go?" said Tom, who did not understand that expression.

"Yes, loosen it! Now you, Bat—the same thing! Good! Heave—haul taut. Let us see, pull it in!"

"Like that?" said Bat.

"Yes, like that. Very good. Come, Hercules—strong. A good pull there!"

To say "strong" to Hercules was, perhaps, imprudent. The giant of course gave a pull that brought down the rope.

"Oh! not so strong, my honest fellow!" cried Dick Sand, smiling. "You are going to bring down the masts!"

"I have hardly pulled," replied Hercules.

"Well, only make believe! You will see that that will be enough! Well, slacken—cast off! Make fast—Make fast—like that! Good! All together! Heave—pull on the braces."

And the whole breadth of the foremast, whose larboard braces had been loosened, turned slowly. The wind then swelling the sails imparted a certain speed to the ship.

Dick Sand then had the jib sheet-ropes loosened. Then he called the blacks aft:

"Behold what is done, my friends, and well done. Now let us attend to the mainmast. But break nothing, Hercules."

"I shall try," replied the colossus, without being willing to promise more.

This second operation was quite easy. The main-boom sheet-rope having been let go gently, the brigantine took the wind more regularly, and added its powerful action to that of the forward sails.

The fore-staff was then set above the brigantine, and, as it is simply brailed up, there was nothing to do but bear on the rope, to haul aboard, then to secure it. But Hercules pulled so hard, along with his friend Acteon, without counting little Jack, who had joined them, that the rope broke off.

All three fell backwards—happily, without hurting themselves. Jack was enchanted.

"That's nothing! that's nothing!" cried the novice. "Fasten the two ends together for this time and hoist softly!"

That was done under Dick Sand's eyes, while he had not yet left the helm. The "Pilgrim" was already sailing rapidly, headed to the east, and there was nothing more to be done but keep it in that direction. Nothing easier, because the wind was favorable, and lurches were not to be feared.

"Good, my friends!" said the novice. "You will be good sailors before the end of the voyage!"

"We shall do our best, Captain Sand," replied Tom.

Mrs. Weldon also complimented those honest men.

Little Jack himself received his share of praise, for he had worked bravely.

"Indeed, I believe, Mr. Jack," said Hercules, smiling, "that it was you who broke the rope. What a good little fist you have. Without you we should have done nothing right."

And little Jack, very proud of himself, shook his friend Hercules' hand vigorously.

The setting of the "Pilgrim's" sails was not yet complete. She still lacked those top-sails whose action is not to be despised under this full-sail movement. Top-sail, royal, stay-sails, would add sensibly to the schooner's speed, and Dick Sand resolved to set them.

This operation would be more difficult than the others, not for the stay-sails, which could be hoisted, hauled aboard and fastened from below, but for the cross-jacks of the foremast. It was necessary to climb to the spars to let them out, and Dick Sand, not wishing to expose any one of his improvised crew, undertook to do it himself.

He then called Tom and put him at the wheel, showing him how he should keep the ship. Then Hercules, Bat, Acteon and Austin being placed, some at the royal halyards, others at those of the top-sails, he proceeded up the mast. To climb the rattlings of the fore-shrouds, then the rattlings of the topmast-shrouds, to gain the spars, that was only play for the young novice. In a minute he was on the foot-rope of the top-sail yard, and he let go the rope-bands which kept the sail bound.

Then he stood on the spars again and climbed on the royal yard, where he let out the sail rapidly.

Dick Sand had finished his task, and seizing one of the starboard backstays, he slid to the deck.

There, under his directions, the two sails were vigorously hauled and fastened, then the two yards hoisted to the block. The stay-sails being set next between the mainmast and the foremast, the work was finished. Hercules had broken nothing this time.

The "Pilgrim" then carried all the sails that composed her rigging. Doubtless Dick Sand could still add the foremast studding-sails to larboard, but it was difficult work under the present circumstances, and should it be necessary to take them in, in case of a squall, it could not be done fast enough. So the novice stopped there.

Tom was relieved from his post at the wheel, which Dick Sand took charge of again.

The breeze freshened. The "Pilgrim," making a slight turn to starboard, glided rapidly over the surface of the sea, leaving behind her a very flat track, which bore witness to the purity of her water-line.

"We are well under way, Mrs. Weldon," then said Dick Sand, "and, now, may God preserve this favorable wind!"

Mrs. Weldon pressed the young man's hand. Then, fatigued with all the emotions of that last hour, she sought her cabin, and fell into a sort of painful drowsiness, which was not sleep.

The new crew remained on the schooner's deck, watching on the forecastle, and ready to obey Dick Sand's orders—that is to say, to change the set of the sails according to the variations of the wind; but so long as the breeze kept both that force and that direction, there would be positively nothing to do.

During all this time what had become of Cousin Benedict?

Cousin Benedict was occupied in studying with a magnifying glass an articulate which he had at last found on board—a simple orthopter, whose head disappeared under the prothorax; an insect with flat elytrums, with round abdomen, with rather long wings, which belonged to the family of the roaches, and to the species of American cockroaches.

It was exactly while ferreting in Negoro's kitchen, that he had made that precious discovery, and at the moment when the cook was going to crush the said insect pitilessly. Thence anger, which, indeed, Negoro took no notice of.

But this Cousin Benedict, did he know what change had taken place on board since the moment when Captain Hull and his companions had commenced that fatal whale-fishing? Yes, certainly. He was even on the deck when the "Pilgrim" arrived in sight of the remains of the whale-boat. The schooner's crew had then perished before his eyes.

To pretend that this catastrophe had not affected him, would be to accuse his heart. That pity for others that all people feel, he had certainly experienced it. He was equally moved by his cousin's situation. He had come to press Mrs. Weldon's hand, as if to say to her: "Do not be afraid. I am here. I am left to you."

Then Cousin Benedict had turned toward his cabin, doubtless so as to reflect on the consequences of this disastrous event, and on the energetic measures that he must take. But on his way he had met the cockroach in question, and his desire was—held, however, against certain entomologists— to prove the cockroaches of the phoraspe species, remarkable for their colors, have very different habits from cockroaches properly so called; he had given himself up to the study, forgetting both that there had been a Captain Hull in command of the "Pilgrim," and that that unfortunate had just perished with his crew. The cockroach absorbed him entirely. He did not admire it less, and he made as much time over it as if that horrible insect had been a golden beetle.

The life on board had then returned to its usual course, though every one would remain for a long time yet under the effects of such a keen and unforeseen catastrophe.

During this day Dick Sand was everywhere, so that everything should be in its place, and that he could be prepared for the smallest contingency. The blacks obeyed him with zeal. The most perfect order reigned on board the "Pilgrim." It might then be hoped that all would go well.

On his side, Negoro made no other attempt to resist Dick Sand's authority. He appeared to have tacitly recognized him. Occupied as usual in his narrow kitchen, he was not seen more than before. Besides, at the least infraction—at the first symptom of insubordination, Dick Sand was determined to send him to the hold for the rest of the passage. At a sign from him, Hercules would take the head cook by the skin of the neck; that would not have taken long. In that case, Nan, who knew how to cook, would replace the cook in his functions. Negoro then could say to himself that he was indispensable, and, as he was closely watched, he seemed unwilling to give any cause of complaint.

The wind, though growing stronger till evening, did not necessitate any change in the "Pilgrim's" sails. Her solid masting, her iron rigging, which was in good condition, would enable her to bear in this condition even a stronger breeze.

During the night it is often the custom to lessen the sails, and particularly to take in the high sails, fore-staff, top-sail, royal, etc. That is prudent, in case some squall of wind should come up suddenly. But Dick Sand believed he could dispense with this precaution. The state of the atmosphere indicated nothing of the kind, and besides, the young novice determined to pass the first night on the deck, intending to have an eye to everything. Then the progress was more rapid, and he longed to be in less desolate parts.

It has been said that the log and the compass were the only instruments which Dick Sand could use, so as to estimate approximately the way made by the "Pilgrim."

During this day the novice threw the log every half-hour, and he noted the indications furnished by the instrument.

As to the instrument which bears the name of compass, there were two on board. One was placed in the binnacle, under the eyes of the man at the helm. Its dial, lighted by day by the diurnal light, by night by two side-lamps, indicated at every moment which way the ship headed—that is, the direction she followed. The other compass was an inverted one, fixed to the bars of the cabin which Captain Hull formerly occupied. By that means, without leaving his chamber, he could always know if the route given was exactly followed, if the man at the helm, from ignorance or negligence, allowed the ship to make too great lurches.

Besides, there is no ship employed in long voyages which does not possess at least two compasses, as she has two chronometers. It is necessary to compare these instruments with each other, and, consequently, control their indications.

The "Pilgrim" was then sufficiently provided for in that respect, and Dick Sand charged his men to take the greatest care of the two compasses, which were so necessary to him.

Now, unfortunately, during the night of the 12th to the 13th of February, while the novice was on watch, and holding the wheel of the helm, a sad accident took place. The inverted compass, which was fastened by a copper ferule to the woodwork of the cabin, broke off and fell on the floor. It was not seen till the next day.

How had the ferule come to break. It was inexplicable enough. It was possible, however, that it was oxydized, and that the pitching and rolling had broken it from the woodwork. Now, indeed, the sea had been rougher during the night. However it was, the compass was broken in such a manner that it could not be repaired.

Dick Sand was much thwarted. Henceforth he was reduced to trust solely to the compass in the binnacle. Very evidently no one was responsible for the breaking of the second compass, but it might have sad consequences. The novice then took every precaution to keep the other compass beyond the reach of every accident.

Till then, with that exception, all went well on board the "Pilgrim."

Mrs. Weldon, seeing Dick Sand's calmness, had regained confidence. It was not that she had ever yielded to despair. Above all, she counted on the goodness of God. Also, as a sincere and pious Catholic, she comforted herself by prayer.

Dick Sand had arranged so as to remain at the helm during the night. He slept five or six hours in the day, and that seemed enough for him, as he did not feel too much fatigued. During this time Tom or his son Bat took his place at the wheel of the helm, and, thanks to his counsels, they were gradually becoming passable steersmen.

Often Mrs. Weldon and the novice talked to each other. Dick Sand willingly took advice from this intelligent and courageous woman. Each day he showed her on the ship's chart the course run, which he took by reckoning, taking into account only the direction and the speed of the ship. "See, Mrs.

Weldon," he often repeated to her, "with these winds blowing, we cannot fail to reach the coast of South America. I should not like to affirm it, but I verily believe that when our vessel shall arrive in sight of land, it will not be far from Valparaiso."

Mrs. Weldon could not doubt the direction of the vessel was right, favored above all by those winds from the northwest. But how far the "Pilgrim" still seemed to be from the American coast! How many dangers between her and the firm land, only counting those which might come from a change in the state of the sea and the sky!

Jack, indifferent like children of his age, had returned to his usual games, running on the deck, amusing himself with Dingo. He found, of course, that his friend Dick was less with him than formerly; but his mother had made him understand that they must leave the young novice entirely to his occupations. Little Jack had given up to these reasons, and no longer disturbed "Captain Sand."

So passed life on board. The blacks did their work intelligently, and each day became more skilful in the sailor's craft. Tom was naturally the boatswain, and it was he, indeed, whom his companions would have chosen for that office. He commanded the watch while the novice rested, and he had with him his son Bat and Austin. Acteon and Hercules formed the other watch, under Dick Sand's direction. By this means, while one steered, the others watched at the prow.

Even though these parts were deserted, and no collision was really to be feared, the novice exacted a rigorous watch during the night. He never sailed without having his lights in position—a green light on the starboard, a red light on the larboard—and in that he acted wisely.

All the time, during those nights which Dick Sand passed entirely at the helm, he occasionally felt an irresistible heaviness over him. His hand then steered by pure instinct. It was the effect of a fatigue of which he did not wish to take account.

Now, it happened that during the night of the 13th to the 14th of February, that Dick Sand was very tired, and was obliged to take a few hours' rest. He was replaced at the helm by old Tom.

The sky was covered with thick clouds, which had gathered with the evening, under the influence of the cold air. It was then very dark, and it was impossible to distinguish the high sails lost in the darkness. Hercules and Acteon were on watch on the forecastle.

Aft, the light from the binnacle only gave a faint gleam, which the metallic apparatus of the wheel reflected softly. The ship's lanterns throwing their lights laterally, left the deck of the vessel in profound darkness.

Toward three o'clock in the morning, a kind of hypnotic phenomenon took place, of which old Tom was not even conscious. His eyes, which were fixed too long on a luminous point of the binnacle, suddenly lost the power of vision, and he fell into a true anæsthetic sleep.

Not only was he incapable of seeing, but if one had touched or pinched him hard he would probably have felt nothing.

So he did not see a shadow which glided over the deck.

It was Negoro.

Arrived aft, the head cook placed under the binnacle a pretty heavy object which he held in hand.

Then, after observing for an instant the luminous index of the compass, he retired without having been seen.

If, the next day, Dick Sand had perceived that object placed by Negoro under the binnacle, he might have hastened to take it away.

In fact, it was a piece of iron, whose influence had just altered the indications of the compass. The magnetic needle had been deviated, and instead of marking the magnetic north, which differs a little from the north of the world, it marked the northeast. It was then, a deviation of four points; in other words, of half a right angle.

Tom soon recovered from his drowsiness. His eyes were fixed on the compass. He believed, he had reason to believe, that the "Pilgrim" was not in the right direction. He then moved the helm so as to head the ship to the east—at least, he thought so.

But, with the deviation of the needle, which he could not suspect, that point, changed by four points, was the southeast.

And thus, while under the action of a favorable wind, the "Pilgrim" was supposed to follow the direction wished for, she sailed with an error of forty-five degrees in her route!

## CHAPTER XI.

### TEMPEST.

During the week which followed that event, from the 14th of February to the 21st, no incident took place on board. The wind from the northwest freshened gradually, and the "Pilgrim" sailed rapidly, making on an average one hundred and sixty miles in twenty-four hours. It was nearly all that could be asked of a vessel of that size.

Dick Sand thought the schooner must be approaching those parts more frequented by the merchant vessels which seek to pass from one hemisphere to the other. The novice was always hoping to encounter one of those ships, and he clearly intended either to transfer his passengers, or to borrow some additional sailors, and perhaps an officer. But, though he watched vigilantly, no ship could be signaled, and the sea was always deserted.

Dick Sand continued to be somewhat astonished at that. He had crossed this part of the Pacific several times during his three fishing voyages to the Southern Seas. Now, in the latitude and longitude where his reckoning put him, it was seldom that some English or American ship did not appear, ascending from Cape Horn toward the equator, or coming toward the extreme point of South America.

But what Dick Sand was ignorant of, what he could not even discover, was that the "Pilgrim" was already in higher latitude—that is to say, more to the south than he supposed. That was so for two reasons:

The first was, that the currents of these parts, whose swiftness the novice could only imperfectly estimate, had contributed—while he could not possibly keep account of them—to throw the ship out of her route.

The second was, that the compass, made inaccurate by Negoro's guilty hand, henceforth only gave incorrect bearings—bearings that, since the loss of the second compass, Dick Sand could not control. So that, believing, and having reason to believe, that he was sailing eastward, in reality, he was sailing southeast. The compass, it was always before his eyes. The log, it was thrown regularly. His two instruments permitted him, in a certain measure, to direct the "Pilgrim," and to estimate the number of miles sailed. But, then, was that sufficient?

However, the novice always did his best to reassure Mrs. Weldon, whom the incidents of this voyage must at times render anxious.

"We shall arrive, we shall arrive!" he repeated. "We shall reach the American coast, here or there; it matters little, on the whole, but we cannot fail to land there!"

"I do not doubt it, Dick."

"Of course, Mrs. Weldon, I should be more at ease if you were not on board—if we had only ourselves to answer for; but——"

"But if I were not on board," replied Mrs. Weldon; "if Cousin Benedict,

Jack, Nan and I, had not taken passage on the 'Pilgrim,' and if, on the other hand, Tom and his companions had not been picked up at sea, Dick, there would be only two men here, you and Negoro! What would have become of you, alone with that wicked man, in whom you cannot have confidence? Yes, my child, what would have become of you?"

"I should have begun," replied Dick Sand, resolutely, "by putting

Negoro where he could not injure me."

"And you would have worked alone?"

"Yes—alone—with the aid of God!"

The firmness of these words was well calculated to encourage Mrs. Weldon. But, nevertheless, while thinking of her little Jack, she often felt uneasy. If the woman would not show what she experienced as a mother, she did not always succeed in preventing some secret anguish for him to rend her heart.

Meanwhile, if the young novice was not sufficiently advanced in his hydrographic studies to make his point, he possessed a true sailor's scent, when the question was "to tell the weather." The appearance of the sky, for one thing; on the other hand, the indications of the barometer, enabled him to be on his guard. Captain Hull, a good meteorologist, had taught him to consult this instrument, whose prognostications are remarkably sure.

Here is, in a few words, what the notices relative to the observation of the barometer contain:

1. When, after a rather long continuance of fine weather, the barometer begins to fall in a sudden and continuous manner, rain will certainly fall; but, if the fine weather has had a long duration, the mercury may fall two or three days in the tube of the barometer before any change in the state of the atmosphere may be perceived. Then, the longer the time between the falling of the mercury and the arrival of the rain, the longer will be the duration of rainy weather.

2. If, on the contrary, during a rainy period which has already had a long duration, the barometer commences to rise slowly and regularly, very certainly fine weather will come, and it will last much longer if a long interval elapses between its arrival and the rising of the barometer.

3. In the two cases given, if the change of weather follows immediately the movement of the barometrical column, that change will last only a very short time.

4. If the barometer rises with slowness and in a continuous manner for two or three days, or even more, it announces fine weather, even when the rain will

not cease during those three days, and vice versa; but if the barometer rises two days or more during the rain, then, the fine weather having come, if it commences to fall again, the fine weather will last a very short time, and vice versa.

5. In the spring and in the autumn, a sudden fall of the barometer presages wind. In the summer, if the weather is very warm, it announces a storm. In winter, after a frost of some duration, a rapid falling of the barometrical column announces a change of wind, accompanied by a thaw and rain; but a rising which happens during a frost which has already lasted a certain time, prognosticates snow.

6. Rapid oscillations of the barometer should never be interpreted as presaging dry or rainy weather of any duration. Those indications are given exclusively by the rising or the falling which takes place in a slow and continuous manner.

7. Toward the end of autumn, if after prolonged rainy and windy weather, the barometer begins to rise, that rising announces the passage of the wind to the north and the approach of the frost.

Such are the general consequences to draw from the indications of this precious instrument.

Dick Sand knew all that perfectly well, as he had ascertained for himself in different circumstances of his sailor's life, which made him very skilful in putting himself on his guard against all contingencies.

Now, just toward the 20th of February, the oscillations of the barometrical column began to preoccupy the young novice, who noted them several times a day with much care. In fact, the barometer began to fall in a slow and continuous manner, which presages rain; but, this rain being delayed, Dick Sand concluded from that, that the bad weather would last. That is what must happen.

But the rain was the wind, and in fact, at that date, the breeze freshened so much that the air was displaced with a velocity of sixty feet a second, say thirty-one miles an hour.

Dick Sand was obliged to take some precautions so as not to risk the

"Pilgrim's" masting and sails.

Already he had the royal, the fore-staff, and the flying-jib taken in, and he resolved to do the same with the top-sail, then take in two reefs in the top-sail.

This last operation must present certain difficulties with a crew of little experience. Hesitation would not do, however, and no one hesitated. Dick Sand, accompanied by Bat and Austin, climbed into the rigging of the foremast, and succeeded, not without trouble, in taking in the top-sail. In less threatening weather he would have left the two yards on the mast, but, foreseeing that he would probably be obliged to level that mast, and perhaps even to lay it down upon the deck, he unrigged the two yards and sent them to the deck. In fact, it is understood that when the wind becomes too strong, not only must the sails be diminished, but also the masting. That is a great relief to the ship, which, carrying less weight above, is no longer so much strained with the rolling and pitching.

This first work accomplished—and it took two hours—Dick Sand and his companions were busy reducing the surface of the top-sail, by taking in two reefs. The "Pilgrim" did not carry, like the majority of modern ships, a double top-sail, which facilitates the operation. It was necessary, then, to work as formerly—that is to say, to run out on the foot-ropes, pull toward you a sail beaten by the wind, and lash it firmly with its reef-lines. It was difficult, long, perilous; but, finally, the diminished top-sail gave less surface to the wind, and the schooner was much relieved.

Dick Sand came down again with Bat and Austin. The "Pilgrim" was then in the sailing condition demanded by that state of the atmosphere which has been qualified as "very stiff."

During the three days which followed, 20th, 21st and 22d of February, the force and direction of the wind were not perceptibly changed. All the time the mercury continued to fall in the barometrical tube, and, on this last day, the novice noted that it kept continually below twenty-eight and seven-tenths inches.

Besides, there was no appearance that the barometer would rise for some time. The aspect of the sky was bad, and extremely windy. Besides, thick fogs covered it constantly. Their stratum was even so deep that the sun was no longer seen, and it would have been difficult to indicate precisely the place of his setting and rising.

Dick Sand began to be anxious. He no longer left the deck; he hardly slept. However, his moral energy enabled him to drive back his fears to the bottom of his heart.

The next day, February 22d, the breeze appeared to decrease a little in the morning, but Dick Sand did not trust in it. He was right, for in the afternoon the wind freshened again, and the sea became rougher.

Toward four o'clock, Negoro, who was rarely seen, left his post and came up on the forecastle. Dingo, doubtless, was sleeping in some corner, for it did not bark as usual.

Negoro, always silent, remained for half an hour observing the horizon.

Long surges succeeded each other without, as yet, being dashed together. However, they were higher than the force of the wind accounted for. One must conclude from that, that there was very bad weather in the west, perhaps at a rather short distance, and that it would not be long in reaching these parts.

Negoro watched that vast extent of sea, which was greatly troubled, around the "Pilgrim." Then his eyes, always cold and dry, turned toward the sky.

The aspect of the sky was disturbing. The vapors moved with very different velocities. The clouds of the upper zone traveled more rapidly than those of the low strata of the atmosphere. The case then must be foreseen, in which those heavy masses would fall, and might change into a tempest, perhaps a hurricane, what was yet only a very stiff breeze—that is to say, a displacement of the air at the rate of forty-three miles an hour.

Whether Negoro was not a man to be frightened, or whether he understood nothing of the threats of the weather, he did not appear to be affected. However, an evil smile glided over his lips. One would say, at the end of his observations, that this state of things was rather calculated to please him than to displease him. One moment he mounted on the bowsprit and crawled as far as the ropes, so as to extend his range of vision, as if he were seeking some indication on the horizon. Then he descended again, and tranquilly, without having pronounced a single word, without having made a gesture, he regained the crew's quarters.

Meanwhile, in the midst of all these fearful conjunctions, there remained one happy circumstance which each one on board ought to remember; it was that this wind, violent as it was or might become, was favorable, and that the "Pilgrim" seemed to be rapidly making the American coast. If, indeed, the weather did not turn to tempest, this navigation would continue to be accomplished without great danger, and the veritable perils would only spring up when the question would be to land on some badly ascertained point of the coast.

That was indeed what Dick Sand was already asking himself. When he should once make the land, how should he act, if he did not encounter some pilot, some one who knew the coast? In case the bad weather should oblige him to seek a port of refuge, what should he do, because that coast was to him absolutely unknown? Indeed, he had not yet to trouble himself with that contingency. However, when the hour should come, he would be obliged to adopt some plan. Well, Dick Sand adopted one.

During the thirteen days which elapsed, from the 24th of February to the 9th of March, the state of the atmosphere did not change in any perceptible manner. The sky was always loaded with heavy fogs. For a few hours the wind went down, then it began to blow again with the same force. Two or three times the barometer rose again, but its oscillation, comprising a dozen lines, was too sudden to announce a change of weather and a return of more manageable winds. Besides the barometrical column fell again almost immediately, and nothing could inspire any hope of the end of that bad weather within a short period.

Terrible storms burst forth also, which very seriously disturbed Dick Sand. Two or three times the lightning struck the waves only a few cable-lengths from the ship. Then the rain fell in torrents, and made those whirlpools of half condensed vapors, which surrounded the "Pilgrim" with a thick mist.

For entire hours the man at the lookout saw nothing, and the ship sailed at random.

Even though the ship, although resting firmly on the waves, was horribly shaken, Mrs. Weldon, fortunately, supported this rolling and pitching without being incommoded. But her little boy was very much tried, and she was obliged to give him all her care.

As to Cousin Benedict, he was no more sick than the American cockroaches which he made his society, and he passed his time in studying, as if he were quietly settled in his study in San Francisco.

Very fortunately, also, Tom and his companions found themselves little sensitive to sea-sickness, and they could continue to come to the young novice's aid—well accustomed, himself, to all those excessive movements of a ship which flies before the weather.

The "Pilgrim" ran rapidly under this reduced sail, and already Dick Sand foresaw that he would be obliged to reduce it again. But he wished to hold out as long as it would be possible to do so without danger. According to his reckoning, the coast ought to be no longer distant. So they watched with care. All the time the novice could hardly trust his companions' eyes to discover the first indications of land. In fact, no matter what good sight he may have, he who is not accustomed to interrogating the sea horizons is not skilful in distinguishing the first contours of a coast, above all in the middle of fogs. So Dick Sand must watch himself, and he often climbed as far as the spars to see better. But no sign yet of the American coast.

This astonished him, and Mrs. Weldon, by some words which escaped him, understood that astonishment.

It was the 9th of March. The novice kept at the prow, sometimes observing the sea and the sky, sometimes looking at the "Pilgrim's" masting, which began to strain under the force of the wind.

"You see nothing yet, Dick?" she asked him, at a moment when he had just left the long lookout.

"Nothing, Mrs. Weldon, nothing," replied the novice; and meanwhile, the horizon seems to clear a little under this violent wind, which is going to blow still harder."

"And, according to you, Dick, the American coast ought not to be distant now."

"It cannot be, Mrs. Weldon, and if anything astonishes me, it is not having made it yet."

"Meanwhile," continued Mrs. Weldon, "the ship has always followed the right course."

"Always, since the wind settled in the northwest," replied Dick Sand; "that is to say, since the day when we lost our unfortunate captain and his crew. That was the 10th of February. We are now on the 9th of March. There have been then, twenty-seven since that."

"But at that period what distance were we from the coast?" asked Mrs. Weldon.

"About four thousand five hundred miles, Mrs. Weldon. If there are things about which I have more than a doubt, I can at least guarantee this figure within about twenty miles."

"And what has been the ship's speed?"

"On an average, a hundred and eighty miles a day since the wind freshened," replied the novice. "So, I am surprised at not being in sight of land. And, what is still more extraordinary, is that we do not meet even a single one of those vessels which generally frequent these parts!"

"Could you not be deceived, Dick," returned Mrs. Weldon, "in estimating the 'Pilgrim's' speed?"

"No, Mrs. Weldon. On that point I could not be mistaken. The log has been thrown every half hour, and I have taken its indications very accurately. Wait, I am going to have it thrown anew, and you will see that we are sailing at this moment at the rate of ten miles an hour, which would give us more than two hundred miles a day."

Dick Sand called Tom, and gave him the order to throw the log, an operation to which the old black was now quite accustomed.

The log, firmly fastened to the end of the line, was brought and sent out.

Twenty-five fathoms were hardly unrolled, when the rope suddenly slackened between Tom's hands.

"Ah! Mr. Dick!" cried he.

"Well, Tom?"

"The rope has broken!"

"Broken!" cried Dick Sand. "And the log is lost!"

Old Tom showed the end of the rope which remained in his hand.

It was only too true. It was not the fastening which had failed. The rope had broken in the middle. And, nevertheless, that rope was of the first quality. It must have been, then, that the strands of the rope at the point of rupture were singularly worn! They were, in fact, and Dick Sand could tell that when he had the end of the rope in his hands! But had they become so by use? was what the novice, become suspicious, asked himself.

However that was, the log was now lost, and Dick Sand had no longer any means of telling exactly the speed of his ship. In the way of instruments, he only possessed one compass, and he did not know that its indications were false.

Mrs. Weldon saw him so saddened by this accident, that she did not wish to insist, and, with a very heavy heart, she retired into her cabin.

But if the "Pilgrim's" speed and consequently the way sailed over could no longer be estimated, it was easy to tell that the ship's headway was not diminishing.

In fact, the next day, March 10th, the barometer fell to twenty-eight and two-tenths inches. It was the announcement of one of those blasts of wind which travel as much as sixty miles an hour.

It became urgent to change once more the state of the sails, so as not to risk the security of the vessel.

Dick Sand resolved to bring down his top-gallant mast and his fore-staff, and to furl his low sails, so as to sail under his foretop-mast stay-sail and the low reef of his top-sail.

He called Tom and his companions to help him in that difficult operation, which, unfortunately, could not be executed with rapidity.

And meanwhile time pressed, for the tempest already declared itself with violence.

Dick Sands, Austin, Acteon, and Bat climbed into the masting, while Tom remained at the wheel, and Hercules on the deck, so as to slacken the ropes, as soon as he was commanded.

After numerous efforts, the fore-staff and the top-gallant mast were gotten down upon the deck, not without these honest men having a hundred times risked being precipitated into the sea, the rolling shook the masting to such an extent. Then, the top-sail having been lessened and the foresail furled, the schooner carried only her foretop-mast stay-sail and the low reef of the top-sail.

Even though her sails were then extremely reduced, the "Pilgrim" continued, none the less, to sail with excessive velocity.

The 12th the weather took a still worse appearance. On that day, at dawn, Dick Sand saw, not without terror, the barometer fall to twenty-seven and nine-tenths inches. It was a real tempest which was raging, and such that the "Pilgrim" could not carry even the little sail she had left.

Dick Sand, seeing that his top-sail was going to be torn, gave the order to furl. But it was in vain. A more violent gust struck the ship at that moment, and tore off the sail. Austin, who was on the yard of the foretop-sail, was struck by the larboard sheet-rope. Wounded, but rather slightly, he could climb down again to the deck.

Dick Sand, extremely anxious, had but one thought. It was that the ship, urged with such fury, was going to be dashed to pieces every moment; for, according to his calculation, the rocks of the coast could not be distant. He then returned to the prow, but he saw nothing which had the appearance of land, and then, came back to the wheel.

A moment after Negoro came on deck. There, suddenly, as if in spite of himself, his arm was extended toward a point of the horizon. One would say that he recognized some high land in the fogs!

Still, once more he smiled wickedly, and without saying anything of what he had been able to see, he returned to his post.

## CHAPTER XII.

### ON THE HORIZON.

At that date the tempest took its most terrible form, that of the hurricane. The wind had set in from the southwest. The air moved with a velocity of ninety miles an hour. It was indeed a hurricane, in fact, one of those terrible windstorms which wrecks all the ships of a roadstead, and which, even on land, the most solid structures cannot resist. Such was the one which, on the 25th of July, 1825, devastated Guadaloupe. When heavy cannons, carrying balls of twenty-four pounds, are raised from their carriages, one may imagine what would become of a ship which has no other point of support than an unsteady sea? And meanwhile, it is to its mobility alone that she may owe her salvation. She yields to the wind, and, provided she is strongly built, she is in a condition to brave the most violent surges. That was the case with the "Pilgrim."

A few minutes after the top-sail had been torn in pieces, the foretop-mast stay-sail was in its turn torn off. Dick Sand must then give up the idea of setting even a storm-jib—a small sail of strong linen, which would make the ship easier to govern.

The "Pilgrim" then ran without canvas, but the wind took effect on her hull, her masts, her rigging, and nothing more was needed to impart to her an excessive velocity. Sometimes even she seemed to emerge from the waves, and it was to be believed that she hardly grazed them. Under these circumstances, the rolling of the ship, tossed about on the enormous billows raised by the tempest, was frightful. There was danger of receiving some monstrous surge aft. Those mountains of water ran faster than the schooner, threatening to strike her stern if she did not rise pretty fast. That is extreme danger for every ship which scuds before the tempest. But what could be done to ward off that contingency? Greater speed could not be imparted to the "Pilgrim," because she would not have kept the smallest piece of canvas. She must then be managed as much as possible by means of the helm, whose action was often powerless.

Dick Sand no longer left the helm. He was lashed by the waist, so as not to be carried away by some surge. Tom and Bat, fastened also, stood near to help him. Hercules and Acteon, bound to the bitts, watched forward. As to Mrs. Weldon, to Little Jack, to Cousin Benedict, to Nan, they remained, by order of the novice, in the aft cabins. Mrs. Weldon would have preferred to have remained on deck, but Dick Sand was strongly opposed to it; it would be exposing herself uselessly.

All the scuttles had been hermetically nailed up. It was hoped that they would resist if some formidable billow should fall on the ship. If, by any mischance, they should yield under the weight of these avalanches, the ship might fill and sink. Very fortunately, also, the stowage had been well attended to, so that, notwithstanding the terrible tossing of the vessel, her cargo was not moved about.

Dick Sand had again reduced the number of hours which he gave to sleep. So Mrs. Weldon began to fear that he would take sick. She made him consent to take some repose.

Now, it was while he was still lying down, during the night of the 13th to the 14th of March, that a new incident took place.

Tom and Bat were aft, when Negoro, who rarely appeared on that part of the deck, drew near, and even seemed to wish to enter into conversation with them; but Tom and his son did not reply to him.

Suddenly, in a violent rolling of the ship, Negoro fell, and he would, doubtless, have been thrown into the sea if he had not held on to the binnacle.

Tom gave a cry, fearing the compass would be broken.

Dick Sand, in a moment of wakefulness, heard that cry, and rushing out of his quarters, he ran aft.

Negoro had already risen, but he held in his hand the piece of iron which he had just taken from under the binnacle, and he hid it before Dick Sand could see it.

Was it, then, Negoro's interest for the magnetic needle to return to its true direction? Yes, for these southwest winds served him now!

"What's the matter?" asked the novice.

"It's that cook of misfortune, who has just fallen on the compass!" replied Tom.

At those words Dick Sand, in the greatest anxiety, leaned over the binnacle. It was in good condition; the compass, lighted by two lamps, rested as usual on its concentric circles.

The young novice was greatly affected. The breaking of the only compass on board would be an irreparable misfortune.

But what Dick Sand could not observe was that, since the taking away of the piece of iron, the needle had returned to its normal position, and indicated exactly the magnetic north as it ought to be under that meridian.

Meanwhile, if Negoro could not be made responsible for a fall which seemed to be involuntary, Dick Sand had reason to be astonished that he was, at that hour, aft in the ship.

"What are you doing there?" he asked him.

"What I please," replied Negoro.

"You say——" cried Dick Sand, who could not restrain his anger.

"I say," replied the head cook, "that there is no rule which forbids walking aft."

"Well, I make that the rule," replied Dick Sand, "and I forbid you, remember, to come aft."

"Indeed!" replied Negoro.

That man, so entirely under self-control, then made a menacing gesture.

The novice drew a revolver from his pocket, and pointed it at the head cook.

"Negoro," said he, "recollect that I am never without this revolver, and that on the first act of insubordination I shall blow out your brains!"

At that moment Negoro felt himself irresistibly bent to the deck.

It was Hercules, who had just simply laid his heavy hand on Negoro's shoulder.

"Captain Sand," said the giant, "do you want me to throw this rascal overboard? He will regale the fishes, who are not hard to please!"

"Not yet," replied Dick Sand.

Negoro rose as soon as the black's hand no longer weighed upon him.

But, in passing Hercules:

"Accursed negro," murmured he, "I'll pay you back!"

Meanwhile, the wind had just changed; at least, it seemed to have veered round forty-five degrees. And, notwithstanding, a singular thing, which struck the novice, nothing in the condition of the sea indicated that change. The ship headed the same way all the time, but the wind and the waves, instead of taking her directly aft, now struck her by the larboard quarter—a very dangerous situation, which exposes a ship to receive bad surges. So Dick Sand was obliged to veer round four points to continue to scud before the tempest.

But, on the other hand, his attention was awakened more than ever. He asked himself if there was not some connection between Negoro's fall and the breaking of the first compass. What did the head cook intend to do there? Had he some interest in putting the second compass out of service also? What could that interest be? There was no explanation of that. Must not Negoro desire, as they all desired, to land on the American coast as soon as possible?

When Dick Sand spoke of this incident to Mrs. Weldon, the latter, though she shared his distrust in a certain measure, could find no plausible motive for what would be criminal premeditation on the part of the head cook.

However, as a matter of prudence, Negoro was well watched. Thereafter he attended to the novice's orders and he did not risk coming aft in the ship, where his duties never called him. Besides, Dingo having been installed there permanently, the cook took earn to keep away.

During all that week the tempest did not abate. The barometer fell again. From the 14th to the 26th of March it was impossible to profit by a single calm to set a few sails. The "Pilgrim" scudded to the northeast with a speed which could not be less than two hundred miles in twenty-four hours, and still the land did not appear!—that land, America, which is thrown like an immense barrier between the Atlantic and the Pacific, over an extent of more than a hundred and twenty degrees!

Dick Sand asked himself if he was not a fool, if he was still in his right mind, if, for so many days, unknown to him, he was not sailing in a false direction. No, he could not find fault with himself on that point. The sun, even though he could not perceive it in the fogs, always rose before him to set behind him. But, then, that land, had it disappeared? That America, on which his vessel would go to pieces, perhaps, where was it, if it was not there? Be it the Southern Continent or the Northern Continent—for anything way possible in that chaos—the "Pilgrim" could not miss either one or the other. What had happened since the beginning of this frightful tempest? What was still going on, as that coast, whether it should prove salvation or destruction, did not appear? Must Dick Sand suppose, then, that he was deceived by his compass, whose indications he could no longer control, because the second compass was lacking to make that control? Truly, he had that fear which the absence of all land might justify.

So, when he was at the helm, Dick Sand did not cease to devour the chart with his eyes. But he interrogated it in vain; it could not give him the solution of an enigma which, in the situation in which Negoro had placed him, was incomprehensible for him, as it would have been for any one else.

On this day, however, the 26th of March, towards eight o'clock in the morning, an incident of the greatest importance took place.

Hercules, on watch forward, gave this cry:

"Land! land!"

Dick Sand sprang to the forecastle. Hercules could not have eyes like a seaman. Was he not mistaken?

"Land?" cried Dick Sand.

"There," replied Hercules, showing an almost imperceptible point on the horizon in the northeast.

They hardly heard each other speak in the midst of the roaring of the sea and the sky.

"You have seen the land?" said the novice.

"Yes," replied Hercules.

And his hand was still stretched out to larboard forward.

The novice looked. He saw nothing.

At that moment, Mrs. Weldon, who had heard the cry given by Hercules, came up on deck, notwithstanding her promise not to come there.

"Madam!" cried Dick Sand.

Mrs. Weldon, unable to make herself heard, tried, for herself, to perceive that land signaled by the black, and she seemed to have concentrated all her life in her eyes.

It must be believed that Hercules's hand indicated badly the point of the horizon which he wished to show: neither Mrs. Weldon nor the novice could see anything.

But, suddenly, Dick Sand in turn stretched out his hand.

"Yes! yes! land!" said he.

A kind of summit had just appeared in an opening in the fog. His sailor's eyes could not deceive him.

"At last!" cried he; "at last!"

He clang feverishly to the netting. Mrs. Weldon, sustained by Hercules, continued to watch that land almost despaired of.

The coast, formed by that high summit, rose at a distance of ten miles to leeward.

The opening being completely made in a breaking of the clouds, they saw it again more distinctly. Doubtless it was some promontory of the American continent. The "Pilgrim," without sails, was not in a condition to head toward it, but it could not fail to make the land there.

That could be only a question of a few hours. Now, it was eight o'clock in the morning. Then, very certainly, before noon the "Pilgrim" would be near the land.

At a sign from Dick Sand, Hercules led Mrs. Weldon aft again, for she could not bear up against the violence of the pitching.

The novice remained forward for another instant, then he returned to the helm, near old Tom.

At last, then, he saw that coast, so slowly made, so ardently desired! but it was now with a feeling of terror.

In fact, in the "Pilgrim's" present condition, that is to say, scudding before the tempest, land to leeward, was shipwreck with all its terrible contingencies.

Two hours passed away. The promontory was then seen off from the ship.

At that moment they saw Negoro come on deck. This time he regarded the coast with extreme attention, shook his head like a man who would know what to believe, and went down again, after pronouncing a name that nobody could hear.

Dick Sand himself sought to perceive the coast, which ought to round off behind the promontory.

Two hours rolled by. The promontory was standing on the larboard stern, but the coast was not yet to be traced.

Meanwhile the sky cleared at the horizon, and a high coast, like the American land, bordered by the immense chain of the Andes, should be visible for more than twenty miles.

Dick Sand took his telescope and moved it slowly over the whole eastern horizon.

Nothing! He could see nothing!

At two o'clock in the afternoon every trace of land had disappeared behind the "Pilgrim." Forward, the telescope could not seize any outline whatsoever of a coast, high or low.

Then a cry escaped Dick Sand. Immediately leaving the deck, he rushed into the cabin, where Mrs. Weldon was with little Jack, Nan, and Cousin Benedict.

"An island! That was only an island!" said he.

"An island, Dick! but what?" asked Mrs. Weldon.

"The chart will tell us," replied the novice.

And running to his berth, he brought the ship's chart.

"There, Mrs. Weldon, there!" said he. "That land which we have seen, it can only be this point, lost in the middle of the Pacific! It can only be the Isle of Paques; there is no other in these parts."

"And we have already left it behind?" asked Mrs. Weldon.

"Yes, well to the windward of us."

Mrs. Weldon looked attentively at the Isle of Paques, which only formed an imperceptible point on the chart.

"And at what distance is it from the American coast?"

"Thirty-five degrees."

"Which makes——"

"About two thousand miles."

"But then the 'Pilgrim' has not sailed, if we are still so far from the continent?"

"Mrs. Weldon," replied Dick Sand, who passed his hand over his forehead for a moment, as if to concentrate his ideas, "I do not know—I cannot explain this incredible delay! No! I cannot—unless the indications of the compass have been false? But that island can only be the Isle of Paques, because we have been obliged to scud before the wind to the northeast, and we must thank Heaven, which has permitted me to mark our position! Yes, it is still two thousand miles from the coast! I know, at last, where the tempest has blown us, and, if it abates, we shall be able to land on the American continent with some chance of safety. Now, at least, our ship is no longer lost on the immensity of the Pacific!"

This confidence, shown by the young novice, was shared by all those who heard him speak. Mrs. Weldon, herself, gave way to it. It seemed, indeed, that these poor people were at the end of their troubles, and that the "Pilgrim," being to the windward of her port, had only to wait for the open sea to enter it! The Isle of Paques—by its true name Vai-Hon—discovered by David in 1686, visited by Cook and Laperouse, is situated 27° south latitude and 112° east longitude. If the schooner had been thus led more than fifteen degrees to the north, that was evidently due to that tempest from the southwest, before which it had been obliged to scud.

Then the "Pilgrim" was still two thousand miles from the coast.

However, under the impetus of that wind which blew like thunder, it

must, in less than ten days, reach some point of the coast of South

America.

But could they not hope, as the novice had said, that the weather would become more manageable, and that it would be possible to set some sail, when they should make the land?

It was still Dick Sand's hope. He said to himself that this hurricane, which had lasted so many days, would end perhaps by "killing itself." And now that, thanks to the appearance of the Isle of Paques, he knew exactly his position, he had reason to believe that, once master of his vessel again, he would know how to lead her to a safe place.

Yes! to have had knowledge of that isolated point in the middle of the sea, as by a providential favor, that had restored confidence to Dick Sand; if he was going all the time at the caprice of a hurricane, which he could not subdue, at least, he was no longer going quite blindfold.

Besides, the "Pilgrim," well-built and rigged, had suffered little during those rude attacks of the tempest. Her damages reduced themselves to the loss of the top-sail and the foretop-mast stay-sail—a loss which it would be easy to repair. Not a drop of water had penetrated through the well-stanched seams of the hull and the deck. The pumps were perfectly free. In this respect there was nothing to fear.

There was, then, this interminable hurricane, whose fury nothing seemed able to moderate. If, in a certain measure, Dick Sand could put his ship in a condition to struggle against the violent storm, he could not order that wind to moderate, those waves to be still, that sky to become serene again. On board, if he was "master after God," outside the ship, God alone commanded the winds and the waves.

## CHAPTER XIII.
## LAND! LAND!

Meanwhile, that confidence with which Dick Sand's heart filled instinctively, was going to be partly justified.

The next day, March 27th, the column of mercury rose in the barometrical tube. The oscillation was neither sudden nor considerable—a few lines only—but the progression seemed likely to continue. The tempest was evidently going to enter its decreasing period, and, if the sea did remain excessively rough, they could tell that the wind was going down, veering slightly to the west.

Dick Sand could not yet think of using any sail. The smallest sail would be carried away. However, he hoped that twenty-four hours would not elapse before it would be possible for him to rig a storm-jib.

During the night, in fact, the wind went down quite noticeably, if they compared it to what it had been till then, and the ship was less tossed by those violent rollings which had threatened to break her in pieces.

The passengers began to appear on deck again. They no longer ran the risk of being carried away by some surge from the sea.

Mrs. Weldon was the first to leave the hatchway where Dick Sand, from prudent motives, had obliged them to shut themselves up during the whole duration of that long tempest. She came to talk with the novice, whom a truly superhuman will had rendered capable of resisting so much fatigue. Thin, pale under his sunburnt complexion, he might well be weakened by the loss of that sleep so necessary at his age. No, his valiant nature resisted everything. Perhaps he would pay dearly some day for that period of trial. But that was not the moment to allow himself to be cast down. Dick Sand had said all that to himself. Mrs. Weldon found him as energetic as he had ever been.

And then he had confidence, that brave Sand, and if confidence does not command itself, at least it commands.

"Dick, my dear child, my captain," said Mrs. Weldon, holding out her hand to the young novice.

"Ah! Mrs. Weldon," exclaimed Dick Sand, smiling, "you disobey your captain. You return on deck, you leave your cabin in spite of his—prayers."

"Yes, I disobey you," replied Mrs. Weldon; "but I have, as it were, a presentiment that the tempest is going down or is going to become calm."

"It is becoming calm, in fact, Mrs. Weldon," replied the novice. "You are not mistaken. The barometer has not fallen since yesterday. The wind has moderated, and I have reason to believe that our hardest trials are over."

"Heaven hears you, Dick. All! you have suffered much, my poor child!

You have done there———"

"Only my duty, Mrs. Weldon."

"But at last will you be able to take some rest?"

"Rest!" replied the novice; "I have no need of rest, Mrs. Weldon. I am well, thank God, and it is necessary for me to keep up to the end. You have called me captain, and I shall remain captain till the moment when all the 'Pilgrim's' passengers shall be in safety."

"Dick," returned Mrs. Weldon, "my husband and I, we shall never forget what you have just done."

"God has done all," replied Dick Sand; "all!"

"My child, I repeat it, that by your moral and physical energy, you have shown yourself a man—a man fit to command, and before long, as soon as your studies are finished—my husband will not contradict me—you will command for the house of James W. Weldon!"

"I—I———" exclaimed Dick Sand, whose eyes filled with tears.

"Dick," replied Mrs. Weldon, "you are already our child by adoption, and now, you are our son, the deliverer of your mother, and of your little brother Jack. My dear Dick, I embrace you for my husband and for myself!"

The courageous woman did not wish to give way while clasping the young novice in her arms, but her heart overflowed. As to Dick Sand's feelings, what pen could do them justice? He asked himself if he could not do more than give his life for his benefactors, and he accepted in advance all the trials which might come upon him in the future.

After this conversation Dick Sand felt stronger. If the wind should become so moderate that he should be able to hoist some canvas, he did not doubt being able to steer his ship to a port where all those which it carried would at last be in safety.

On the 29th, the wind having moderated a little, Dick Sand thought of setting the foresail and the top-sail, consequently to increase the speed of the "Pilgrim" while directing her course.

"Come, Tom; come, my friends!" cried he, when he went on deck at daybreak; "come, I need your arms!"

"We are ready, Captain Sand," replied old Tom.

"Ready for everything," added Hercules. "There was nothing to do during that tempest, and I begin to grow rusty."

"You should have blown with your big mouth," said little Jack; "I bet you would have been as strong as the wind!"

"That is an idea, Jack," replied Dick Sand, laughing. "When there is a calm we shall make Hercules blow on the sails."

"At your service, Mister Dick!" replied the brave black, inflating his cheeks like a gigantic Boreas.

"Now, my friends," continued the novice, we are to begin by binding a spare sail to the yard, because our top-sail was carried away in the hurricane. It will be difficult, perhaps, but it must be done."

"It shall be done!" replied Acteon.

"Can I help you?" asked little Jack, always ready to work.

"Yes, my Jack," replied the novice. "You will take your place at the wheel, with our friend Bat, and you will help him to steer."

If little Jack was proud of being assistant helmsman on the "Pilgrim," it is superfluous to say so.

"Now to work," continued Dick Sand, "and we must expose ourselves as little as possible."

The blacks, guided by the novice, went to work at once. To fasten a top-sail to its yard presented some difficulties for Tom and his companions. First the rolled up sail must be hoisted, then fastened to the yard.

However, Dick Sand commanded so well, and was so well obeyed, that after an hour's work the sail was fastened to its yard, the yard hoisted, and the top-sail properly set with two reefs.

As to the foresail and the second jib, which had been furled before the tempest, those sails were set without a great deal of trouble, in spite of the force of the wind.

At last, on that day, at ten o'clock in the morning, the "Pilgrim" was sailing under her foresail, her top-sail, and her jib.

Dick Sand had not judged it prudent to set more sail. The canvas which he carried ought to assure him, as long as the wind did not moderate, a speed of at least two hundred miles in twenty-four hours, and he did not need any greater to reach the American coast before ten days.

The novice was indeed satisfied when, returning to the wheel, he again took his post, after thanking Master Jack, assistant helmsman of the "Pilgrim." He was no longer at the mercy of the waves. He was making headway. His joy will be understood by all those who are somewhat familiar with the things of the sea.

The next day the clouds still ran with the same velocity, but they left large openings between them, through which the rays of the sun made their way to the surface of the waters. The "Pilgrim" was at times overspread with them. A good thing is that vivifying light! Sometimes it was extinguished behind a large mass of vapors which came up in the east, then it reappeared, to disappear again, but the weather was becoming fine again.

The scuttles had been opened to ventilate the interior of the ship. A salubrious air penetrated the hold, the rear hatchway, the crew's quarters. They put the wet sails to dry, stretching them out in the sun. The deck was also cleaned. Dick Sand did not wish his ship to arrive in port without having made a bit of toilet. Without overworking the crew, a few hours spent each day at that work would bring it to a good end.

Though the novice could no longer throw the log, he was so accustomed to estimating the headway of a ship that he could take a close account of her speed. He had then no doubt of reaching land before seven days, and he gave that opinion to Mrs. Weldon, after showing her, on the chart, the probable position of the ship.

"Well, at what point of the coast shall we arrive, my dear Dick?" she asked him.

"Here, Mrs. Weldon," replied the novice, indicating that long coast line which extends from Peru to Chili. "I do not know how to be more exact. Here is the Isle of Paques, that we have left behind in the west, and, by the direction of the wind, which has been constant, I conclude that we shall reach land in the east. Ports are quite numerous on that coast, but to name the one we shall have in view when we make the land is impossible at this moment."

"Well, Dick, whichever it may be, that port will be welcome."

"Yes, Mrs. Weldon, and you will certainly find there the means to return promptly to San Francisco. The Pacific Navigation Company has a very well organized service on this coast. Its steamers touch at the principal points of the coast; nothing will be easier than to take passage for California."

"Then you do not count on bringing the 'Pilgrim' to San Francisco?" asked Mrs. Weldon.

"Yes, after having put you on shore, Mrs. Weldon. If we can procure an officer and a crew, we are going to discharge our cargo at Valparaiso, as Captain Hull would have done. Then we shall return to our own port. But that would delay you too much, and, though very sorry to be separated from you ——"

"Well, Dick," replied Mrs. Weldon, "we shall see later what must be done. Tell me, you seem to fear the dangers which the land presents."

"In fact, they are to be feared," replied the novice, "but I am always hoping to meet some ship in these parts, and I am even very much surprised at not seeing any. If only one should pass, we would enter into communication with her; she would give us our exact situation, which would greatly facilitate our arrival in sight of land."

"Are there not pilots who do service along this coast?" asked Mrs. Weldon.

"There ought to be," replied Dick Sand, "but much nearer land. We must then continue to approach it."

"And if we do not meet a pilot?" asked Mrs. Weldon, who kept on questioning him in order to know how the young novice would prepare for all contingencies.

"In that case, Mrs. Weldon, either the weather will be clear, the wind moderate, and I shall endeavor to sail up the coast sufficiently near to find a refuge, or the wind will be stronger, and then——"

"Then what will you do, Dick?"

"Then, in the present condition of the 'Pilgrim,'" replied Dick Sand, "once near the land, it will be very difficult to set off again."

"What will you do?" repeated Mrs. Weldon.

"I shall be forced to run my ship aground," replied the novice, whose brow darkened for a moment. "Ah! it is a hard extremity. God grant that we may not be reduced to that. But, I repeat it, Mrs. Weldon, the appearance of the sky is reassuring, and it is impossible for a vessel or a pilot-boat not to meet us. Then, good hope. We are headed for the land, we shall see it before long."

Yes, to run a ship aground is a last extremity, to which the most energetic sailor does not resort without fear! Thus, Dick Sand did not wish to foresee it, while he had some chances of escaping it.

For several days there were, in the state of the atmosphere, alternatives which, anew, made the novice very uneasy. The wind kept in the condition of a stiff breeze all the time, and certain oscillations of the barometrical column indicated that it tended to freshen. Dick Sand then asked himself, not without apprehension, if he would be again forced to scud without sails. He had so much interest in keeping at least his top-sail, that he resolved to do so so long as it was not likely to be carried away. But, to secure the solidity of the masts, he had the shrouds and backstays hauled taut. Above all, all unnecessary risk must be avoided, as the situation would become one of the gravest, if the "Pilgrim" should be disabled by losing her masts.

Once or twice, also, the barometer rising gave reason to fear that the wind might change point for point; that is to say, that it might pass to the east. It would then be necessary to sail close to the wind!

A new anxiety for Dick Sand. What should he do with a contrary wind? Tack about? But if he was obliged to come to that, what new delays and what risks of being thrown into the offing.

Happily those fears were not realized. The wind, after shifting for several days, blowing sometimes from the north, sometimes from the south, settled definitely in the west. But it was always a strong breeze, almost a gale, which strained the masting.

It was the 5th of April. So, then, more than two months had already elapsed since the "Pilgrim" had left New Zealand. For twenty days a contrary wind and long calms had retarded her course. Then she was in a favorable condition to reach land rapidly. Her speed must even have been very considerable during the tempest. Dick Sand estimated its average at not less than two hundred miles a day! How, then, had he not yet made the coast? Did it flee before the "Pilgrim?" It was absolutely inexplicable.

And, nevertheless, no land was signaled, though one of the blacks kept watch constantly in the crossbars.

Dick Sand often ascended there himself. There, with a telescope to his eyes, he sought to discover some appearance of mountains. The Andes chain is very high. It was there in the zone of the clouds that he must seek some peak, emerging from the vapors of the horizon.

Several times Tom and his companions were deceived by false indications of land. They were only vapors of an odd form, which rose in the background. It happened sometimes that these honest men were obstinate in their belief; but, after a certain time, they were forced to acknowledge that they had been dupes of an optical illusion. The pretended land, moved away, changed form and finished by disappearing completely.

On the 6th of April there was no longer any doubt possible.

It was eight o'clock in the morning. Dick Sand had just ascended into the bars. At that moment the fogs were condensed under the first rays of the sun, and the horizon was pretty clearly defined.

From Dick Sand's lips escaped at last the so long expected cry:

"Land! land before us!"

At that cry every one ran on deck, little Jack, curious as folks are at that age, Mrs. Weldon, whose trials were going to cease with the landing, Tom and his companions, who were at last going to set foot again on the American continent, Cousin Benedict himself, who had great hope of picking up quite a rich collection of new insects for himself.

Negoro, alone, did not appear.

Each then saw what Dick Sand had seen, some very distinctly, others with the eyes of faith. But on the part of the novice, so accustomed to observe sea horizons, there was no error possible, and an hour after, it must be allowed he was not deceived.

At a distance of about four miles to the east stretched a rather low coast, or at least what appeared such. It must be commanded behind by the high chain of the Andes, but the last zone of clouds did not allow the summits to be perceived.

The "Pilgrim" sailed directly and rapidly to this coast, which grew larger to the eye.

Two hours after it was only three miles away.

This part of the coast ended in the northeast by a pretty high cape, which covered a sort of roadstead protected from land winds. On the contrary, in the southeast, it lengthened out like a thin peninsula.

A few trees crowned a succession of low cliffs, which were then clearly defined under the sky. But it was evident, the geographical character of the country being given, that the high mountain chain of the Andes formed their background.

Moreover, no habitation in sight, no port, no river mouth, which might serve as a harbor for a vessel.

At that moment the "Pilgrim" was running right on the land. With the reduced sail which she carried, the winds driving her to the coast, Dick Sand would not be able to set off from it.

In front lay a long band of reefs, on which the sea was foaming all white. They saw the waves unfurl half way up the cliffs. There must be a monstrous surf there.

Dick Sand, after remaining on the forecastle to observe the coast, returned aft, and, without saying a word, he took the helm.

The wind was freshening all the time. The schooner was soon only a mile from the shore.

Dick Sand then perceived a sort of little cove, into which he resolved to steer; but, before reaching it, he must cross a line of reefs, among which it would be difficult to follow a channel. The surf indicated that the water was shallow everywhere.

At that moment Dingo, who was going backwards and forwards on the deck, dashed forward, and, looking at the land, gave some lamentable barks. One would say that the dog recognized the coast, and that its instinct recalled some sad remembrance.

Negoro must have heard it, for an irresistible sentiment led him out of his cabin; and although he had reason to fear the dog, he came almost immediately to lean on the netting.

Very fortunately for him Dingo, whose sad barks were all the time being addressed to that land, did not perceive him.

Negoro looked at that furious surf, and that did not appear to frighten him. Mrs. Weldon, who was looking at him, thought she saw his face redden a little, and that for an instant his features were contracted.

Then, did Negoro know this point of the continent where the winds were driving the "Pilgrim?"

At that moment Dick Sand left the wheel, which he gave back to old Tom.

For a last time he came to look at the cove, which gradually opened.

Then:

"Mrs. Weldon," said he, in a firm voice, "I have no longer any hope of finding a harbor! Before half an hour, in spite of all my efforts, the 'Pilgrim' will be on the reefs! We must run aground! I shall not bring the ship into port! I am forced to lose her to save you! But, between your safety and hers, I do not hesitate!"

"You have done all that depended on you, Dick?" asked Mrs. Weldon.

"All," replied the young novice.

And at once he made his preparations for stranding the ship.

First of all, Mrs. Weldon, Jack, Cousin Benedict and Nan, must put on life-preservers. Dick Sand, Tom and the blacks, good swimmers, also took measures to gain the coast, in case they should be precipitated into the sea.

Hercules would take charge of Mrs. Weldon. The novice took little Jack under his care.

Cousin Benedict, very tranquil, however, reappeared on the deck with his entomologist box strapped to his shoulder. The novice commended him to Bat and Austin. As to Negoro, his singular calmness said plainly enough that he had no need of anybody's aid.

Dick Sand, by a supreme precaution, had also brought on the forecastle ten barrels of the cargo containing whale's oil.

That oil, properly poured the moment the "Pilgrim" would be in the surf, ought to calm the sea for an instant, in lubricating, so to say, the molecules of water, and that operation would perhaps facilitate the ship's passage between the reefs. Dick Sand did not wish to neglect anything which might secure the common safety.

All these precautions taken, the novice returned to take his place at the wheel.

The "Pilgrim" was only two cables' lengths from the coast, that is, almost touching the reefs, her starboard side already bathed in the white foam of the surf. Each moment the novice thought that the vessel's keel was going to strike some rocky bottom.

Suddenly, Dick Sand knew, by a change in the color of the water, that a channel lengthened out among the reefs. He must enter it bravely without hesitating, so as to make the coast as near as possible to the shore.

The novice did not hesitate. A movement of the helm thrust the ship into the narrow and sinuous channel. In this place the sea was still more furious, and the waves dashed on the deck.

The blacks were posted forward, near the barrels, waiting for the novice's orders.

"Pour the oil—pour!" exclaimed Dick Sand.

Under this oil, which was poured on it in quantities, the sea grew calm, as by enchantment, only to become more terrible again a moment after.

The "Pilgrim" glided rapidly over those lubricated waters and headed straight for the shore.

Suddenly a shock took place. The ship, lifted by a formidable wave, had just stranded, and her masting had fallen without wounding anybody.

The "Pilgrim's" hull, damaged by the collision, was invaded by the water with extreme violence. But the shore was only half a cable's length off, and a chain of small blackish rocks enabled it to be reached quite easily.

So, ten minutes after, all those carried by the "Pilgrim" had landed at the foot of the cliff.

## CHAPTER XIV.

### THE BEST TO DO.

So then, after a voyage long delayed by calms, then favored by winds from the northwest and from the southwest—a voyage which had not lasted less than seventy-four days—the "Pilgrim" had just run aground!

However, Mrs. Weldon. and her companions thanked Providence, because they were in safety. In fact, it was on a continent, and not on one of the fatal isles of Polynesia, that the tempest had thrown them. Their return to their country, from any point of South America on which they should land, ought not, it seemed, to present serious difficulties.

As to the "Pilgrim," she was lost. She was only a carcass without value, of which the surf was going to disperse the débris in a few hours. It would be impossible to save anything. But if Dick Sand had not that joy of bringing back a vessel intact to his ship-owner, at least, thanks to him, those who sailed in her were safe and sound on some hospitable coast, and among them, the wife and child of James W. Weldon.

As to the question of knowing on what part of the American coast the schooner had been wrecked, they might dispute it for a long time. Was it, as Dick Sand must suppose, on the shore of Peru? Perhaps, for he knew, even by the bearings of the Isle of Paques, that the "Pilgrim" had been thrown to the northeast under the action of the winds; and also, without doubt, under the influence of the currents of the equatorial zone. From the forty-third degree of latitude, it had, indeed, been possible to drift to the fifteenth.

It was then important to determine, as soon as possible, the precise point of the coast where the schooner had just been lost. Granted that this coast was that of Peru, ports, towns and villages were not lacking, and consequently it would be easy to gain some inhabited place. As to this part of the coast, it seemed deserted.

It was a narrow beach, strewed with black rocks, shut off by a cliff of medium height, very irregularly cut up by large funnels due to the rupture of the rock. Here and there a few gentle declivities gave access to its crest.

In the north, at a quarter of a mile from the stranding place, was the mouth of a little river, which could not have been perceived from the offing. On its banks hung numerous rhizomas, sorts of mangroves, essentially distinct from their congeners of India.

The crest of the cliff—that was soon discovered—was overhung by a thick forest, whose verdant masses undulated before the eyes, and extended as far as the mountains in the background. There, if Cousin Benedict had been a botanist, how many trees, new to him, would not have failed to provoke his admiration.

There were high baobabs—to which, however, an extraordinary longevity has been falsely attributed—the bark of which resembles Egyptian syenite, Bourbon palms, white pines, tamarind-trees, pepper-plants of a peculiar species, and a hundred other plants that an American is not accustomed to see in the northern region of the New Continent.

But, a circumstance rather curious, among those forest productions one would not meet a single specimen of that numerous family of palm-trees which counts more than a thousand species, spread in profusion over almost the whole surface of the globe.

Above the sea-shore a great number of very noisy birds were flying, which belonged for the greater part to different varieties of swallows, of black plumage, with a steel-blue shade, but of a light chestnut color on the upper part of the head. Here and there also rose some partridges, with necks entirely white, and of a gray color.

Mrs. Weldon and Dick Sand observed that these different birds did not appear to be at all wild. They approached without fearing anything. Then, had they not yet learned to fear the presence of man, and was this coast so deserted that the detonation of a firearm had never been heard there?

At the edge of the rocks were walking some pelicans of the species of "pelican minor," occupied in filling with little fish the sack which they carry between the branches of their lower jaw. Some gulls, coming from the offing, commenced to fly about around the "Pilgrim."

Those birds were the only living creatures that seemed to frequent this part of the coast, without counting, indeed, numbers of interesting insects that Cousin Benedict would well know how to discover. But, however little Jack would have it, one could not ask them the name of the country; in order to learn it, it would be necessary to address some native. There were none there, or at least, there was not one to be seen. No habitation, hut, or cabin, neither in the north, beyond the little river, nor in the south, nor finally on the upper part of the cliff, in the midst of the trees of the thick forest. No smoke ascended into the air, no indication, mark, or imprint indicated that this portion of the continent was visited by human beings. Dick Sand continued to be very much surprised.

"Where are we? Where can we be?" he asked himself. "What! nobody to speak to?"

Nobody, in truth, and surely, if any native had approached, Dingo would have scented him, and announced him by a bark. The dog went backward and forward on the strand, his nose to the ground, his tail down, growling secretly —certainly very singular behavior—but neither betraying the approach of man nor of any animal whatsoever.

"Dick, look at Dingo!" said Mrs. Weldon.

"Yes, that is very strange," replied the novice. "It seems as if he were trying to recover a scent."

"Very strange, indeed," murmured Mrs. Weldon; then, continuing, "what is Negoro doing?" she asked.

"He is doing what Dingo is doing," replied Dick Sand. "He goes, he comes! After all, he is free here. I have no longer the right to control him. His service ended with the stranding of the Pilgrim.'"

In fact, Negoro surveyed the strand, turned back, and looked at the shore and the cliff like a man trying to recall recollections and to fix them. Did he, then, know this country? He would probably have refused to reply to that question if it had been asked. The best thing was still to have nothing to do with that very unsociable personage. Dick Sand soon saw him walk from the side of the little river, and when Negoro had disappeared on the other side of the cliff, he ceased to think of him.

Dingo had indeed barked when the cook had arrived on the steep bank, but became silent almost immediately.

It was necessary, now, to consider the most pressing wants. Now, the most pressing was to find a refuge, a shelter of some kind, where they could install themselves for the time, and partake of some nourishment. Then they would take counsel, and they would decide what it would be convenient to do.

As to food, they had not to trouble themselves. Without speaking of the resources which the country must offer, the ship's store-room had emptied itself for the benefit of the survivors of the shipwreck. The surf had thrown here and there among the rocks, then uncovered by the ebb-tide, a great quantity of objects. Tom and his companions had already picked up some barrels of biscuit, boxes of alimentary preserves, cases of dried meat. The water not having yet damaged them, food for the little troop was secured for more time, doubtless, than they would require to reach a town or a village. In that respect there was nothing to fear. These different waifs, already put in a safe place, could no longer be taken back by a rising sea.

Neither was sweet water lacking. First of all Dick Sand had taken care to send Hercules to the little river for a few pints. But it was a cask which the vigorous negro brought back on his shoulder, after having filled it with water fresh and pure, which the ebb of the tide left perfectly drinkable.

As to a fire, if it were necessary to light one, dead wood was not lacking in the neighborhood, and the roots of the old mangroves ought to furnish all the fuel of which they would have need. Old Tom, an ardent smoker, was provided with a certain quantity of German tinder, well preserved in a box hermetically closed, and when they wanted it, he would only have to strike the tinder-box with the flint of the strand.

It remained, then, to discover the hole in which the little troop would lie down, in case they must take one night's rest before setting out.

And, indeed, it was little Jack who found the bedroom in question, While trotting about at the foot of the cliff, he discovered, behind a turn of the rock, one of those grottoes well polished, well hollowed out, which the sea herself digs, when the waves, enlarged by the tempest, beat the coast.

The young child was delighted. He called his mother with cries of joy, and triumphantly showed her his discovery.

"Good, my Jack!" replied Mrs. Weldon. "If we were Robinson Crusoes, destined to live a long time on this shore, we should not forget to give your name to that grotto!"

The grotto was only from ten to twelve feet long, and as many wide; but, in little Jack's eyes, it was an enormous cavern. At all events, it must suffice to contain the shipwrecked ones; and, as Mrs. Weldon and Nan noted with satisfaction, it was very dry. The moon being then in her first quarter, they need not fear that those neap-tides would reach the foot of the cliff, and the grotto in consequence. Then, nothing more was needed for a few hours' rest.

Ten minutes after everybody was stretched out on a carpet of sea-weed. Negoro himself thought he must rejoin the little troop and take his part of the repast, which was going to be made in common. Doubtless he had not judged it proper to venture alone under the thick forest, through which the winding river made its way.

It was one o'clock in the afternoon. The preserved meat, the biscuit, the sweet water, with the addition of a few drops of rum, of which Bat had saved a quarter cask, made the requisites for this repast. But if Negoro took part in it, he did not at all mingle in the conversation, in which were discussed the measures demanded by the situation of the shipwrecked. All the time, without appearing to do so, he listened to it, and doubtless profited by what he heard.

During this time Dingo, who had not been forgotten, watched outside the grotto. They could be at ease. No living being would show himself on the strand without the faithful animal giving the alarm.

Mrs. Weldon, holding her little Jack, half lying and almost asleep on her lap, began to speak.

"Dick, my friend," said she, "in the name of all, I thank you for the devotion that you have shown us till now; but we do not consider you free yet. You will be our guide on land, as you were our captain at sea. We place every confidence in you. Speak, then! What must we do?"

Mrs. Weldon, old Nan, Tom and his companions, all had their eyes fixed on the young novice. Negoro himself looked at him with a singular persistence. Evidently, what Dick Sand was going to reply interested him very particularly.

Dick Sand reflected for a few moments. Then:

"Mrs. Weldon," said he, "the important thing is to know, first, where we are. I believe that our ship can only have made the land on that portion of the American sea-coast which forms the Peruvian shore. The winds and currents must have carried her as far as that latitude. But are we here in some southern province of Peru, that is to say on the least inhabited part which borders upon the pampas? Maybe so. I would even willingly believe it, seeing this beach so desolate, and, it must be, but little frequented. In that case, we might be very far from the nearest town, which would be unfortunate."

"Well, what is to be done?" repeated Mrs. Weldon.

"My advice," replied Dick Sand, "would be not to leave this shelter till we know our situation. To-morrow, after a night's rest, two of us could go to discover it. They would endeavor, without going too far, to meet some natives, to inform themselves from them, and return to the grotto. It is not possible that, in a radius of ten or twelve miles, we find nobody."

"To separate!" said Mrs. Weldon.

"That seems necessary to me," replied the novice. "If no information can be picked up, if, as is not impossible, the country is absolutely desolate, well, we shall consider some other way of extricating ourselves."

"And which of us shall go to explore?" asked Mrs. Weldon, after a moment's reflection.

"That is yet to be decided," replied Dick Sand. "At all events, I think that you, Mrs. Weldon, Jack, Mr. Benedict, and Nan, ought not to quit this grotto. Bat, Hercules, Acteon, and Austin should remain near you, while Tom and I should go forward. Negoro, doubtless, will prefer to remain here?" added Dick Sand, looking at the head-cook.

"Probably," replied Negoro, who was not a man to commit himself any more than that.

"We should take Dingo with us," continued the novice. "He would be useful to us during our exploration."

Dingo, hearing his name pronounced, reappeared at the entrance of the grotto, and seemed to approve of Dick Sand's projects by a little bark.

Since the novice had made this proposition, Mrs. Weldon remained pensive. Her repugnance to the idea of a separation, even short, was very serious. Might it not happen that the shipwreck of the "Pilgrim" would soon be known to the Indian tribes who frequented the sea-shore, either to the north or to the south, and in case some plunderers of the wrecks thrown on the shore should present themselves, was it not better for all to be united to repulse them?

That objection, made to the novice's proposition, truly merited a discussion.

It fell, however, before Dick Sand's arguments, who observed that the Indians ought not to be confounded with the savages of Africa or Polynesia, and any aggression on their part was probably not to be feared. But to entangle themselves in this country without even knowing to what province of South America it belonged, nor at what distance the nearest town of that province was situated, was to expose themselves to many fatigues. Doubtless separation might have its inconveniences, but far less than marching blindly into the midst of a forest which appeared to stretch as far as the base of the mountains.

"Besides," repeated Dick Sand, persistently, "I cannot admit that this separation will be of long duration, and I even affirm that it will not be so. After two days, at the most, if Tom and I have come across neither habitation nor inhabitant, we shall return to the grotto. But that is too improbable, and we shall not have advanced twenty miles into the interior of the country before we shall evidently be satisfied about its geographical situation. I may be mistaken in my calculation, after all, because the means of fixing it astronomically have failed me, and it is not impossible for us to be in a higher or lower latitude."

"Yes—you are certainly right, my child," replied Mrs. Weldon, in great anxiety.

"And you, Mr. Benedict," asked Dick Sand, "what do you think of this project?"

"I?" replied Cousin Benedict.

"Yes; what is your advice?"

"I have no advice," replied Cousin Benedict. "I find everything proposed, good, and I shall do everything that you wish. Do you wish to remain here one day or two? that suits me, and I shall employ my time in studying this shore from a purely entomological point of view."

"Do, then, according to your wish," said Mrs. Weldon to Dick Sand. "We shall remain here, and you shall depart with old Tom."

"That is agreed upon," said Cousin Benedict, in the most tranquil manner in the world. "As for me, I am going to pay a visit to the insects of the country."

"Do not go far away, Mr. Benedict," said the novice. "We urge you strongly not to do it."

"Do not be uneasy, my boy."

"And above all, do not bring back too many musquitoes," added old Tom.

A few moments after, the entomologist, his precious tin box strapped to his shoulders, left the grotto.

Almost at the same time Negoro abandoned it also. It appeared quite natural to that man to, be always occupied with himself. But, while Cousin Benedict clambered up the slopes of the cliff to go to explore the border of the forest, he, turning round toward the river, went away with slow steps and disappeared, a second time ascending the steep bank.

Jack slept all the time. Mrs. Weldon, leaving him on Nan's knees, then descended toward the strand. Dick Sand and his companions followed her. The question was, to see if the state of the sea then would permit them to go as far as the "Pilgrim's" hull, where there were still many objects which might be useful to the little troop.

The rocks on which the schooner had been wrecked were now dry. In the midst of the débris of all kinds stood the ship's carcass, which the high sea had partly covered again. That astonished Dick Sand, for he knew that the tides are only very moderate on the American sea-shore of the Pacific. But, after all, this phenomenon might be explained by the fury of the wind which beat the coast.

On seeing their ship again, Mrs. Weldon and her companions experienced a painful impression. It was there that they had lived for long days, there that they had suffered. The aspect of that poor ship, half broken, having neither mast nor sails, lying on her side like a being deprived of life, sadly grieved their hearts. But they must visit this hull, before the sea should come to finish demolishing it.

Dick Sand and the blacks could easily make their way into the interior, after having hoisted themselves on deck by means of the ropes which hung over the "Pilgrim's" side. While Tom, Hercules, Bat, and Austin employed themselves in taking from the storeroom all that might be useful, as much eatables as liquids, the novice made his way into the arsenal. Thanks to God, the water had not invaded this part of the ship, whose rear had remained out of the water after the stranding.

There Dick Sand found four guns in good condition, excellent Remingtons from Purdy & Co.'s factory, as well as a hundred cartridges, carefully shut up in their cartridge-boxes. There was material to arm his little band, and put it in a state of defense, if, contrary to all expectation, the Indians attacked him on the way.

The novice did not neglect to take a pocket-lantern; but the ship's charts, laid in a forward quarter and damaged by the water, were beyond use.

There were also in the "Pilgrim's" arsenal some of those solid cutlasses which serve to cut up whales. Dick Sand chose six, destined to complete the arming of his companions, and he did not forget to bring an inoffensive child's gun, which belonged to little Jack.

As to the other objects still held by the ship, they had either been dispersed, or they could no longer be used. Besides, it was useless to overburden themselves for the few days the journey would last. In food, in arms, in munitions, they were more than provided for. Meanwhile, Dick Sand, by Mrs. Weldon's advice, did not neglect to take all the money which he found on board—about five hundred dollars.

That was a small sum, indeed! Mrs. Weldon had carried a larger amount herself and she did not find it again.

Who, then, except Negoro, had been able to visit the ship before them and to lay hands on Captain Hull's and Mrs. Weldon's reserve? No one but he, surely, could be suspected. However, Dick Sand hesitated a moment. All that he knew and all that he saw of him was that everything was to be feared from that concentrated nature, from whom the misfortunes of others could snatch a smile. Yes, Negoro was an evil being, but must they conclude from that that he was a criminal? It was painful to Dick Sand's character to go as far as that. And, meanwhile, could suspicion rest on any other? No, those honest negroes had not left the grotto for an instant, while Negoro had wandered over the beach. He alone must be guilty. Dick Sand then resolved to question Negoro, and, if necessary, have him searched when he returned. He wished to know decidedly what to believe.

The sun was then going down to the horizon. At that date he had not yet crossed the equator to carry heat and light into the northern hemisphere, but he was approaching it. He fell, then, almost perpendicularly to that circular line where the sea and the sky meet. Twilight was short, darkness fell promptly—which confirmed the novice in the thought that he had landed on a point of the coast situated between the tropic of Capricorn and the equator.

Mrs. Weldon, Dick Sand, and the blacks then returned to the grotto, where they must take some hours' rest.

"The night will still be stormy," observed Tom, pointing to the horizon laden with heavy clouds.

"Yes," replied Dick Sand, "there is a strong breeze blowing up. But what matter, at present? Our poor ship is lost, and the tempest can no longer reach us?"

"God's will be done!" said Mrs. Weldon.

It was agreed that during that night, which would be very dark, each of the blacks would watch turn about at the entrance to the grotto. They could, besides, count upon Dingo to keep a careful watch.

They then perceived that Cousin Benedict had not returned.

Hercules called him with all the strength of his powerful lungs, and almost immediately they saw the entomologist coming down the slopes of the cliff, at the risk of breaking his neck.

Cousin Benedict was literally furious. He had not found a single new insect in the forest—no, not one—which was fit to figure in his collection. Scorpions, scolopendras, and other myriapodes, as many as he could wish, and even more, were discovered. And we know that Cousin Benedict did not interest himself in myriapodes.

"It was not worth the trouble," added he, "to travel five or six thousand miles, to have braved the tempest, to be wrecked on the coast, and not meet one of those American hexapodes, which do honor to an entomological museum! No; the game was not worth the candle!"

As a conclusion, Cousin Benedict asked to go away. He did not wish to remain another hour on that detested shore.

Mrs. Weldon calmed her large child. They made him hope that he would be more fortunate the next day, and all went to lie down in the grotto, to sleep there till sunrise, when Tom observed that Negoro had not yet returned, though night had arrived.

"Where can he be?" asked Mrs. Weldon.

"What matter!" said Bat.

"On the contrary, it does matter," replied Mrs. Weldon. "I should prefer having that man still near us."

"Doubtless, Mrs. Weldon," replied Dick Sand; "but if he has forsaken our company voluntarily, I do not see how we could oblige him to rejoin us. Who knows but he has his reasons for avoiding us forever?"

And taking Mrs. Weldon aside, Dick Sand confided to her his suspicions. He was not astonished to find that she had them also. Only they differed on one point.

"If Negoro reappears," said Mrs. Weldon, "he will have put the product of his theft in a safe place. Take my advice. What we had better do, not being able to convict him, will be to hide our suspicions from him, and let him believe that we are his dupes."

Mrs. Weldon was right. Dick Sand took her advice.

However, Negoro was called several times.

He did not reply. Either he was still too far away to hear, or he did not wish to return.

The blacks did not regret being rid of his presence; but, as Mrs. Weldon had just said, perhaps he was still more to be feared afar than near. And, moreover, how explain that Negoro would venture alone into that unknown country? Had he then lost his way, and on this dark night was he vainly seeking the way to the grotto?

Mrs. Weldon and Dick Sand did not know what to think. However it was, they could not, in order to wait for Negoro, deprive themselves of a repose so necessary to all.

At that moment the dog, which was running on the strand, barked aloud.

"What is the matter with Dingo?" asked Mrs. Weldon.

"We must, indeed, find out," replied the novice. "Perhaps it is Negoro coming back."

At once Hercules, Bat, Austin, and Dick Sand took their way to the mouth of the river.

But, arrived at the bank, they neither saw nor heard anything. Dingo now was silent.

Dick Sand and the blacks returned to the grotto.

The going to sleep was organized as well as possible. Each of the blacks prepared himself to watch in turn outside. But Mrs. Weldon, uneasy, could not sleep. It seemed to her that this land so ardently desired did not give her what she had been led to hope for, security for hers, and rest for herself.

## CHAPTER XV.

### HARRIS.

The next day, April 7th, Austin, who was on guard at sunrise, saw Dingo run barking to the little river. Almost immediately Mrs. Weldon, Dick Sand and the blacks came out of the grotto.

Decidedly there was something there.

"Dingo has scented a living creature, man or beast," said the novice.

"At all events it was not Negoro," observed Tom, "for Dingo would bark with fury."

"If it is not Negoro, where can he be?" asked Mrs. Weldon, giving Dick Sand a look which was only understood by him; "and if it is not he, who, then, is it?"

"We are going to see, Mrs. Weldon," replied the novice. Then, addressing Bat, Austin, and Hercules, "Arm yourselves, my friends, and come!"

Each of the blacks took a gun and a cutlass, as Dick Sand had done. A cartridge was slipped into the breech of the Remingtons, and, thus armed, all four went to the bank of the river.

Mrs. Weldon, Tom, and Acteon remained at the entrance of the grotto, where little Jack and Nan still rested by themselves.

The sun was then rising. His rays, intercepted by the high mountains in the east, did not reach the cliff directly; but as far as the western horizon, the sea sparkled under the first fires of day.

Dick Sand and his companions followed the strand of the shore, the curve of which joined the mouth of the river.

There Dingo, motionless, and as if on guard, was continually barking.

It was evident that he saw or scented some native.

And, in fact, it was no longer against Negoro, against its enemy on board the ship, that the dog had a grudge this time.

At that moment a man turned the last plane of the cliff. He advanced prudently to the strand, and, by his familiar gestures, he sought to calm Dingo. They saw that he did not care to face the anger of the vigorous animal.

"It is not Negoro!" said Hercules.

"We cannot lose by the change," replied Bat.

"No," said the novice. "It is probably some native, who will spare us the ennui of a separation. We are at last going to know exactly where we are."

And all four, putting their guns back on their shoulders, went rapidly toward the unknown.

The latter, on seeing them approach, at first gave signs of the greatest surprise. Very certainly, he did not expect to meet strangers on that part of the coast. Evidently, also, he had not yet perceived the remains of the "Pilgrim," otherwise the presence of the shipwrecked would very naturally be explained to him. Besides, during the night the surf had finished demolishing the ship's hull; there was nothing left but the wrecks that floated in the offing.

At the first moment the unknown, seeing four armed men marching toward him, made a movement as if he would retrace his steps. He carried a gun in a shoulder-belt, which passed rapidly into his hand, and from his hand to his shoulder. They felt that he was not reassured.

Dick Sand made a gesture of salutation, which doubtless the unknown understood, for, after some hesitation, he continued to advance.

Dick Sand could then examine him with attention.

He was a vigorous man, forty years old at the most, his eyes bright, his hair and beard gray, his skin sunburnt like that of a nomad who has always lived in the open air, in the forest, or on the plain. A kind of blouse of tanned skin served him for a close coat, a large hat covered his head, leather boots came up above his knees, and spurs with large rowels sounded from their high heels.

What Dick Sand noticed at first—and which was so, in fact—was that he had before him, not one of those Indians, habitual rovers over the pampas, but one of those adventurers of foreign blood, often not very commendable, who are frequently met with in those distant countries.

It also seemed, by his rather familiar attitude, by the reddish color of a few hairs of his beard, that this unknown must be of Anglo-Saxon origin. At all events, he was neither an Indian nor a Spaniard.

And that appeared certain, when in answer to Dick Sand, who said to him in English, "Welcome!" he replied in the same language and without any accent.

"Welcome yourself, my young friend," said the unknown, advancing toward the novice, whose hand he pressed.

As to the blacks, he contented himself with making a gesture to them without speaking to them.

"You are English?" he asked the novice.

"Americans," replied Dick Sand.

"From the South?"

"From the North."

This reply seemed to please the unknown, who shook the novice's hand more vigorously and this time in very a American manner.

"And may I know, my young friend," he asked, "how you find yourself on this coast?"

But, at that moment, without waiting till the novice had replied to his question, the unknown took off his hat and bowed.

Mrs. Weldon had advanced as far as the steep bank, and she then found herself facing him.

It was she who replied to this question.

"Sir," said she, "we are shipwrecked ones whose ship was broken to pieces yesterday on these reefs."

An expression of pity spread over the unknown's face, whose eyes sought the vessel which had been stranded.

"There is nothing left of our ship," added the novice. "The surf has finished the work of demolishing it during the night."

"And our first question," continued Mrs. Weldon, "will be to ask you where we are."

"But you are on the sea-coast of South America," replied the unknown, who appeared surprised at the question. "Can you have any doubt about that?"

"Yes, sir, for the tempest had been able to make us deviate from our route," replied Dick Sand. "But I shall ask where we are more exactly. On the coast of Peru, I think."

"No, my young friend, no! A little more to the south! You are wrecked on the Bolivian coast."

"Ah!" exclaimed Dick Sand.

"And you are even on that southern part of Bolivia which borders on

Chili."

"Then what is that cape?" asked Dick Sand, pointing to the promontory on the north.

"I cannot tell you the name," replied the unknown, "for if I know the country in the interior pretty well from having often traversed it, it is my first visit to this shore."

Dick Sand reflected on what he had just learned. That only half astonished him, for his calculation might have, and indeed must have, deceived him, concerning the currents; but the error was not considerable. In fact, he believed himself somewhere between the twenty-seventh and the thirtieth parallel, from the bearings he had taken from the Isle of Paques, and it was on the twenty-fifth parallel that he was wrecked. There was no impossibility in the "Pilgrim's" having deviated by relatively small digression, in such a long passage.

Besides, there was no reason to doubt the unknown's assertions, and, as that coast was that of lower Bolivia there was nothing astonishing in its being so deserted.

"Sir," then said Dick Sand, "after your reply I must conclude that we are at a rather great distance from Lima."

"Oh! Lima is far away—over there—in the north!"

Mrs. Weldon, made suspicious first of all by Negoro's disappearance, observed the newly-arrived with extreme attention; but she could discover nothing, either in his attitude or in his manner of expressing himself which could lead her to suspect his good faith.

"Sir," said she, "without doubt my question is not rash. You do not seem to be of Peruvian origin?"

"I am American as you are, madam," said the unknown, who waited for an instant for the American lady to tell him her name.

"Mrs. Weldon," replied the latter.

"I? My name is Harris and I was born in South Carolina. But here it is twenty years since I left my country for the pampas of Bolivia, and it gives me pleasure to see compatriots."

"You live in this part of the province, Mr. Harris?" again asked Mrs. Weldon.

"No, Mrs. Weldon," replied Harris, "I live in the South, on the Chilian frontier; but at this present moment I am going to Atacama, in the northeast."

"Are we then on the borders of the desert of that name?" asked Dick Sand.

"Precisely, my young friend, and this desert extends far beyond the mountains which shut off the horizon."

"The desert of Atacama?" repeated Dick Sand.

"Yes," replied Harris. "This desert is like a country by itself, in this vast South America, from which it differs in many respects. It is, at the same time, the most curious and the least known portion of this continent."

"And you travel alone?" asked Mrs. Weldon.

"Oh, it is not the first time that I have taken this journey!" replied the American. "There is, two hundred miles from here, an important farm, the Farm of San Felice, which belongs to one of my brothers, and it is to his house that I am going for my trade. If you wish to follow me you will be well received, and the means of transport to gain the town of Atacama will not fail you. My brother will be happy to furnish, them."

These offers, made freely, could only prepossess in favor of the

American, who immediately continued, addressing Mrs. Weldon:

"These blacks are your slaves?"

And he pointed to Tom and his companions.

"We have no longer any slaves in the United States," replied Mrs. Weldon, quickly. "The North abolished slavery long ago, and the South has been obliged to follow the example of the North!"

"Ah! that is so," replied Harris. "I had forgotten that the war of 1862 had decided that grave question. I ask those honest men's pardon for it," added Harris, with that delicate irony which a Southerner must put into his language when speaking to blacks. "But on seeing those gentlemen in your service, I believed——"

"They are not, and have never been, in my service, sir," replied Mrs. Weldon, gravely.

"We should be honored in serving you, Mrs. Weldon," then said old Tom. "But, as Mr. Harris knows, we do not belong to anybody. I have been a slave myself, it is true, and sold as such in Africa, when I was only six years old; but my son Bat, here, was born of an enfranchised father, and, as to our companions, they were born of free parents."

"I can only congratulate you about it," replied Harris, in a tone which

Mrs. Weldon did not find sufficiently serious. "In this land of

Bolivia, also, we have no slaves. Then you have nothing to fear, and

you can go about as freely here as in the New England States."

At that moment little Jack, followed by Nan, came out of the grotto rubbing his eyes. Then, perceiving his mother, he ran to her. Mrs. Weldon embraced him tenderly.

"The charming little boy!" said the American, approaching Jack.

"It is my son," replied Mrs. Weldon.

"Oh, Mrs. Weldon, you must have been doubly tried, because your child has been exposed to so many dangers."

"God has brought him out of them safe and sound, as He has us, Mr.

Harris," replied Mrs. Weldon.

"Will you permit me to kiss him on his pretty cheeks?" asked Harris.

"Willingly," replied Mrs. Weldon.

But Mr. Harris's face, it appeared, did not please little Jack, for he clung more closely to his mother.

"Hold!" said Harris, "you do not want me to embrace you? You are afraid of me, my good little man?"

"Excuse him, sir," Mrs. Weldon hastened to say. "It is timidity on his part."

"Good! we shall become better acquainted," replied Harris. "Once at the Farm, he will amuse himself mounting a gentle pony, which will tell him good things of me."

But the offer of the gentle pony did not succeed in cajoling Jack any more than the proposition to embrace Mr. Harris.

Mrs. Weldon, thus opposed, hastened to change the conversation. They must not offend a man who had so obligingly offered his services.

During this time Dick Sand was reflecting on the proposition which had been made to them so opportunely, to gain the Farm of San Felice. It was, as Harris had said, a journey of over two hundred miles, sometimes through forests, sometimes through plains—a very fatiguing journey, certainly, because there were absolutely no means of transport.

The young novice then presented some observations to that effect, and waited for the reply the American was going to make.

"The journey is a little long, indeed," replied Harris, "but I have there, a few hundred feet behind the steep bank, a horse which I count on offering to Mrs. Weldon and her son. For us, there is nothing difficult, nor even very fatiguing in making the journey on foot. Besides, when I spoke of two hundred miles, it was by following, as I have already done, the course of this river. But if we go through the forest, our distance will be shortened by at least eighty miles. Now, at the rate of ten miles a day, it seems to me that we shall arrive at the Farm without too much distress."

Mrs. Weldon thanked the American.

"You cannot thank me better than by accepting," replied Harris. "Though I have never crossed this forest, I do not believe I shall be embarrassed in finding the way, being sufficiently accustomed to the pampas. But there is a graver question—that of food. I have only what is barely enough for myself while on the way to the Farm of San Felice."

"Mr. Harris," replied Mrs. Weldon, "fortunately we have food in more than sufficient quantity, and we shall be happy to share with you."

"Well, Mrs. Weldon, it seems to me that all is arranged for the best, and that we have only to set out."

Harris went toward the steep bank, with the intention of going to take his horse from the place where he had left it, when Dick Sand stopped him again, by asking him a question.

To abandon the sea-coast, to force his way into the interior of the country, under that interminable forest, did not please the young novice. The sailor reappeared in him, and either to ascend or descend the coast would be more to his mind.

"Mr. Harris," said he, "instead of traveling for one hundred and twenty miles in the Desert of Atacama, why not follow the coast? Distance for distance, would it not be better worth while to seek to reach the nearest town, either north or south?"

"But my young friend," replied Harris, frowning slightly, "it seems to me that on this coast, which I know very imperfectly, there is no town nearer than three or four hundred miles."

"To the north, yes," replied Dick Sand; "but to the south——"

"To the south," replied the American, "we must descend as far as Chili. Now, the distance is almost as long, and, in your place, I should not like to pass near the pampas of the Argentine Republic. As to me, to my great regret, I could not accompany you there."

"The ships which go from Chili to Peru, do they not pass, then, in sight of this coast?" asked Mrs. Weldon.

"No," replied Harris. "They keep much more out at sea, and you ought not to meet any of them."

"Truly," replied Mrs. Weldon. "Well, Dick, have you still some question to ask Mr. Harris?"

"A single one, Mrs. Weldon," replied the novice, who experienced some difficulty in giving up. "I shall ask Mr. Harris in what port he thinks we shall be able to find a ship to bring us back to San Francisco?"

"Faith, my young friend, I could not tell you," replied the American. "All that I know is, that at the Farm of San Felice we will furnish you with the means of gaining the town of Atacama, and from there——"

"Mr. Harris," then said Mrs. Weldon, "do not believe that Dick Sand hesitates to accept your offers."

"No, Mrs. Weldon, no; surely I do not hesitate," replied the young novice; "but I cannot help regretting not being stranded a few degrees farther north or farther south. We should have been in proximity to a port, and that circumstance, in facilitating our return to our country, would prevent us from taxing Mr. Harris's good will."

"Do not fear imposing upon me, Mrs. Weldon," returned Harris. "I repeat to you that too rarely have I occasion to find myself again in the presence of my compatriots. For me it is a real pleasure to oblige you."

"We accept your offer, Mr. Harris," replied Mrs. Weldon; "but I should not wish, however, to deprive you of your horse. I am a good walker——"

"And I am a very good walker," replied Harris, bowing. "Accustomed to long journeys across the pampas, it is not I who will keep back our caravan. No, Mrs. Weldon, you and your little Jack will use this horse. Besides, it is possible that we may meet some of the farm servants on the way, and, as they will be mounted—well, they will yield their horses to us."

Dick Sand saw well that in making new objections he would oppose Mrs. Weldon.

"Mr. Harris," said he, "when do we set out?"

"Even to-day, my young friend," replied Harris. "The bad season commences with the month of April, and it is of the utmost importance for you to reach the farm of San Felice first. Finally, the way across the forest is the shortest, and perhaps the safest. It is less exposed than the coast to the incursions of wandering Indians, who are indefatigable robbers."

"Tom, my friends," replied Dick Sand, turning to the blacks, "it only remains for us to make preparations for departure. Let us select, then, from among the provisions on hand, those which can be most easily transported, and let us make packs, of which each will take his share."

"Mr. Dick," said Hercules, "if you wish, I shall carry the whole load very well."

"No, my brave Hercules," replied the novice; "it will be better for us all to share the burden."

"You are a strong companion, Hercules," then said Harris, who looked at the negro as if the latter were for sale. "In the markets of Africa you would be worth a good price."

"I am worth what I am worth," replied Hercules, laughing, "and the buyers will only have to run well, if they wish to catch me."

All was agreed upon, and to hasten the departure, each went to work. However, they had only to think of feeding the little troop for the journey from the sea-coast to the farm, that is to say, for a march of ten days.

"But, before setting out, Mr. Harris," said Mrs. Weldon, "before accepting your hospitality, I beg you to accept ours. We offer it to you with our best wishes."

"I accept, Mrs. Weldon; I accept with eagerness," replied Harris, gayly.

"In a few minutes our breakfast will be ready."

"Good, Mrs. Weldon. I am going to profit by those ten minutes to go and get my horse and bring it here. He will have breakfasted, he will."

"Do you want me to go with you, sir?" asked Dick Sand.

"As you please, my young friend," replied Harris. "Come; I shall make you acquainted with the lower course of this river."

Both set out.

During this time, Hercules was sent in search of the entomologist. Faith, Cousin Benedict was very uneasy indeed about what was passing around him.

He was then wandering on the summit of the cliff in quest of an "unfindable" insect, which, however, he did not find.

Hercules brought him back against his will. Mrs. Weldon informed him that departure was decided upon, and that, for ten days, they must travel to the interior of the country.

Cousin Benedict replied that he was ready to set out, and that he would not ask better than to cross America entirely, provided they would let him "collect" on the way.

Mrs. Weldon then occupied herself, with Nan's assistance, in preparing a comfortable repast—a good precaution before setting out.

During this time, Harris, accompanied by Dick Sand, had turned the angle of the cliff. Both followed the high bank, over a space of three hundred steps. There, a horse, tied to a tree, gave joyous neighing at the approach of his master.

It was a vigorous beast, of a species that Dick Sand could not recognize. Neck and shoulders long, loins short, and hindquarters stretched out, shoulders flat, forehead almost pointed. This horse offered, however, distinctive signs of those races to which we attribute an Arabian origin.

"You see, my young friend," said Harris, "that it is a strong animal, and you may count on it not failing you on the route."

Harris detached his horse, took it by the bridle, and descended the steep bank again, preceding Dick Sand. The latter had thrown a rapid glance, as well over the river as toward the forest which shut up its two banks. But he saw nothing of a nature to make him uneasy.

However, when he had rejoined the American, he suddenly gave him the following question, which the latter could little expect:

"Mr. Harris," he asked, "you have not met a Portuguese, named Negoro, in the night?"

"Negoro?" replied Harris, in the tone of a man who does not understand what is said. "Who is this Negoro?"

"He was the cook on board," replied Dick Sand, "and he has disappeared."

"Drowned, perhaps," said Harris.

"No, no," replied Dick Sand. "Yesterday evening he was still with us, but during the night he has left us, and he has probably ascended the steep bank of this river. So I asked you, who have come from that side, if you had not met him."

"I have met nobody," replied the American; "and if your cook has ventured alone into the forest, he runs a great risk of going astray. Perhaps we shall overtake him on the way."

"Yes; perhaps!" replied Dick Sand.

When the two returned to the grotto, breakfast was ready. It was composed, like the supper of the evening before, of alimentary conserves, of corned beef and of biscuit. Harris did honor to it, like a man whom nature had endowed with a great appetite.

"Let us go," said he; "I see that we shall not die of hunger on the way! I shall not say as much for that poor devil of a Portuguese, of whom our young friend has spoken."

"Ah!" said Mrs. Weldon, "Dick Sand has told you that we have not seen Negoro again?"

"Yes, Mrs. Weldon," replied the novice. "I desired to know if Mr. Harris had not met him."

"No," replied Harris; "so let us leave that deserter where he is, and think of our departure—whenever you are ready, Mrs. Weldon."

Each took the pack which was intended for him. Mrs. Weldon, assisted by Hercules, placed herself on the horse, and the ungrateful little Jack, with his gun strapped on his back, straddled the animal without even thinking of thanking him who had put that excellent beast at his disposal. Jack, placed before his mother, then said to her that he would know how to lead the gentleman's horse very well.

They then gave him the bridle to hold, and he did not doubt that he was the veritable head of the caravan.

## CHAPTER XVI.

### ON THE WAY.

It was not without a certain apprehension—nothing seemed to justify it, however—that Dick Sand, three hundred steps from the steep bank of the river, penetrated into the thick forest, the difficult paths of which he and his companions were going to follow for ten days. On the contrary, Mrs. Weldon herself, a woman and a mother, whom the perils would make doubly anxious, had every confidence. Two very serious motives had contributed to reassure her; first, because this region of the pampas was neither very formidable on account of the natives, nor on account of the animals which were found there; next, because, under the direction of Harris, of a guide so sure of himself as the American appeared to be, they could not be afraid of going astray.

Here is the order of proceeding, which, as far as possible, would be observed during the journey:

Dick Sand and Harris, both armed, one with his long gun, the other with a Remington, kept at the head of the little troop.

Then came Bat and Austin, also armed, each with a gun and a cutlass.

Behind them followed Mrs. Weldon and little Jack, on horseback; then

Nan and Tom.

In the rear, Acteon, armed with the fourth Remington, and Hercules, with a hatchet in his belt, closed the march.

Dingo went backwards and forwards, and, as Dick Sand remarked, always like an uneasy dog seeking a scent. The dog's ways had visibly changed since the "Pilgrim's" shipwreck had cast it on this sea-coast. It seemed agitated, and almost incessantly it kept up a dull grumbling, rather lamentable than furious. That was remarked by all, though no one could explain it.

As to Cousin Benedict, it had been as impossible to assign him an order of marching as Dingo. Unless he had been held by a string, he would not have kept it. His tin box strapped to his shoulder, his net in his hand, his large magnifying glass suspended to his neck, sometimes behind, sometimes in front, he scampered away among the high herbs, watching for orthopters or any other insect in "pter," at the risk of being bit by some venomous serpent.

During the first hour Mrs. Weldon, uneasy, called him back twenty times. It was no use.

"Cousin Benedict," she finished by saying to him, "I beg you very seriously not to go far away, and I urge you for the last time to pay attention to my entreaties."

"Meanwhile, cousin," replied the intractable entomologist, "when I perceive an insect?"

"When you perceive an insect," replied Mrs. Weldon, "you would do well to let it go in peace, or you will put me under the necessity of taking your box away from you."

"Take away my box!" cried Cousin Benedict, as if it were a question of snatching away his heart.

"Your box and your net," added Mrs. Weldon, pitilessly.

"My net, cousin! And why not my glasses? You will not dare! No; you will not dare!"

"Even, your glasses, which I forgot. I thank you, Cousin Benedict, for reminding me that I have that means of making you blind, and, in that way, forcing you to be wise."

This triple menace had the effect of making him keep quiet—this unsubmissive cousin—for about an hour. Then he began to go away again, and, as he would do the same, even without net, without box, and without glasses, they were obliged to let him do as he pleased. But Hercules undertook to watch him closely—which quite naturally became one of his duties—and it was agreed that he would act with Cousin Benedict as the latter would with an insect; that is, that he would catch him, if necessary, and bring him back as delicately as the other would with the rarest of the lepidopters.

That rule made, they troubled themselves no more about Cousin Benedict.

The little troop, it has been seen, was well armed, and guarded itself carefully. But, as Harris repeated, there was no encounter to fear except with wandering Indians, and they would probably see none.

At all events, the precautions taken would suffice to keep them respectful.

The paths which wound across the thick forest did not merit that name. They were rather the tracks of animals than the tracks of men. They could only be followed with difficulty. So, in fixing the average distance that the little troop would make in a march of twelve hours at only five or six miles, Harris had calculated wisely.

The weather, however, was very fine. The sun mounted toward the zenith, spreading in waves his almost perpendicular rays. On the plain this heat would be unbearable, Harris took care to remark; but, under those impenetrable branches, they bore it easily and with impunity.

The greater part of the trees of this forest were unknown, as well to

Mrs. Weldon as to her companions, black or white.

However, an expert would remark that they were more remarkable for their quality than for their height. Here, it was the "banhinia," or iron wood; there, the "molompi," identical with the "pterocarpe," a solid and light wood, fit for making the spoons used in sugar manufactories or oars, from the trunk of which exuded an abundant resin; further on, "fusticks," or yellow wood, well supplied with coloring materials, and lignum-vitæs, measuring as much as twelve feet in diameter, but inferior in quality to the ordinary lignum-vitæs.

While walking, Dick Sand asked Harris the name of these different trees.

"Then you have never been on the coast of South America?" Harris asked him before replying to his question.

"Never," replied the novice; "never, during my voyages, have I had occasion to visit these coasts, and to say the truth, I do not believe that anybody who knew about them has ever spoken to me of them."

"But have you at least explored the coasts of Colombia, those of Chili, or of Patagonia?"

"No, never."

"But perhaps Mrs. Weldon has visited this part of the new continent?" asked Harris. "Americans do not fear voyages, and doubtless——"

"No, Mr. Harris," replied Mrs. Weldon. "The commercial interests of my husband have never called him except to New Zealand, and I have not had to accompany him elsewhere. Not one of us, then, knows this portion of lower Bolivia."

"Well, Mrs. Weldon, you and your companions will see a singular country, which contrasts strangely with the regions of Peru, of Brazil, or of the Argentine Republic. Its flora and fauna would astonish a naturalist. Ah! we may say that you have been shipwrecked at a good place, and if we may ever thank chance——"

"I wish to believe that it is not chance which has led us here, but

God, Mr. Harris."

"God! Yes! God!" replied Harris, in the tone of a man who takes little account of providential intervention in the things of this world.

Then, since nobody in the little troop knew either the country or its productions, Harris took a pleasure in naming pleasantly the most curious trees of the forest.

In truth, it was a pity that, in Cousin Benedict's case, the entomologist was not supplemented by the botanist! If, up to this time, he had hardly found insects either rare or new, he might have made fine discoveries in botany. There was, in profusion, vegetation of all heights, the existence of which in the tropical forests of the New World had not been yet ascertained. Cousin Benedict would certainly have attached his name to some discovery of this kind. But he did not like botany—he knew nothing about it. He even, quite naturally, held flowers in aversion, under the pretext that some of them permit themselves to imprison the insects in their corollas, and poison them with their venomous juices.

At times, the forest became marshy. They felt under foot quite a network of liquid threads, which would feed the affluents of the little river. Some of the rills, somewhat large, could only be crossed by choosing fordable places.

On their banks grew tufts of reeds, to which Harris gave the name of papyrus. He was not mistaken, and those herbaceous plants grew abundantly below the damp banks.

Then, the marsh passed, thickets of trees again covered the narrow routes of the forest.

Harris made Mrs. Weldon and Dick Sand remark some very fine ebony-trees, much larger than the common ebony-tree, which furnish a wood much blacker and much stronger than that of commerce. Then there were mango-trees, still numerous, though they were rather far from the sea. A kind of fur of white moss climbed them as far as the branches. Their thick shade and their delicious fruit made them precious trees, and meanwhile, according to Harris, not a native would dare to propagate the species. "Whoever plants a mango-tree dies!" Such is the superstitious maxim of the country.

During the second half of this first day of the journey, the little troop, after the midday halt, began to ascend land slightly inclined. They were not as yet the slopes of the chain of the first plane, but a sort of undulating plateau which connected the plain with the mountain.

There the trees, a little less compact, sometimes clustered in groups, would have rendered the march easier, if the soil had not been invaded by herbaceous plants. One might believe himself in the jungles of Oriental India. Vegetation appeared to be less luxuriant than in the lower valley of the little river, but it was still superior to that of the temperate regions of the Old or of the New World.

Indigo was growing there in profusion, and, according to Harris, this leguminous plant passed with reason for the most usurping plant of the country. If a field came to be abandoned, this parasite, as much despised as the thistle or the nettle, took possession of it immediately.

One tree seemed lacking in this forest, which ought to be very common in this part of the new continent; it was the caoutchouc-tree. In fact, the "ficus primoides," the "castilloa elastica," the "cecropia peltats," the "collophora utilis," the "cameraria letifolia," and above all, the "syphonia elastica," which belong to different families, abound in the provinces of South America. And meanwhile, a rather singular thing, there was not a single one to be seen.

Now, Dick Sand had particularly promised his friend Jack to show him some caoutchouc trees. So a great deception for the little boy, who figured to himself that gourds, speaking babies, articulate punchinellos, and elastic balloons grew quite naturally on those trees. He complained.

"Patience, my good little man," replied Harris. "We shall find some of those caoutchoucs, and by hundreds, in the neighborhood of the farm."

"Handsome ones, very elastic?" asked little Jack.

"The most elastic there are. Hold! while waiting, do you want a good fruit to take away your thirst?" And, while speaking, Harris went to gather from a tree some fruits, which seemed to be as pleasant to the taste as those from the peach-tree.

"Are you very sure, Mr. Harris," asked Mrs. Weldon, "that this fruit can do no harm?"

"Mrs. Weldon, I am going to convince you," replied the American, who took a large mouthful of one of those fruits. "It is a mango."

And little Jack, without any more pressing, followed Harris's example, He declared that it was very good, "those pears," and the tree was at once put under contribution.

Those mangos belonged to a species whose fruit is ripe in March and April, others being so only in September, and, consequently, their mangos were just in time.

"Yes, it is good, good, good!" said little Jack, with his mouth full. "But my friend Dick has promised me caoutchoucs, if I was very good, and I want caoutchoucs!"

"You will have them, Jack," replied Mrs. Weldon, "because Mr. Harris assures you of it."

"But that is not all," went on Jack. "My friend Dick has promised me some other thing!"

"What then, has friend Dick promised?" asked Harris, smiling.

"Some humming-birds, sir."

"And you shall have some humming-birds, my good little man, but farther on—farther on," replied Harris.

The fact is that little Jack had a right to claim some of these charming creatures, for he was now in a country where they should abound. The Indians, who know how to weave their feathers artistically, have lavished the most poetical names on those jewels of the flying race. They call them either the "rays" or the "hairs of the sun." Here, it is "the little king of the flowers;"

there, "the celestial flower that comes in its flight to caress the terrestrial flower." It is again "the bouquet of jewels, which sparkles in the fire of the day." It can be believed that their imagination would know how to furnish a new poetical appellation for each of the one hundred and fifty species which constitute this marvelous tribe of humming-birds.

Meanwhile, however numerous these humming-birds might be in the forests of Bolivia, little Jack was obliged to still content himself with Harris's promise. According to the American, they were still too close to the coast, and the humming-birds did not like these deserts so near the ocean. The presence of man did not frighten them at the "hacienda;" they heard nothing all day but their cry of "teretere" and the murmur of their wings, similar to that of a spinning-wheel.

"Ah! how I should like to be there!" cried little Jack.

The surest method of getting there—to the "hacienda" of San Felice—was not to stop on the road. Mrs. Weldon and her companions only took the time absolutely necessary for repose.

The aspect of the forest already changed. Between the less crowded trees large clearings opened here and there. The sun, piercing the green carpet, then showed its structure of red, syenite granite, similar to slabs of lapis-lazuli. On some heights the sarsaparilla abounded, a plant with fleshy tubercles, which formed an inextricable tangle. The forest, with the narrow paths, was better for them.

Before sunset the little troop were about eight miles from the point of departure. This journey had been made without accident, and even without great fatigue. It is true, it was the first journey on the march, and no doubt the following halting places would be rougher.

By a common consent they decided to make a halt at this place. The question then was, not to establish a real camp, but to simply organize a resting-place. One man on guard, relieved every two hours, would suffice to watch during the night, neither the natives nor the deer being truly formidable.

They found nothing better for shelter than an enormous mango-tree, whose large branches, very bushy, formed a kind of natural veranda. If necessary, they could nestle in the branches.

Only, on the arrival of the little troop, a deafening concert arose from the top of the tree.

The mango served as a perch for a colony of gray parrots, prattling, quarrelsome, ferocious birds, which set upon living birds, and those who would judge them from their congeners which Europe keeps in cages, would be singularly mistaken.

These parrots jabbered with such a noise that Dick Sand thought of firing at them to oblige them to be silent, or to put them to flight. But Harris dissuaded him, under the pretext that in these solitudes it was better not to disclose his presence by the detonation of a fire-arm.

"Let us pass along without noise," he said, "and we shall pass along without danger."

Supper was prepared at once, without any need of proceeding to cook food. It was composed of conserves and biscuit. A little rill, which wound under the plants, furnished drinkable water, which they did not drink without improving it with a few drops of rum. As to dessert, the mango was there with its juicy fruit, which the parrots did not allow to be picked without protesting with their abominable cries.

At the end of the supper it began to be dark. The shade rose slowly from the ground to the tops of the trees, from which the foliage soon stood out like a fine tracery on the more luminous background of the sky. The first stars seemed to be shining flowers, which twinkled at the end of the last branches. The wind went down with the night, and no longer trembled in the branches of the trees. The parrots themselves had become mute. Nature was going to rest, and inviting every living being to follow her in this deep sleep.

Preparations for retiring had to be of a very primitive character.

"Shall we not light a large fire for the night?" Dick Sand asked the American.

"What's the good?" replied Harris. "Fortunately the nights are not cold, and this enormous mango will preserve the soil from all evaporation. We have neither cold nor dampness to fear. I repeat, my young friend, what I told you just now. Let us move along incognito. No more fire than gunshots, if possible."

"I believe, indeed," then said Mrs. Weldon, "that we have nothing to fear from the Indians—even from those wanderers of the woods, of whom you have spoken, Mr. Harris. But, are there not other four-footed wanderers, that the sight of a fire would help to keep at a distance?"

"Mrs. Weldon," replied the American, "you do too much honor to the deer of this country. Indeed, they fear man more than he fears them."

"We are in a wood," said Jack, "and there is always beasts in the woods."

"There are woods and woods, my good little man, as there are beasts and beasts," replied Harris, laughing. "Imagine that you are in the middle of a large park. Truly, it is not without reason that the Indians say of this country, 'Es como el pariso!' It is like an earthly paradise!"

"Then there are serpents?" said Jack.

"No, my Jack," replied Mrs. Weldon, "there are no serpents, and you may sleep tranquilly."

"And lions?" asked Jack.

"Not the ghost of a lion, my good little man," replied Harris.

"Tigers, then?"

"Ask your mama if she has ever heard tell of tigers on this continent."

"Never," replied Mrs. Weldon.

"Good!" said Cousin Benedict, who, by chance, was listening to the conversation: "if there are neither lions nor tigers in the New World, which is perfectly true, we at least encounter cougars and jaguars."

"Are they bad?" asked little Jack.

"Phew!" replied Harris; "a native has little fear of attacking those animals, and we are strong. Stay! Hercules would be strong enough to crush two jaguars at once, one in each hand!"

"You will watch well, Hercules," then said little Jack, "and if a beast comes to bite us———"

"It is I who will bite it, Mr. Jack!" replied Hercules, showing his mouth, armed with superb teeth.

"Yes, you will watch, Hercules," said the novice, "but your companions and I will relieve you, turn about."

"No, Mr. Dick," replied Acteon, "Hercules, Bat, Austin, and I, we four will be enough for this labor. You must rest the whole night."

"Thank you, Acteon," replied Dick Sand, "but I ought to———"

"No! let those brave men do it, my dear Dick!" then said Mrs. Weldon.

"I, also; I shall watch!" added little Jack, whose eyelids were already closing.

"Yes, my Jack, yes, you will watch!" replied his mother, who did not wish to contradict him.

"But," the little boy said again, "if there are no lions, if there are no tigers in the forest, there are wolves!"

"Oh! wolves in jest!" replied the American. "They are not even wolves, but kinds of foxes, or rather of those dogs of the woods which they call 'guaras.'"

"And those guaras, they bite?" asked little Jack.

"Bah! Dingo would make only one mouthful of those beasts!"

"Never mind," replied Jack, with a last yawn; "guaras are wolves, because they are called wolves!"

And with that Jack fell asleep peaceably in Nan's arms, beside the trunk of the mango. Mrs. Weldon, lying near her, gave a last kiss to her little boy, and her tired eyes quickly closed for the night.

A few moments later Hercules brought back to the camp Cousin Benedict, who had just gone off to commence a chase for pyrophores. They are "cocuyos," or luminous flies, which the stylish put in their hair, like so many living gems. These insects which throw a bright and bluish light from two spots situated at the base of their corselet, are very numerous in South America. Cousin Benedict then counted on making a large collection, but Hercules did not leave him time, and, in spite of his recriminations, the negro brought him to the halting-place. That was because, when Hercules had orders, he executed them with military preciseness, which, no doubt, prevented the incarceration of a notable quantity of luminous flies in the entomologist's tin box.

A few moments after, with the exception of the giant, who was watching, all were reposing in a profound sleep.

## CHAPTER XVII.

### A HUNDRED MILES IN TWO DAYS.

Generally, travelers or ramblers in the woods, who have slept in the forests under the lovely stars, are awakened by howlings as fantastic as disagreeable. There is everything in this morning concert: clucking, grunting, croaking, sneering, barking, and almost "speaking," if one may make use of this word, which completes the series of different noises.

There are the monkeys who thus salute the daybreak. There we meet the little "marikina," the marmoset with a speckled mask; the "mono gris," the skin of which the Indians use to recover the batteries of their guns; the "sagous," recognizable from their long bunches of hair, and many others, specimens of this numerous family.

Of these various four-handed animals, the most remarkable are decidedly the "gueribas," with curling tails and a face like Beelzebub. When the sun rises, the oldest of the band, with an imposing and mysterious voice, sings a monotonous psalm. It is the baritone of the troop. The young tenors repeat after him the morning symphony. The Indians say then that the "gueribas" recite their pater-nosters.

But, on this day, it seemed that the monkeys did not offer their prayer, for no one heard them; and, meanwhile, their voice is loud, for it is produced by the rapid vibration of a kind of bony drum, formed by a swelling of the hyoides bone in the neck.

In short, for one reason or for another, neither the "gueribas," nor the "sagous," nor any other four-handed animals of this immense forest, sang, on this morning, their usual concert.

This would not have satisfied the wandering Indians. Not that these natives appreciate this kind of strange choral music, but they willingly give chase to the monkeys, and if they do, it is because the flesh of this animal is excellent, above all, when it is smoke-dried.

Dick Sand, of course, could not be familiar with the habits of the "gueribas," neither were his companions, or this not hearing them would have undoubtedly been a subject of surprise. They awoke then, one after the other, much refreshed by these few hours of repose, which no alarm had come to disturb.

Little Jack was not the last to stretch his arms. His first question was, to ask if Hercules had eaten a wolf during the night. No wolf had shown himself, and consequently Hercules had not yet breakfasted.

All, besides, were fasting like him, and after the morning prayer, Nan occupied herself preparing the repast.

The bill of fare was that of the supper of the night before, but with appetites sharpened by the morning air of the forest, no one dreamed of being difficult to please. It was necessary, above all, to gather strength for a good day's march, and they did it. For the first time, perhaps, Cousin Benedict comprehended that to eat was not an action indifferent or useless to life; only, he declared that he had not come to "visit" this country to walk with his hands in his pockets, and that, if Hercules prevented him from chasing the "cocuyos," and other luminous flies, Hercules would have some trouble with him.

This threat did not seem to frighten the giant to any great extent. However, Mrs. Weldon took him aside and told him that, perhaps, he might allow his big baby to run to the right and left, but on condition that he did not lose sight of him. It would not do to completely sever Cousin Benedict from the pleasures so natural to his age.

At seven o'clock in the morning, the little troop took up their journey toward the east, preserving the order of march that had been adopted the previous day. It was always the forest. On this virgin soil, where the heat and the moisture agreed to produce vegetation, it might well be thought that the reign of growth appeared in all its power. The parallel of this vast plateau was almost confounded with tropical latitudes, and, during certain months in summer, the sun, in passing to the zenith, darted its perpendicular rays there. There was, therefore, an enormous quantity of imprisoned heat in this earth, of which the subsoil preserved the damp. Also, nothing could be more magnificent than this succession of forests, or rather this interminable forest.

Meanwhile, Dick Sand had not failed to observe this—that, according to Harris, they were in the region of the pampas. Now, pampas is a word from the "quichna" language, which signifies a plain. Now, if his recollections did not deceive him, he believed that these plains presented the following characteristics: Lack of water, absence of trees, a failure of stones, an almost luxuriant abundance of thistles during the rainy season, thistles which became almost shrubby with the warm season, and then formed impenetrable thickets; then, also, dwarf trees, thorny shrubs, the whole giving to these plains a rather arid and desolate aspect.

Now, it had not been thus, since the little troop, guided by the American, had left the coast. The forest had not ceased to spread to the limits of the horizon. No, this was not the pampas, such as the young novice had imagined them. Had nature, as Harris had told him, been able to make a region apart from the plateau of Atacama, of which he knew nothing, if it did not form one of the most vast deserts of South America, between the Andes and the Pacific Ocean?

On that day Dick Sand propounded some questions on this subject, and expressed to the American the surprise he felt at this singular appearance of the pampas.

But he was quickly undeceived by Harris, who gave him the most exact details about this part of Bolivia, thus witnessing to his great knowledge of the country.

"You are right, my young friend," he said to the novice. "The true pampa is indeed such as the books of travels have depicted it to you, that is, a plain rather arid, and the crossing of which is often difficult. It recalls our savannahs of North America—except that these are a little marshy. Yes, such is indeed the pampa of the Rio Colorado, such are the "llanos" of the Orinoco and of Venezuela. But here, we are in a country, the appearance of which even astonishes me. It is true, it is the first time I have followed this route across the plateau, a route which has the advantage of shortening our journey. But, if I have not yet seen it, I know that it presents an extraordinary contrast to the veritable pampa. As to this one, you would find it again, not between the Cordilleras of the west and the high chain of the Andes, but beyond the mountains, over all that eastern part of the continent which extends as far as the Atlantic."

"Must we then clear the Andes range?" Dick Sand asked, quickly.

"No, my young friend, no," replied the American, smiling. "So I said: You would find it again, and not: You will find it again. Be reassured, we shall not leave this plateau, the greatest elevations of which do not exceed fifteen hundred feet. Ah! if it had been necessary to cross the Cordilleras with only the means of transport at our disposal, I should never have drawn you into such an undertaking."

"In fact," replied Dick Sand, "it would be better to ascend or descend the coast."

"Oh! a hundred times!" replied Harris. "But the Farm of San Felice is situated on this side of the Cordilleras. So, then, our journey, neither in its first nor in its second part, will offer any real difficulty."

"And you do not fear going astray in these forests, which you cross for the first time?" asked Dick Sand.

"No, my young friend, no," replied Harris. "I know indeed that this forest is like an immense sea, or rather like the bottom of a sea, where a sailor himself could not take the latitude nor recognize his position. But accustomed to traveling in the woods, I know how to find my route only by the inclination of certain trees, by the direction of their leaves, by the movement or the composition of the soil, by a thousand details which escape you! Be sure of it, I will lead you, you and yours, where you ought to go!"

All these things were said very clearly by Harris. Dick Sand and he, at the head of the troop, often talked without any one mingling in their conversation. If the novice felt some doubts that the American did not always succeed in scattering, he preferred to keep them to himself.

The 8th, 9th, 10th, 11th, and 12th of April passed in this manner, without any incident to mark the journey. They did not make more than eight to nine miles in twelve hours. The times consecrated to eating or repose came at regular intervals, and though a little fatigue was felt already, the sanitary condition was still very satisfactory.

Little Jack began to suffer a little from this life in the woods, to which he was not accustomed, and which was becoming very monotonous for him. And then all the promises which had been made him had not been kept. The caoutchouc jumping-jacks, the humming-birds, all those seemed constantly to recede. There had also been a question of showing him the most beautiful parrots in the world, and they ought not to be wanting in these rich forests. Where, then, were the popinjays with green plumage, almost all originally from these countries, the aras, with naked cheeks, with long pointed tails, with glittering colors, whose paws never rest on the earth, and the "caminds," which are more peculiar to tropical countries, and the many-colored she-parrots, with feathered faces, and finally all those prattling birds which, according to the Indians, still speak the language of extinct tribes?

Of parrots, little Jack only saw ash-gray jakos, with red tails, which abounded under the trees. But these jakos were not new to him. They have transported them into all parts of the world. On the two continents they fill the houses with their insupportable chattering, and, of all the family of the "psittacius," they are the ones which learn to speak most easily.

It must be said, besides, that if Jack was not contented, Cousin Benedict was no more so. He had been allowed to wander a little to the right or to the left during the march. However, he had not found any insect which was fit to enrich his collection. Even the "pyrophores" obstinately refused to show themselves to him, and attract him by the phosphorescences of their corselet. Nature seemed truly to mock the unhappy entomologist, whose temper was becoming cross.

For four days more the march toward the northeast was continued in the same way. On the 16th of April the distance traversed from the coast could not be estimated at less than one hundred miles. If Harris had not gone astray—and he affirmed it without hesitation—the Farm of San Felice was no more than twenty miles from the halting place of that day. Before forty-eight hours the little troop then would have a comfortable shelter where its members could at last repose from their fatigues.

Meanwhile, though the plateau had been almost entirely crossed in its middle part, not a native, not a wanderer had been encountered under the immense forest.

More than once, without saying anything about it, Dick Sand regretted being unable to go ashore on some other point of the coast. More to the south, or more to the north, villages, hamlets, or plantations would not have been lacking, and long before this Mrs. Weldon and her companions would have found an asylum.

But, if the country seemed to be abandoned by man, animals showed themselves more frequently during these last days. At times was heard a kind of long, plaintive cry, that Harris attributed to some of those large tardi-grades, habitual denizens of those vast wooded regions, named "ais."

On that day, also, during the midday halt, a hissing passed through the air, which made Mrs. Weldon very uneasy, because it was so strange.

"What is that?'" she asked, rising hastily.

"A serpent!" cried Dick Sand, who gun, in hand, threw himself before

Mrs. Weldon.

They might fear, in fact, that some reptile would glide among the plants to the halting place. It would be nothing astonishing if it were one of those enormous "sucurus," kinds of boas, which sometimes measure forty feet in length.

But Harris reminded Dick Sand that the blacks were already following, and he reassured Mrs. Weldon.

According to him, that hissing could not be produced by a "sucuru," because that serpent does not hiss; but he indicated the presence of several inoffensive quadrupeds, rather numerous in that country.

"Be reassured, then," said he, "and make no movement which may frighten those animals."

"But what are they?" asked Dick Sand, who made it like a law of conscience to interrogate and make the American speak—who, however, never required pressing before replying.

"They are antelopes, my young friend," replied Harris.

"Oh! how I should like to see them!" cried Jack.

"That is very difficult, my good little man," replied the American, "very difficult."

"Perhaps we may try to approach than—those hissing antelopes?" returned Dick Sand.

"Oh! you will not take three steps," replied the American, shaking his head, "before the whole band will take flight. I beg of you, then, not to trouble yourself."

But Dick Sand had his reasons for being curious. He wished to see, and, gun in hand, he glided among the herbs. Immediately a dozen graceful gazelles, with small, sharp horns, passed with the rapidity of a water-spout. Their hair, bright red, looked like a cloud of fire under the tall underwood of the forest.

"I had warned you," said Harris, when the novice returned to take his place.

Those antelopes were so light of foot, that it had been truly impossible to distinguish them; but it was not so with another troop of animals which was signaled the same day. Those could be seen—imperfectly, it is true—but their apparition led to a rather singular discussion between Harris and some of his companions.

The little troop, about four o'clock in the afternoon, had stopped for a moment near an opening in the woods, when three or four animals of great height went out of a thicket a hundred steps off, and scampered away at once with remarkable speed.

In spite of the American's recommendations, this time the novice, having quickly shouldered his gun, fired at one of these animals. But at the moment when the charge was going off, the weapon had been rapidly turned aside by Harris, and Dick Sand, skilful as he was, had missed his aim.

"No firing; no firing!" said the American.

"Ah, now, but those are giraffes!" cried Dick Sand, without otherwise replying to Harris's observation.

"Giraffes!" repeated Jack, standing up on the horse's saddle. "Where are they, the large beasts?"

"Giraffes!" replied Mrs. Weldon. "You are mistaken, my dear Dick. There are no giraffes in America."

"Indeed," said Harris, who appeared rather surprised, "there cannot be any giraffes in this country."

"What, then?" said Dick Sand.

"I really do not know what to think," replied Harris. "Have not your eyes deceived you, my young friend, and are not those animals more likely to be ostriches?"

"Ostriches!" repeated Dick Sand and Mrs. Weldon, looking at each other in great surprise.

"Yes, only ostriches," repeated Harris.

"But ostriches are birds," returned Dick Sand, "and consequently they have only two feet."

"Well," replied Harris, "I indeed thought I saw that those animals, which have just made off so rapidly, were bipeds."

"Bipeds!" replied the novice.

"Indeed it seemed to me that I saw animals with four legs," then said Mrs. Weldon.

"I also," added old Tom; then Bat, Acteon, and Austin confirmed those words.

"Ostriches with four legs!" cried Harris, with a burst of laughter.

"That would be ridiculous!"

"So," returned Dick Sand, "we have believed they were giraffes, and not ostriches."

"No, my young friend, no," said Harris. "You have certainly seen badly. That is explained by the rapidity with which those animals have flown away. Besides, it has happened more than once that hunters have been deceived like you, and in the best faith in the world."

What the American said was very plausible. Between an ostrich of great height and a giraffe of medium height, seen at a certain distance, it is easy to make a mistake. If it were a question of a beak or a nose, both are none the less joined to the end of a long neck turned backward, and, strictly speaking, it may be said that an ostrich is only a half giraffe. It only needs the hind legs. Then, this biped and this quadruped, passing rapidly, on a sudden may, very properly, be taken one for the other.

Besides, the best proof that Mrs. Weldon and the others were mistaken was that there are no giraffes in America.

Dick Sand then made this reflection:

"But I believed that ostriches were not met with in the New World any more than giraffes."

"Yes, my young friend," replied Harris; "and, indeed, South America possesses a peculiar species. To this species belongs the 'nandon,' which you have just seen."

Harris spoke the truth. The "nandon" is a long-legged bird, rather common in the plains of South America, and its flesh, when it is young, is good to eat.

This strong animal, whose height sometimes exceeds two meters, has a straight beak; wings long, and formed of tufted feathers of a bluish shade; feet formed of three claws, furnished with nails—which essentially distinguishes it from the ostriches of Africa.

These very exact details were given by Harris, who appeared to be very strongly posted on the manners of the "nandons."

Mrs. Weldon and her companions were obliged to acknowledge that they had been deceived.

"Besides," added Harris, "possibly we may encounter another band of these ostriches. Well, next time look better, and no longer allow yourselves to takes birds for quadrupeds! But above all, my young friend, do not forget my recommendations, and do not fire on any animal whatsoever. We have no need of hunting to procure food, and no detonation of a fire-arm must announce our presence in this forest."

Meanwhile Dick Sand remained pensive. Once more a doubt had just arisen on his mind.

The next day, April 17th, the march was continued, and the American affirmed that twenty-four hours would not pass before the little troop should be installed at the Farm of San Felice.

"There, Mrs. Weldon," added he, "you will receive all the care necessary to your position, and a few days' rest will quite restore you. Perhaps you will not find at this farm the luxury to which you are accustomed in your residence in San Francisco, but you will see that our improved lands in the interior do not lack what is comfortable. We are not absolutely savages."

"Mr. Harris," replied Mrs. Weldon, "if we have only thanks to offer you for your generous resort, at least we shall offer them to you with all our hearts. Yes! It is time for us to arrive there!"

"You are very much fatigued, Mrs. Weldon?"

"I, no matter!" replied Mrs. Weldon; "but I perceive that my little Jack is gradually becoming exhausted! The fever begins to affect him at certain hours!"

"Yes," replied Harris, "and although the climate of this plateau is very healthful, it must be acknowledged that in March and April intermittent fevers reign."

"Doubtless," then said Dick Sand, "but also Nature, who is always and everywhere provident, has put the remedy near the evil!"

"And how is that, my young friend?" asked Harris, who did not seem to understand.

"Are we not, then, in the region of the quinquinas?" replied Dick Sand.

"In fact," said Harris, "you are perfectly right. The trees which furnish, the precious febrifuge bark are native here."

"I am even astonished," added Dick Sand, "that we have not yet seen a single one."

"Ah! my young friend," replied Harris, "those trees are not easy to distinguish. Though they are often of great height, though their leaves are large, their flowers rosy and odoriferous, we do not discover them easily. It is rarely that they grow in groups. They are rather scattered through the forests, and the Indians who collect the quinquina can only recognize them by their foliage, always green."

"Mr. Harris," said Mrs. Weldon, "if you see one of those trees you will show it to me."

"Certainly, Mrs. Weldon, but at the farm you will find some sulphate of quinine. That is worth still more to break the fever than the simple bark of the tree."

Formerly, this bark was only reduced to powder, which bore the name of "Jesuits' Powder," because, in 1649, the Jesuits of Rome received a considerable quantity from their mission in America.

This last day of the journey passed without other incident. Evening came and the halt was organized for the whole night as usual. Till then it had not rained, but the weather was preparing to change, for a warm mist rose from the soil and soon found a thick fog.

They were touching, in fact, on the rainy season. Fortunately, the next day, a comfortable shelter would be hospitably offered to the little troop. There were only a few hours to elapse.

Though, according to Harris, who could only establish his calculation by the time which the journey had lasted, they could not be more than six miles from the farm, the ordinary precautions were taken for the night. Tom and his companions would watch one after the other. Dick Sand insisted that nothing should be neglected in that respect. Less than ever, would he depart from his habitual prudence, for a terrible suspicion was incrusted in his mind; but he did not wish to say anything yet.

The retiring to rest had been made at the feet of a group of large trees. Fatigue aiding, Mrs. Weldon and hers were already asleep, when they were awakened by a great cry.

"Eh! what's the matter?" asked Dick Sand, quickly, who was on his feet first of all.

"It is I! it is I who have cried!" replied Cousin Benedict.

"And what is the matter with you?" asked Mrs. Weldon.

"I have just been bit!"

"By a serpent?" asked Mrs. Weldon, with alarm.

"No, no! It was not a serpent, but an insect," replied Cousin Benedict.

"Ah! I have it! I have it!"

"Well, crush your insect," said Harris, "and let us sleep, Mr. Benedict!"

"Crush an insect!" cried Cousin Benedict. "Not so! I must see what it is!"

"Some mosquito!" said Harris, shrugging his shoulders.

"No! It is a fly," replied Cousin Benedict, "and a fly which ought to be very curious!"

Dick Sand had lit a little portable lantern, and he approached Cousin Benedict.

"Divine goodness!" cried the latter. "Behold what consoles me for all my deceptions! I have, then, at last made a discovery!"

The honest man was raving. He looked at his fly in triumph. He would willingly kiss it.

"But what is it, then?" asked Mrs. Weldon.

"A dipter, cousin, a famous dipter!" And Cousin Benedict showed a fly smaller than a bee, of a dull color, streaked with yellow on the lower part of its body.

"And this fly is not venomous?" asked Mrs. Weldon.

"No, cousin, no; at least not for man. But for animals, for antelopes, for buffaloes, even for elephants, it is another thing. Ah! adorable insect!"

"At last," asked Dick Sand, "will you tell us, Mr. Benedict, what is this fly?"

"This fly," replied the entomologist, "this fly that I hold between my fingers, this fly—it is a tsetse! It is that famous dipter that is the honor of a country, and, till now, no one has ever found a tsetse in America!"

Dick Sand did not dare to ask Cousin Benedict in what part of the world this redoubtable tsetse was only to be met. And when his companions, after this incident, had returned to their interrupted sleep, Dick Sand, in spite of the fatigue which overwhelmed him, did not close his eyes the whole night.

## CHAPTER XVIII.

### THE TERRIBLE WORD.

It was time to arrive. Extreme lassitude made it impossible for Mrs. Weldon to continue any longer a journey made under such painful conditions. Her little boy, crimson during the fits of fever, very pale during the intermissions, was pitiable to see. His mother extremely anxious, had not been willing to leave Jack even in the care of the good Nan. She held him, half-lying, in her arms.

Yes, it was time to arrive. But, to trust to the American, on the very evening of this day which was breaking—the evening of the 18th of April, the little troop should finally reach the shelter of the "hacienda" of San Felice.

Twelve days' journey for a woman, twelve nights passed in the open air; it was enough to overwhelm Mrs. Weldon, energetic as she was. But, for a child, it was worse, and the sight of little Jack sick, and without the most ordinary cares, had sufficed to crush her.

Dick Sand, Nan, Tom, and his companions had supported the fatigues of the journey better.

Their provisions, although they were commencing to get exhausted, had not become injured, and their condition was satisfactory.

As for Harris, he seemed made for the difficulties of these long journeys across the forests, and it did not appear that fatigue could affect him. Only, in proportion as he neared the farm, Dick Sand observed that he was more preoccupied and less frank in behavior than before. The contrary would have been more natural. This was, at least, the opinion of the young novice, who had now become more than suspicious of the American. And meanwhile, what interest could Harris have in deceiving them? Dick Sand could not have explained it, but he watched their guide more closely.

The American probably felt himself suspected by Dick Sand, and, no doubt, it was this mistrust which made him still more taciturn with "his young friend."

The march had been resumed.

In the forest, less thick, the trees were scattered in groups, and no longer formed impenetrable masses. Was it, then, the true pampas of which Harris had spoken?

During the first hours of the day, no accident happened to aggravate the anxieties that Dick Sand felt. Only two facts were observed by him. Perhaps they were not very important, but in these actual junctures, no detail could be neglected.

It was the behavior of Dingo which, above all, attracted more especially the young man's attention.

In fact the dog, which, during all this journey, had seemed to be following a scent, became quite different, and that almost suddenly. Until then, his nose to the ground, generally smelling the herbs or the shrubs, he either kept quiet, or he made a sort of sad, barking noise, like an expression of grief or of regret.

Now, on this day, the barking of the singular animal became like bursts, sometimes furious, such as they formerly were when Negoro appeared on the deck of the "Pilgrim." A suspicion crossed suddenly Dick Sand's mind, and it was confirmed by Tom, who said to him:

"How very singular, Mr. Dick! Dingo no longer smells the ground as he did yesterday! His nose is in the air, he is agitated, his hair stands up! One would think he scented in the distance——"

"Negoro, is it not so?" replied Dick Sand, who seized the old black's arm, and signed to him to speak in a low voice.

"Negoro, Mr. Dick! May it not be that he has followed our steps?"

"Yes, Tom; and that at this moment even he may not be very far from us."

"But why?" said Tom.

"Either Negoro does not know this country," went on Dick Sand, "and then he would have every interest in not losing sight of us——"

"Or?" said Tom, who anxiously regarded the novice.

"Or," replied Dick Sand, "he does know it, and then he——"

"But how should Negoro know this country? He has never come here!"

"Has he never been here?" murmured Dick Sand.

"It is an incontestable fact that Dingo acts as if this man whom he detests were near us!"

Then, interrupting himself to call the dog, which, after some hesitation, came to him:

"Eh!" said he; "Negoro! Negoro!"

A furious barking was Dingo's reply. This name had its usual effect upon him, and he darted forward, as if Negoro had been hidden behind some thicket.

Harris had witnessed all this scene. With his lips a little drawn, he approached the novice.

"What did you ask Dingo then?" said he.

"Oh, not much, Mr. Harris," replied old Tom, jokingly. "We asked him for news of the ship-companion whom we have lost!"

"Ah!" said the American, "the Portuguese, the ship's cook of whom you have already spoken to me?"

"Yes." replied Tom. "One would say, to hear Dingo, that Negoro is in the vicinity."

"How could he get as far as this?" replied Harris.

"He never was in this country that I know of; at least, he concealed it from us," replied Tom.

"It would be astonishing," said Harris. "But, if you wish, we will beat these thickets. It is possible that this poor devil has need of help; that he is in distress."

"It is useless, Mr. Harris," replied Dick Sand. "If Negoro has known how to come as far as this, he will know how to go farther. He is a man to keep out of trouble."

"As you please," replied Harris.

"Let us go. Dingo, be quiet," added Dick Sand, briefly, so as to end the conversation.

The second observation made by the novice was in connection with the American horse. He did not appear to "feel the stable," as do animals of his species. He did not suck in the air; he did not hasten his speed; he did not dilate his nostrils; he uttered none of the neighings that indicate the end of a journey. To observe him well, he appeared to be as indifferent as if the farm, to which he had gone several times, however, and which he ought to know, had been several hundreds of miles away.

"That is not a horse near home," thought the young novice.

And, meanwhile, according to what Harris had said the evening before, there only remained six miles to go, and, of these last six miles, at five o'clock in the evening four had been certainly cleared.

Now, if the horse felt nothing of the stable, of which he should have great need, nothing besides announced the approaches to a great clearing, such as the Farm of San Felice must be.

Mrs. Weldon, indifferent as she then was to what did not concern her child, was struck at seeing the country still so desolate. What! not a native, not a farm-servant, at such a short distance! Harris must be wild! No! she repulsed this idea. A new delay would have been the death of her little Jack!

Meanwhile, Harris always kept in advance, but he seemed to observe the depths of the wood, and looked to the right and left, like a man who was not sure of himself—nor of his road.

Mrs. Weldon shut her eyes so as not to see him.

After a plain a mile in extent, the forest, without being as dense as in the west, had reappeared, and the little troop was again lost under the great trees.

At six o'clock in the evening they had reached a thicket, which appeared to have recently given passage to a band of powerful animals. Dick Sand looked around him very attentively. At a distance winch far surpassed the human height, the branches were torn off or broken. At the same time the herbs, roughly scattered, exhibited on the soil, a little marshy, prints of steps which could not be those of jaguars, or cougars.

Were these, then, the "ais," or some other tardi-graves, whose feet had thus marked the soil? But how, then, explain the break in the branches at such a height?

Elephants might have, without doubt, left such imprints, stamped these large traces, made a similar hole in the impenetrable underwood. But elephants are not found in America. These enormous thick-skinned quadrupeds are not natives of the New World. As yet, they have never been acclimated there.

The hypothesis that elephants had passed there was absolutely inadmissible.

However that might be, Dick Sand hardly knew how much this inexplicable fact gave him to think about. He did not even question the American on this point. What could he expect from a man who had tried to make him take giraffes for ostriches? Harris would have given him some explanation, more or less imaginative, which would not have changed the situation.

At all events, Dick had formed his opinion of Harris. He felt in him a traitor! He only awaited an occasion to unmask his disloyalty, to have the right to do it, and everything told him that this opportunity was near.

But what could be Harris's secret end? What future, then, awaited the survivors of the "Pilgrim?" Dick Sand repeated to himself that his responsibility had not ceased with the shipwreck. It was more than ever necessary for him to provide for the safety of those whom the waves had thrown on this coast! This woman, this young child, these blacks—all his companions in misfortune—it was he alone who must save them! But, if he could attempt anything on board ship, if he could act on the sea, here, in the midst of the terrible trials which he foresaw, what part could he take?

Dick Sand would not shut his eyes before the frightful reality that each instant made more indisputable. In this juncture he again became the captain of fifteen years, as he had been on the "Pilgrim." But he would not say anything which could alarm the poor mother before the moment for action had arrived.

And he said nothing, not even when, arrived on the bank of a rather large stream, preceding the little troop about one hundred feet, he perceived enormous animals, which threw themselves under the large plants on the brink.

"Hippopotami! hippopotami!" he was going to exclaim.

And they were, indeed, these thick-skinned animals, with a big head, a large, swollen snout, a mouth armed with teeth which extend a foot beyond it —animals which are squat on their short limbs, the skin of which, unprovided with hair, is of a tawny red. Hippopotami in America!

They continued to march during the whole day, but painfully. Fatigue commenced to retard even the most robust. It was truly time to arrive, or they would be forced to stop.

Mrs. Weldon, wholly occupied with her little Jack, did not perhaps feel the fatigue, but her strength was exhausted. All, more or less, were tired. Dick Sand, resisted by a supreme moral energy, caused by the sentiment of duty.

Toward four o'clock in the evening, old Tom found, in the grass, an object which attracted his attention. It was an arm, a kind of knife, of a particular shape, formed of a large, curved blade, set in a square, ivory handle, rather roughly ornamented. Tom carried this knife to Dick Sand, who took it, examined it, and, finally, showed it to the American, saying:

"No doubt the natives are not very far off."

"That is so," replied Harris, "and meanwhile——"

"Meanwhile?" repeated Dick Sand, who now steadily looked Harris in the face.

"We should be very near the farm," replied Harris, hesitating, "and I do not recognize——"

"You are then astray?" quickly asked Dick Sand.

"Astray! no. The farm cannot be more than three miles away, now. But, I wished to take the shortest road through the forest, and perhaps I have made a little mistake!"

"Perhaps," replied Dick Sand.

"I would do well, I think, to go in advance," said Harris.

"No, Mr. Harris, we will not separate," replied Dick Sand, in a decided tone.

"As you will," replied the American. "But, during the night, it will be difficult for me to guide you."

"Never mind that!" replied Dick Sand. "We are going to halt. Mrs. Weldon will consent to pass a last night under the trees, and to-morrow, when it is broad daylight, we will proceed on our journey! Two or three miles still, that will be an hour's walk!"

"Be it so," replied Harris.

At that moment Dingo commenced to bark furiously.

"Here, Dingo, here!" cried Dick Sand. "You know well that no one is there, and that we are in the desert!"

This last halt was then decided upon.

Mrs. Weldon let her companions work without saying a word. Her little Jack was sleeping in her arms, made drowsy by the fever.

They sought the best place to pass the night. This was under a large bunch of trees, where Dick Sand thought of disposing all for their rest. But old Tom, who was helping him in these preparations, stopped suddenly, crying out:

"Mr. Dick! look! look!"

"What is it, old Tom?" asked Dick Sand, in the calm tone of a man who attends to everything.

"There—there!" cried Tom; "on those trees—blood stains!—and—on the ground—mutilated limbs!"

Dick Sand rushed toward the spot indicated by old Tom. Then, returning to him: "Silence, Tom, silence!" said he.

In fact, there on the ground were hands cut off, and above these human remains were several broken forks, and a chain in pieces!

Happily, Mrs. Weldon had seen nothing of this horrible spectacle.

As for Harris, he kept at a distance, and any one observing him at this moment would have been struck at the change made in him. His face had something ferocious in it.

Dingo had rejoined Dick Sand, and before these bloody remains, he barked with rage.

The novice had hard work to drive him away.

Meanwhile, old Tom, at the sight of these forks, of this broken chain, had remained motionless, as if his feet were rooted in the soil. His eyes were wide open, his hands clenched; he stared, murmuring these incoherent words:

"I have seen—already seen—these forks—when little—I have seen!"

And no doubt the memories of his early infancy returned to him vaguely.

He tried to recall them. He was going to speak.

"Be silent, Tom!" repeated Dick Sand. "For Mrs. Weldon's sake, for all our sakes, be silent!"

And the novice led the old black away.

Another halting place was chosen, at some distance, and all was arranged for the night.

The repast was prepared, but they hardly touched it. Fatigue took away their hunger. All were under an indefinable impression of anxiety which bordered on terror.

Darkness came gradually: soon it was profound. The sky was covered with great stormy clouds. Between the trees in the western horizon they saw some flashes of heat lightning. The wind had fallen; not a leaf moved on the trees. An absolute silence succeeded the noises of the day, and it might be believed that the heavy atmosphere, saturated with electricity, was becoming unfit for the transmission of sounds.

Dick Sand, Austin, and Bat watched together. They tried to see, to hear, during this very dark night, if any light whatsoever, or any suspicious noise should strike their eyes or their ears. Nothing troubled either the calm or the obscurity of the forest.

Tom, not sleepy, but absorbed in his remembrances, his head bent, remained quiet, as if he had been struck by some sudden blow.

Mrs. Weldon rocked her child in her arms, and only thought of him.

Only Cousin Benedict slept, perhaps, for he alone did not suffer from the common impression. His faculty for looking forward did not go so far.

Suddenly, about eleven o'clock, a prolonged and grave roaring was heard, with which was mingled a sort of sharper shuddering. Tom stood up and stretched out his hand toward a dense thicket, a mile or more distant.

Dick Sand seized his arm, but he could not prevent Tom from crying in a loud voice: "The lion! the lion!"

This roaring, which he had so often heard in his infancy, the old black had just recognized it.

"The lion!" he repeated.

Dick Sand, incapable of controlling himself longer, rushed, cutlass in hand, to the place occupied by Harris.

Harris was no longer there, and his horse had disappeared with him.

A sort of revelation took place in Dick Sand's mind. He was not where he had believed he was!

So it was not on the American coast that the "Pilgrim" had gone ashore! It was not the Isle of Paques, whose bearing the novice had taken at sea, but some other island situated exactly to the west of this continent, as the Isle of Paques is situated to the west of America.

The compass had deceived him during a part of the voyage, we know why! Led away by the tempest over a false route, he must have doubled Cape Horn, and from the Pacific Ocean he had passed into the Atlantic! The speed of his ship, which he could only imperfectly estimate, had been doubled, unknown to him, by the force of the hurricane!

Behold why the caoutchouc trees, the quinquinas, the products of South

America were missing in this country, which was neither the plateau of

Atacama nor the Bolivian pampa!

Yes, they were giraffes, not ostriches, which had fled away in the opening! They were elephants that had crossed the thick underwood! They were hippopotami whose repose Dick Sand had troubled under the large plants! It was the tsetse, that dipter picked up by Benedict, the formidable tsetse under whose stings the animals of the caravans perish!

Finally, it was, indeed, the roaring of the lion that had just sounded through the forest! And those forks, those chains, that knife of singular form, they were the tools of the slave-trader! Those mutilated hands, they were the hands of captives!

The Portuguese Negoro, and the American Harris, must be in collusion!

And those terrible words guessed by Dick Sand, finally escaped his lips:

"Africa! Equatorial Africa! Africa of the slave-trade and the slaves!"

\*\*\*\*

# PART II

## CHAPTER I.
## THE SLAVE TRADE.

The slave trade! Nobody is ignorant of the significance of this word, which should never have found a place in human language. This abominable traffic, for a long time practised to the profit of the European nations which possessed colonies beyond the sea, has been already forbidden for many years. Meanwhile it is always going on a large scale, and principally in Central Africa. Even in this nineteenth century the signature of a few States, calling themselves Christians, are still missing from the Act for the Abolition of Slavery.

We might believe that the trade is no longer carried on; that this buying and this selling of human creatures has ceased: it is not so, and that is what the reader must know if he wishes to become more deeply interested in the second part of this history. He must learn what these men-hunts actually are still, these hunts which threaten to depopulate a whole continent for the maintenance of a few slave colonies; where and how these barbarous captures are executed; how much blood they cost; how they provoke incendiarism and pillage; finally, for whose profit they are made.

It is in the fifteenth century only that we see the trade in blacks carried on for the first time. Behold under what circumstances it was established:

The Mussulmans, after being expelled from Spain, took refuge beyond the Strait on the coast of Africa. The Portuguese, who then occupied that part of the coast, pursued them with fury. A certain number of those fugitives were made prisoners and brought back to Portugal. Reduced to slavery, they constituted the first nucleus of African slaves which has been formed in Western Europe since the Christian Era.

But those Mussulmans belonged, for the most part, to rich families, who wished to buy them back for gold. The Portuguese refused to accept a ransom, however large it might be. They had only to make foreign gold. What they lacked were the arms so indispensable then for the work of the growing colonies, and, to say it all, the arms of the slave.

The Mussulman families, being unable to buy back their captive relatives, then offered to exchange them for a much larger number of black Africans, whom it was only too easy to carry off. The offer was accepted by the Portuguese, who found that exchange to their advantage, and thus the slave trade was founded in Europe.

Toward the end of the sixteenth century this odious traffic was generally admitted, and it was not repugnant to the still barbarous manners. All the States protected it so as to colonize more rapidly and more surely the isles of the New World. In fact, the slaves of black origin could resist the climate, where the badly acclimated whites, still unfit to support the heat of intertropical climates, would have perished by thousands. The transport of negroes to the American colonies was then carried on regularly by special vessels, and this branch of transatlantic commerce led to the creation of important stations on different points of the African coast. The "merchandise" cost little in the country of production, and the returns were considerable.

But, necessary as was the foundation of the colonies beyond the sea from all points of view, it could not justify those markets for human flesh. Generous voices soon made themselves heard, which protested against the trade in blacks, and demanded from the European governments a decree of abolition in the name of the principles of humanity.

In 1751, the Quakers put themselves at the head of the abolition movement, even in the heart of that North America where, a hundred years later, the War of Secession was to burst forth, to which this question of slavery was not a foreign one. Different States in the North—Virginia, Connecticut, Massachusetts, Pennsylvania—decreed the abolition of the slave trade, and freed the slaves brought to their territories at great expense.

But the campaign commenced by the Quakers did not limit itself to the northern provinces of the New World. Slaveholders were warmly attacked beyond the Atlantic. France and England, more particularly, recruited partisans for this just cause. "Let the colonies perish rather than a principle!" Such was the generous command which resounded through all the Old World, and, in spite of the great political and commercial interests engaged in the question, it was effectively transmitted through Europe.

The impetus was given. In 1807, England abolished the slave-trade in her colonies, and France followed her example in 1814. The two powerful nations exchanged a treaty on this subject—a treaty confirmed by Napoleon during the Hundred Days.

However, that was as yet only a purely theoretical declaration. The slave-ships did not cease to cross the seas, and to dispose of their "ebony cargoes" in colonial ports.

More practical measures must be taken in order to put an end to this commerce. The United States, in 1820, and England, in 1824, declared the slave trade an act of piracy, and those who practised it pirates. As such, they drew on themselves the penalty of death, and they were pursued to the end. France soon adhered to the new treaty; but the States of South America, and the Spanish and Portuguese colonies, did not join in the Act of Abolition. The exportation of blacks then continued to their profit, notwithstanding the right of search generally recognized, which was limited to the verification of the flag of suspicious vessels.

Meanwhile, the new Law of Abolition had not a retroactive effect. No more new slaves were made, but the old ones had not yet recovered their liberty.

It was under those circumstances that England set an example. In May, 1833, a general declaration emancipated all the blacks in the colonies of Great Britain, and in August, 1838, six hundred and seventy thousand slaves were declared free.

Ten years later, in 1848, the Republic emancipated the slaves of the French colonies, say about two hundred and sixty thousand blacks. In 1861, the war which broke out between the Federals and Confederates, of the United States, finishing the work of emancipation, extended it to all North America.

The three great powers had then accomplished this work of humanity. At the present hour, the trade is no longer carried on, except for the benefit of the Spanish and Portuguese colonies, and to satisfy the wants of the populations of the Orient, Turks, or Arabs. Brazil, if she has not yet restored her old slaves to liberty, at least no longer receives new ones, and the children of the blacks are born free there.

It is in the interior of Africa, in the prosecution of those bloody wars, waged by the African chiefs among themselves for this man-hunt, that entire tribes are reduced to slavery. Two opposite directions are then given to the caravans: one to the west, toward the Portuguese colony of Angola; the other to the east, on the Mozambique. Of these unfortunate beings, of whom only a small portion arrive at their destination, some are exported, it may be to Cuba, it may be to Madagascar; others to the Arab or Turkish provinces of Asia, to Mecca, or to Muscat. The English and French cruisers can only prevent this traffic to a small extent, as it is so difficult to obtain an effective surveillance over such far-extended coasts.

But the figures of these odious exportations, are they still considerable?

Yes! The number of slaves who arrive at the coast is estimated at not less than eighty thousand; and this number, it appears, only represents the tenth of natives massacred.

After these dreadful butcheries the devastated fields are deserted, the burnt villages are without inhabitants, the rivers carry down dead bodies, deer occupy the country. Livingstone, the day after one of these men-hunts, no longer recognized the provinces he had visited a few months before. All the other travelers—Grant, Speke, Burton, Cameron, and Stanley—do not speak otherwise of this wooded plateau of Central Africa, the principal theater of the wars between the chiefs. In the region of the great lakes, over all that vast country which feeds the market of Zanzibar, in Bornou and Fezzan, farther south, on the banks of the Nyassa and the Zambesi, farther west, in the districts of the upper Zaire, which the daring Stanley has just crossed, is seen the same spectacle—ruins, massacres, depopulation. Then will slavery in Africa only end with the disappearance of the black race; and will it be with this race as it is with the Australian race, or the race in New Holland?

But the market of the Spanish and Portuguese colonies will close some day. That outlet will be wanting. Civilized nations can no longer tolerate the slave trade!

Yes, without doubt; and this year even, 1878, ought to see the enfranchisement of all the slaves still possessed by Christian States. However, for long years to come the Mussulman nations will maintain this traffic, which depopulates the African continent. It is for them, in fact, that the most important emigration of the blacks is made, as the number of natives snatched from their provinces and brought to the eastern coast annually exceeds forty thousand. Long before the expedition to Egypt the negroes of the Seunaar were sold by thousands to the negroes of the Darfour, and reciprocally. General Bonaparte was able to buy a pretty large number of these blacks, of whom he made organized soldiers, like the Mamelukes. Since then, during this century, of which four-fifths have now passed away, commerce in slaves has not diminished in Africa. On the contrary.

And, in fact, Islamism is favorable to the slave trade. The black slave must replace the white slave of former times, in Turkish provinces. So contractors of every origin pursue this execrable traffic on a large scale. They thus carry a supplement of population to those races, which are dying out and will disappear some day, because they do not regenerate themselves by labor. These slaves, as in the time of Bonaparte, often become soldiers. With certain nations of the upper Niger, they compose the half of the armies of the African chiefs. Under these circumstances, their fate is not sensibly inferior to that of free men. Besides, when the slave is not a soldier, he is money which has circulation; even in Egypt and at Bornou, officers and functionaries are paid in that money. William Lejean has seen it and has told of it.

Such is, then, the actual state of the trade.

Must it be added that a number of agents of the great European powers are not ashamed to show a deplorable indulgence for this commerce.

Nevertheless, nothing is truer; while the cruisers watch the coasts of the Atlantic and the Indian Oceans, the traffic goes on regularly in the interior, the caravans walk on under the eyes of certain functionaries, and massacres, where ten blacks perish to furnish one slave, take place at stated periods!

So it will now be understood how terrible were those words just pronounced by Dick Sand.

"Africa! Equatorial Africa! Africa of slave-traders and slaves!"

And he was not deceived; it was Africa with all its dangers, for his companions and for himself.

But on what part of the African continent had an inexplicable fatality landed him? Evidently on the western coast, and as an aggravating circumstance, the young novice was forced to think that the "Pilgrim" was thrown on precisely that part of the coast of Angola where the caravans, which clear all that part of Africa, arrive.

In fact it was there. It was that country which Cameron on the south and Stanley on the north were going to cross a few years later, and at the price of what efforts! Of this vast territory, which is composed of three provinces, Benguela, Congo, and Angola, there was but little known then except the coast. It extends from the Nourse, in the south, as far as the Zaire in the north, and the two principal towns form two ports, Benguela and St. Paul' de Loanda, the capital of the colony which set off from the kingdom of Portugal.

In the interior this country was then almost unknown. Few travelers had dared to venture there. A pernicious climate, warm and damp lands, which engender fevers, barbarous natives, some of whom are still cannibals, a permanent state of war between tribes, the slave-traders' suspicion of every stranger who seeks to discover the secrets of their infamous commerce; such are the difficulties to surmount, the dangers to overcome in this province of Angola, one of the most dangerous of equatorial Africa.

Tuckey, in 1816, had ascended the Congo beyond the Yellala Falls; but over an extent of two hundred miles at the most. This simple halting-place could not give a definite knowledge of the country, and nevertheless, it had caused the death of the greater part of the savants and officers who composed the expedition. Thirty-seven years later, Dr. Livingstone had advanced from the Cape of Good Hope as far as the upper Zambesi. Thence, in the month of November, with a hardihood which has never been surpassed, he traversed Africa from the south to the northwest, cleared the Coango, one of the branches of the Congo, and on the 31st of May, 1854, arrived at St. Paul de Loanda. It was the first view in the unknown of the great Portuguese Colony.

Eighteen years after, two daring discoverers crossed Africa from the east to the west, and arrived, one south, the other north, of Angola, after unheard-of difficulties.

The first, according to the date, was a lieutenant in the English navy, Verney-Howet Cameron. In 1872, there was reason to fear that the expedition of the American, Stanley, was in great danger. It had been sent to the great lake region in search of Livingstone. Lieutenant Cameron offered to go over the same road.

The offer was accepted. Cameron, accompanied by Dr. Dillon, Lieutenant Cecil Murphy and Robert Moffat, a nephew of Livingstone, started from Zanzibar. After having crossed Ougogo, he met Livingstone's faithful servants carrying their master's body to the eastern coast. He continued his route to the west, with the unconquerable desire to pass from one coast to the other.

He crossed Ounyanyembe, Ougounda, and Kahouele, where he collected the great traveler's papers. Having passed over Tanganyika, and the Bambarre mountains, he reached Loualaba, but could not descend its course. After having visited all the provinces devastated by war and depopulated by the slave trade, Kilemmba, Ouroua, the sources of the Lomane, Oulouda, Lovale, and having crossed the Coanza and the immense forests in which Harris has just entrapped Dick Sand and his companions, the energetic Cameron finally perceived the Atlantic Ocean and arrived at Saint Philip of Benguela. This journey of three years and four months had cost the lives of his two companions, Dr. Dillon and Robert Moffat.

Henry Moreland Stanley, the American, almost immediately succeeded the Englishman, Cameron, on the road of discoveries. We know that this intrepid correspondent of the New York Herald, sent in search of Livingstone, had found him on October 30th, 1871, at Oujiji, on Lake Tanganyika. Having so happily accomplished his object for the sake of humanity, Stanley determined to pursue his journey in the interest of geographical science. His object then was to gain a complete knowledge of Loualaba, of which he had only had a glimpse.

Cameron was then lost in the provinces of Central Africa, when, in November, 1874, Stanley quitted Bagamoga, on the eastern coast. Twenty-one months after, August 24th, 1876, he abandoned Oujiji, which was decimated by an epidemic of smallpox. In seventy-four days he effected the passage of the lake at N'yangwe, a great slave market, which had been already visited by Livingstone and Cameron. Here he witnessed the most horrible scenes, practised in the Maroungou and Manyouema countries by the officers of the Sultan of Zanzibar.

Stanley then took measures to explore the course of the Loualaba and to descend it as far as its mouth. One hundred and forty bearers, engaged at

N'yangwe, and nineteen boats, formed the material and the force of his expedition.

From the very start he had to fight the cannibals of Ougouson. From the start, also, he had to attend to the carrying of boats, so as to pass insuperable cataracts.

Under the equator, at the point where the Loualaba makes a bend to the northeast, fifty-four boats, manned by several hundred natives, attacked Stanley's little fleet, which succeeded in putting them to flight. Then the courageous American, reascending as far as the second degree of northern latitude, ascertained that the Loualaba was the upper Zaire, or Congo, and that by following its course he could descend directly to the sea.

This he did, fighting nearly every day against the tribes that lived near the river. On June 3d, 1877, at the passage of the cataracts of Massassa, he lost one of his companions, Francis Pocock. July 18th he was drawn with his boat into the falls of M'belo, and only escaped death by a miracle.

Finally, August 6th, Henry Stanley arrived at the village of Ni-Sanda, four days' journey from the coast.

Two days after, at Banza-M'bouko, he found the provisions sent by two merchants from Emboma.

He finally rested at this little coast town, aged, at thirty-five years, by overfatigue and privations, after an entire passage of the African continent, which had taken two years and nine months of his life.

However, the course of the Loualaba was explored as far as the Atlantic; and if the Nile is the great artery of the North, if the Zambesi is the great artery of the East, we now know that Africa still possesses in the West the third of the largest rivers in the world—a river which, in a course of two thousand, nine hundred miles, under the names of Loualaba, Zaire, and Congo, unites the lake region with the Atlantic Ocean.

However, between these two books of travel—Stanley's and Cameron's—the province of Angola is somewhat better known in this year than in 1873, at that period when the "Pilgrim" was lost on the African coast. It was well known that it was the seat of the western slave-trade, thanks to its important markets of Bihe, Cassange, and Kazounde.

It was into this country that Dick Sand had been drawn, more than one hundred miles from the coast, with a woman exhausted by fatigue and grief, a dying child, and some companions of African descent, the prey, as everything indicated, to the rapacity of slave merchants.

Yes, it was Africa, and not that America where neither the natives, nor the deer, nor the climate are very formidable. It was not that favorable region, situated between the Cordilleras and the coast, where straggling villages abound, and where missions are hospitably opened to all travelers.

They were far away, those provinces of Peru and Bolivia, where the tempest would have surely carried the "Pilgrim," if a criminal hand had not changed its course, where the shipwrecked ones would have found so many facilities for returning to their country.

It was the terrible Angola, not even that part of the coast inspected by the Portuguese authorities, but the interior of the colony, which is crossed by caravans of slaves under the whip of the driver.

What did Dick Sand know of this country where treason had thrown him? Very little; what the missionaries of the sixteenth and seventeenth centuries had said of it; what the Portuguese merchants, who frequented the road from St. Paul de Loanda to the Zaïre, by way of San Salvador, knew of it; what Dr. Livingstone had written about it, after his journey of 1853, and that would have been sufficient to overwhelm a soul less strong than his.

Truly, the situation was terrible.


## CHAPTER II.

## HARRIS AND NEGORO.


The day after that on which Dick Sand and his companions had established their last halt in the forest, two men met together about three miles from there, as it had been previously arranged between them.

These two men were Harris and Negoro; and we are going to see now what chance had brought together, on the coast of Angola, the Portuguese come from New Zealand, and the American, whom the business of trader obliged to often traverse this province of Western Africa.

Harris and Negoro were seated at the foot of an enormous banyan, on the steep bank of an impetuous stream, which ran between a double hedge of papyrus.

The conversation commenced, for the Portuguese and the American had just met, and at first they dwelt on the deeds which had been accomplished during these last hours.

"And so, Harris," said Negoro, "you have not been able to draw this little troop of Captain Sand, as they call this novice of fifteen years, any farther into

Angola?"

"No, comrade," replied Harris; "and it is even astonishing that I have succeeded in leading him a hundred miles at least from the coast. Several days ago my young friend, Dick Sand, looked at me with an anxious air, his suspicions gradually changed into certainties—and faith—"

"Another hundred miles, Harris, and those people would be still more surely in our hands! However, they must not escape us!"

"Ah! How could they?" replied Harris, shrugging his shoulders. "I repeat it, Negoro, there was only time to part company with them. Ten times have I read in my young friend's eyes that he was tempted to send a ball into my breast, and I have too bad a stomach to digest those prunes which weigh a dozen to the pound."

"Good!" returned Negoro; "I also have an account to settle with this novice."

"And you shall settle it at your ease, with interest, comrade. As to me, during the first three days of the journey I succeeded very well in making him take this province for the Desert of Atacama, which I visited formerly. But the child claimed his caoutchoucs and his humming-birds. The mother demanded her quinquinas. The cousin was crazy to find cocuyos. Faith, I was at the end of my imagination, and after with great difficulty making them swallow ostriches for giraffes—a god-send, indeed, Negoro!—I no longer knew what to invent. Besides, I well saw that my young friend no longer accepted my explanations. Then we fell on elephants' prints. The hippopotami were added to the party. And you know, Negoro, hippopotami and elephants in America are like honest men in the penitentiaries of Benguela. Finally, to finish me, there was the old black, who must find forks and chains at the foot of a tree. Slaves had freed themselves from them to flee. At the same moment the lion roared, starting the company, and it is not easy to pass off that roaring for the mewing of an inoffensive cat. I then had only time to spring on my horse and make my way here."

"I understand," replied Negoro. "Nevertheless, I would wish to hold them a hundred miles further in the province.'"

"One does what he can, comrade," replied Harris. "As to you, who followed our caravan from the coast, you have done well to keep your distance. They felt you were there. There is a certain Dingo that does not seem to love you. What have you done to that animal?"

"Nothing," replied Negoro; "but before long it will receive a ball in the head."

"As you would have received one from Dick Sand, if you had shown ever so little of your person within two hundred feet of his gun. Ah! how well he fires, my young friend; and, between you and me, I am obliged to admit that he is, in his way, a fine boy."

"No matter how fine he is, Harris, he will pay dear for his insolence," replied Negoro, whose countenance expressed implacable cruelty.

"Good," murmured Harris, "my comrade remains just the same as I have always known him! Voyages have not injured him!"

Then, after a moment's silence: "Ah, there, Negoro," continued he, "when I met you so fortunately there below, at the scene of the shipwreck, at the mouth of the Longa, you only had time to recommend those honest people to me, while begging me to lead them as far as possible across this pretended Bolivia. You have not told me what you have been doing these two years! Two years, comrade, in our chance existence, is a long time. One fine day, after having taken charge of a caravan of slaves on old Alvez's account—whose very humble agents we are—you left Cassange, and have not been heard of since! I have thought that you had some disagreement with the English cruiser, and that you were hung!"

"I came very near it, Harris."

"That will come, Negoro."

"Thank you!"

"What would you have?" replied Harris, with an indifference quite philosophical; "it is one of the chances of the trade! We do not carry on the slave-trade on the coast of Africa without running the risk of dying elsewhere than in our beds! So, you have been taken?"

"Yes!"

"By the English?"

"No! By the Portuguese."

"Before or after having delivered your cargo?" asked Harris.

"After—," replied Negoro, who had hesitated a little about replying. "These Portuguese now make difficulties. They want no more slavery, though they have used it so long to their profit. I was denounced —watched. They took me—"

"And condemned—"

"Me to finish my days in the penitentiary of St. Paul de Loanda."

"A thousand devils!" exclaimed Harris. "That is an unhealthy place for men accustomed, like us, to live in the open air. As to me, perhaps I should prefer being hung."

"One does not escape from the gallows," replied Negoro; "but from prison—"

"You were able to make your escape?"

"Yes, Harris. Only fifteen days after being put in prison. I was able to hide myself at the bottom of the hold of an English steamer, sailing for Auckland, of New Zealand. A barrel of water and a case of conserves, between which I had intruded, furnished me with food and drink during the whole passage. Oh! I suffered terribly, from not being willing to show myself when we were at sea. But, if I had been imprudent enough to do it, I would have been confined again at the bottom of the hold, and, voluntarily or not, the torture would be the same. Besides, on my arrival at Auckland, they would have returned me again to the English authorities, and finally brought me back to the penitentiary of Loanda, or, perhaps, hung me, as you said. That was why I preferred to travel incognito."

"And without paying your passage!" exclaimed Harris, laughing. "Ah! that is not considerate, comrade, to be fed and carried gratis!"

"Yes," returned Negoro, "but thirty days' passage at the bottom of the hold—"

"At last that was over, Negoro. You set out for New Zealand, in the land of the Maoris. But you have returned. Was the return made under the same circumstances?"

"Not so, Harris. You may well believe that, over there, I had only one idea—to return to Angola and take up my trade of slave-trader again."

"Yes," replied Harris, "one loves his trade—from habit."

"For eighteen months—"

Having pronounced those last words, Negoro stopped suddenly. He seized his companion's arm, and listened.

"Harris," said he, lowering his voice, "was there not a trembling in that papyrus bush?"

"Yes, indeed," replied Harris, seizing his gun, always ready to fire.

Negoro and he stood up, looked around them, and listened with the greatest attention.

"There is nothing there," said Harris. "It is this brook, swelled by the storm, which runs more noisily. For two years, comrade, you have been unaccustomed to the noises of the forest, but you will get used to them again. Continue, then, the narration of your adventures. When I understand the past, we shall talk of the future."

Negoro and Harris sat down again at the foot of the banyan. The

Portuguese continued, in these terms:

"For eighteen months I vegetated in Auckland. When the steamer arrived there I was able to leave it without being seen; but not a piastre, not a dollar in my pocket! In order to live I had to follow all trades—"

"Even the trade of an honest man, Negoro?"

"As you say, Harris."

"Poor boy!"

"Now, I was always waiting for an opportunity, which was long coming, when the 'Pilgrim,' a whaler, arrived at the port of Auckland."

"That vessel which went ashore on the coast of Angola?"

"Even the same, Harris, and on which Mrs. Weldon, her child, and her cousin were going to take passage. Now, as an old sailor, having even been second on board a slave ship, I was not out of my element in taking service on a ship. I then presented myself to the 'Pilgrim's' captain, but the crew was made up. Very fortunately for me, the schooner's cook had deserted. Now, he is no sailor who does not know how to cook. I offered myself as head cook. For want of a better, I was accepted. A few days after, the 'Pilgrim' had lost sight of the land of New Zealand."

"But," asked Harris, "according to what my young friend has told me, the 'Pilgrim' did not set sail at all for the coast of Africa. How then has she arrived here?"

"Dick Sand ought not to be able to understand it yet, and perhaps he will never understand it," replied Negoro; "but I am going to explain to you what has passed, Harris, and you will be able to tell it again to your young friend, if it pleases you to do so."

"How, then?" replied Harris. "Speak, comrade, speak!"

"The 'Pilgrim,'" continued Negoro, "as on the way to Valparaiso. When I went on board, I only intended to go to Chili. It was always a good half of the way between New Zealand and Angola, and I was drawing nearer Africa's coast by several thousand miles. But it so happened that only three weeks after leaving Auckland, Captain Hull, who commanded the 'Pilgrim,' disappeared with all his crew, while chasing a whale. On that day, then, only two sailors remained on board—the novice and the cook, Negoro."

"And you took command of the ship?" asked Harris.

"I had that idea at first, but I saw that they distrusted me. There were live strong blacks on board, free men. I would not have been the master, and, on reflection, I remained what I was at the departure—the 'Pilgrim's' cook."

"Then it was chance that led this ship to the coast of Africa?"

"No, Harris," replied Negoro; "there has been no chance in all this adventure except meeting you, in one of your journeys, just on that part of the coast where the 'Pilgrim' was wrecked. But as to coming in sight of Angola, it was by my will, my secret will, that that was done. Your young friend, still much of a novice in navigation, could only tell his position by means of the log and the compass. Well, one day, the log went to the bottom. One night the compass was made false, and the 'Pilgrim,' driven by a violent tempest, took the wrong route. The length of the voyage, inexplicable to Dick Sand, would be the same to the most experienced seaman. Without the novice knowing or even suspecting it, Cape Horn was doubled, but I, Harris, I recognized it in the midst of the fogs. Then, thanks to me, the needle in the compass took its true direction again, and the ship, blown to the northeast by that frightful hurricane, has just been cast on the coast of Africa, just on this land of Angola which I wished to reach."

"And even at that moment, Negoro," replied Harris, "chance had led me

there to receive you, and guide those honest people to the interior.

They believed themselves—they could only believe themselves in

America. It was easy for me to make them take this province for lower

Bolivia, to which it has really some resemblance."

"Yes, they believed it, as your young friend believed they had made the Isle of Paques, when they passed in sight of Tristan d'Acunha."

"Anybody would be deceived by it, Negoro."

"I know it, Harris, and I even counted on profiting by that error. Finally, behold Mrs. Weldon and her companions one hundred miles in the interior of this Africa, where I wanted to bring them!"

"But," replied Harris, "they know now where they are."

"Ah! what matter at present!" cried Negoro.

"And what will you do with them?" asked Harris.

"What will I do with them?" replied Negoro. "Before telling you, Harris, give me news of our master, the slave-trader, Alvez, whom I have not seen for two years."

"Oh, the old rascal is remarkably well," replied Harris, "and he will be enchanted to see you again."

"Is he at the Bihe market?" asked Negoro.

"No, comrade, he has been at his establishment at Kazounde for a year."

"And business is lively?"

"Yes, a thousand devils!" exclaimed Harris, "although the slave trade becomes more and more difficult, at least on this coast. The Portuguese authorities on one side, and the English cruisers on the other, limit exportations. There are few places, except in the environs of Mossamedes, to the south of Angola, that the shipping of blacks can now be made with any chance of success. So, at this time, the pens are filled with slaves, waiting for the ships which ought to carry them to Spanish colonies. As to passing them by Benguela, or St. Paul de Loanda, that is not possible. The governors no longer understand reason, no more do the chiefs (title given to the Portuguese governors of secondary establishments). We must, then, return to the factories of the interior. This is what old Alvez intends to do. He will go from the Nyangwe and Tanganyika side to change his stuffs for ivory and slaves. Business is always profitable with upper Egypt and the Mozambique coast, which furnishes all Madagascar. But I fear the time will come when the trade can be no longer carried on. The English are making great progress in the interior of Africa. The missionaries advance and work against us. That Livingstone, curse him, after exploring the lake region, is going, they say, to travel toward Angola. Then they speak of a Lieutenant Cameron, who proposes to cross the continent from east to west. They also fear that the American, Stanley, wishes to do as much. All these visits will end by damaging our operations, Negoro, and if we care for our own interests, not one of those visitors will return to relate in Europe what he has had the indiscretion to come to see in Africa."

Would not one say, to hear them, the rascals, that they were speaking like honest merchants whose affairs were momentarily cramped by a commercial crisis? Who would believe that, instead of sacks of coffee or casks of sugar, they were talking of human beings to export like merchandise? These traders have no other idea of right or wrong. The moral sense is entirely lacking in them, and if they had any, how quickly they would lose it among the frightful atrocities of the African slave trade.

But where Harris was right, was when he said that civilization was gradually penetrating those savage countries in the wake of those hardy travelers, whose names are indissoluble linked to the discoveries of Equatorial Africa. At the head, David Livingstone, after him, Grant, Speke, Burton, Cameron, Stanley, those heroes will leave imperishable names as benefactors of humanity.

When their conversation reached that point, Harris knew what the last two years of Negoro's life had been. The trader Alvez's old agent, the escaped prisoner from the Loanda penitentiary, reappeared the same as Harris had always known him, that is, ready to do anything. But what plan Negoro intended to take in regard to the shipwrecked from the "Pilgrim," Harris did not yet know. He asked his accomplice about it.

"And now," said he, "what are you going to do with those people?"

"I shall make two parties of them," replied Negoro, like a man whose plan had been long formed, "those whom I shall sell as slaves, and those whom _____"

The Portuguese did not finish, but his ferocious physiognomy spoke plainly enough.

"Which will you sell?" asked Harris.

"Those blacks who accompany Mrs. Weldon," replied Negoro. "Old Tom is not perhaps of much value, but the others are four strong fellows, who will bring a high price in the Kazounde market."

"I well believe it, Negoro," replied Harris. "Four negroes, well made, accustomed to work, have very little resemblance to those brutes which come to us from the interior. Certainly, you will sell them at a high price. Slaves, born in America, and exported to the markets of Angola; that is rare merchandise! But," added the American, "you have not told me if there was any money on board the 'Pilgrim.'"

"Oh! a few hundred dollars only, which I have succeeded in saving.

Fortunately, I count on certain returns."

"Which, then, comrade?" asked Harris, with curiosity.

"Nothing!" replied Negoro, who appeared to regret having spoken more than he intended.

"It now remains to take possession of all that high-priced merchandise," said Harris.

"Is it, then, so difficult?" asked Negoro.

"No, comrade. Ten miles from here, on the Coanza, a caravan of slaves is encamped, conducted by the Arab, Ibn Hamis. He only awaits my return to take the road for Kazounde. There are more native soldiers there than are needed to capture Dick Sand and his companions. It will be sufficient for my young friend to conceive the idea of going to the Coanza."

"But will he get that idea?" asked Negoro.

"Surely," replied Harris, "because he is intelligent, and cannot suspect the danger that awaits him. Dick Sand would not think of returning to the coast by the way we have followed together. He would be lost among these immense forests. He will seek, then, I am sure, to reach one of the rivers that flow toward the coast, so as to descend it on a raft. He has no other plan to take, and I know he will take it."

"Yes, perhaps so," replied Negoro, who was reflecting.

"It is not 'perhaps so,' it is 'assuredly so,' that must be said," continued Harris. "Do you see, Negoro? It is as if I had appointed a rendezvous with my young friend on the banks of the Coanza."

"Well, then," replied Negoro, "let us go. I know Dick Sand. He will not delay an hour, and we must get before him."

"Let us start, comrade."

Harris and Negoro both stood up, when the noise that had before attracted the Portuguese's attention was renewed. It was a trembling of the stems between the high papyrus.

Negoro stopped, and seized Harris's hand.

Suddenly a low barking was heard. A dog appeared at the foot of the bank, with its mouth open, ready to spring.

"Dingo!" cried Harris.

"Ah! this time it shall not escape me!" replied Negoro.

Dingo was going to jump upon him, when Negoro, seizing Harris's gun, quickly put it to his shoulder and fired.

A long howl of pain replied to the detonation, and Dingo disappeared between the double row of bushes that bordered the brook.

Negoro descended at once to the bottom of the bank.

Drops of blood stained some of the papyrus stems, and a long red track was left on the pebbles of the brook.

"At last that cursed animal is paid off!" exclaimed Negoro.

Harris had been present at this whole scene without saying a word.

"Ah now, Negoro," said he, "that dog had a particular grudge against you."

"It seemed so, Harris, but it will have a grudge against me no longer!"

"And why did it detest you so much, comrade?"

"Oh! an old affair to settle between it and me."

"An old affair?" replied Harris.

Negoro said no more about it, and Harris concluded that the Portuguese had been silent on some past adventure, but he did not insist on knowing it.

A few moments later, both, descending the course of the brook, went toward the Coanza, across the forest.

## CHAPTER III.

## ON THE MARCH.

Africa! That name so terrible under the present circumstances, that name which he must now substitute for that of America, was not for an instant out of Dick Sand's thoughts. When the young novice traced back the last weeks, it was to ask himself how the "Pilgrim" had ended by reaching this dangerous shore, how it had doubled Cape Horn, and passed from one ocean to the other! He could now explain to himself why, in spite of the rapid motion of his vessel, land was so long coming in sight, because the length of the distance which he should have made to reach the American coast had been doubled without his knowledge.

"Africa! Africa!" Dick Sand repeated.

Then, suddenly, while he called up with tenacious mind all the incidents of this inexplicable voyage, he felt that his compass must have been injured. He remembered, too, that the first compass had been broken, and that the log-line had snapped—a fact which had made it impossible for him to establish the speed of the "Pilgrim."

"Yes," thought he, "there remained but one compass on board, one only, the indications of which I could not control! And one night I was awakened by a cry from old Tom. Negoro was there, aft. He had just fallen on the binnacle. May he not have put it out of order?"

Dick Sand was growing enlightened. He had his finger on the truth. He now understood all that was ambiguous in Negoro's conduct. He saw his hand in this chain of incidents which had led to the loss of the "Pilgrim," and had so fearfully endangered those on board of her.

But what, then, was this miserable man? Had he been a sailor and known so well how to hide the fact? Was he capable of contriving this odious plot which had thrown the ship on the coast of Africa?

At any rate, if obscure points still existed in the past, the present could offer no more of them. The young novice knew only too well that he was in Africa, and very probably in the fatal province of Angola, more than a hundred miles from the coast. He also knew that Harris's treason could no longer be doubted. From this fact, the most simple logic led him to conclude that the American and the Portuguese had long known each other, that a fatal chance had united them on this coast, and that a plan had been concerted between them, the result of which would be dreadful for the survivors of the "Pilgrim."

And now, why these odious actions? That Negoro wished, at all hazards, to seize Tom and his companions, and sell them for slaves in this slave-trading country, might be admitted. That the Portuguese, moved by a sentiment of hatred, would seek to be revenged on him, Dick Sand, who had treated him as he deserved, might also be conceived. But Mrs. Weldon, this mother, and this young child—what would the wretch do with them? If Dick Sand could have overheard a little of the conversation between Harris and Negoro, he would have known what to expect, and what dangers menaced Mrs. Weldon, the blacks, and himself.

The situation was frightful, but the young novice did not yield under it. Captain on board, he remained captain on land. He must save Mrs. Weldon, little Jack, all those whose fate Heaven had placed in his hands. His task was only commencing. He would accomplish it to the end.

After two or three hours, during which the present and the future were summed up in his mind, with their good and their evil chances—the last, alas! the most numerous—Dick Sand rose, firm and resolved.

The first glimmer of light then touched the summits of the forest. With the exception of the novice and Tom, all slept. Dick Sand approached the old black.

"Tom," he said to him, in a low tone, "you have recognized the roaring of the lion, you have remembered the instruments of the slave-traders. You know that we are in Africa!"

"Yes, Mr. Dick, I know it."

"Well, Tom, not a word of all that, neither to Mrs. Weldon nor to your companions. We must be the only ones to know, the only ones to have any fears."

"Alone—in fact. It is necessary," replied Tom.

"Tom," continued the novice, "we have to watch more carefully than ever. We are in an enemy's country—and what enemies! what a country! To keep our companions on their guard, it will be enough to tell them that we have been betrayed by Harris. They will think that we fear an attack from wandering Indians, and that will suffice."

"You can count absolutely on their courage and devotion, Mr. Dick."

"I know it, as I count on your good sense and your experience. You will come to my help, old Tom?"

"Always, and everywhere, Mr. Dick."

Dick Sand's plan was accepted and approved by the old black. If Harris were detected in open treason before the hour for action, at least the young novice and his companions were not in fear of any immediate danger. In fact, it was the discovery of the irons abandoned by some slaves, and the roaring of the lion, that had caused the American's sudden disappearance.

He knew that he was discovered, and he had fled probably before the little party which he guided had reached the place where an attack had been arranged. As for Negoro, whose presence Dingo had certainly recognized during these last days of the march, he must have rejoined Harris, so as to consult with him. At any rate, several hours would pass before Dick Sand and his friends would be assailed, and it was necessary to profit by them.

The only plan was to regain the coast as quickly as possible. This coast, as the young novice had every reason to believe, was that of Angola. After having reached it, Dick Sand would try to gain, either to the north or to the south, the Portuguese settlements, where his companions could await in safety some opportunity to return to their country.

But, to effect this return to the coast, should they take the road already passed over? Dick Sand did not think so, and in that he was going to agree with Harris, who had clearly foreseen that circumstances would oblige the young novice to shorten the road.

In fact, it would have been difficult, not to say imprudent, to recommence this difficult journey through the forest, which, besides, could only tend to bring them out at the place they had started from. This would also allow Negoro's accomplices to follow an assured track. The only thing they could do was to cross a river, without leaving any traces, and, later on, to descend its course. At the same time, there was less to fear from an attack by animals, which by a happy chance had so far kept at a good distance. Even the animosity of the natives, under these circumstances, seemed less important. Once embarked on a solid raft, Dick Sand and his companions, being well armed, would be in the best condition to defend themselves. The whole thing was to find the river.

It must be added that, given the actual state of Mrs. Weldon and her little Jack, this mode of traveling would be the most suitable. Arms would not fail to carry the sick child. Lacking Harris's horse, they could even make a litter of branches, on which Mrs. Weldon could be borne. But this would require two men out of five, and Dick Sand wished, with good reason, that all his companions might be free in their movements in case of a sudden attack.

And then, in descending the current of a river, the young novice would find himself in his element!

The question now was, whether a navigable stream of water existed in the neighborhood. Dick Sand thought it probable, and for this reason: The river which emptied into the Atlantic at the place where the "Pilgrim" had stranded could not ascend much to the north, nor much to the east, of the province, because a chain of mountains quite close to them—those which they had mistaken for the Cordilleras—shut in the horizon on these two sides. Then, either the river descended from these heights, or it made a bend toward the south, and, in these two cases, Dick Sand could not take long to find the course. Perhaps, even before reaching the river—for it had a right to this qualification, being a direct tributary of the ocean—one of its affluents would be met with which would suffice for the transport of the little party.

At any rate, a stream of some sort could not be far away.

In fact, during the last miles of the journey the nature of the earth had been modified. The declivities diminished and became damp. Here and there ran narrow streams, which indicated that the sub-soil enclosed everywhere a watery network. During the last day's march the caravan had kept along one of these rivulets, whose waters, reddened with oxyde of iron, eat away its steep, worn banks. To find it again could not take long, or be very difficult. Evidently they could not descend its impetuous course, but it would be easy to follow it to its junction with a more considerable, possibly a navigable, affluent.

Such was the very simple plan which Dick Sand determined upon, after having conferred with old Tom.

Day came, all their companions gradually awoke. Mrs. Weldon placed little Jack in Nan's arms. The child was drowsy and faded-looking during the intermittent periods, and was sad to see.

Mrs. Weldon approached Dick Sand. "Dick," she asked, after a steady glance, "where is Harris? I do not perceive him."

The young novice thought that, while letting his companions believe that they were treading on the soil of Bolivia, it would not do to hide from them the American's treason. So he said, without hesitation: "Harris is no longer here."

"Has he, then, gone ahead?" asked Mrs. Weldon. "He has fled, Mrs. Weldon," replied Dick Sand. "This Harris is a traitor, and it is according to Negoro's plan that he led us this far." "For what motive?" quickly asked Mrs. Weldon. "I do not know," replied Dick Sand; "but what I do know is, that we must return, without delay, to the coast."

"That man—a traitor!" repeated Mrs. Weldon. "I had a presentiment of it! And you think, Dick, that he is in league with Negoro?"

"That may be, Mrs. Weldon. The wretch is on our track. Chance has brought these two scoundrels together, and—"

"And I hope that they will not be separated when I find them again!" said Hercules. "I will break the head of one against the other's head!" added the giant, holding out his formidable fists.

"But my child!" cried Mrs. Weldon. "The care that I hoped to find for him at the farm of San Felice—"

"Jack will get well," said old Tom, "when he approaches the more healthy part of the coast."

"Dick," remarked Mrs. Weldon, "you are sure that this Harris has betrayed us?"

"Yes, Mrs. Weldon," replied the young novice, who would have liked to avoid any explanation on this subject.

He also hastened to add, while looking at the old black:

"This very night Tom and I discovered his treason, and if he had not jumped on his horse and fled, I would have killed him."

"So this farm—"

"There is neither farm, nor village, nor settlement in the neighborhood," replied Dick Sand. "Mrs. Weldon, I repeat to you, we must return to the coast."

"By the same road, Dick?"

"No, Mrs. Weldon, but by descending a river which will take us to the sea without fatigue and without danger. A few more miles on foot, and I do not doubt—"

"Oh, I am strong, Dick!" replied Mrs. Weldon, who struggled against her own weakness. "I will walk! I will carry my child!"

"We are here, Mrs. Weldon," said Bat, "and we will carry you!"

"Yes. yes," added Austin. "Two branches of a tree, foliage laid across."

"Thanks, my friends," replied Mrs. Weldon; "but I want to march. I will march. Forward!"

"Forward!" exclaimed the young novice.

"Give me Jack," said Hercules, who took the child from Nan's arms.

"When I am not carrying something, I am tired."

The brave negro gently took in his strong arms the little sleeping boy, who did not even wake.

Their arms were carefully examined. What remained of the provisions was placed in one package, so as to be carried by one man. Austin threw it on his back, and his companions thus became free in their movements.

Cousin Benedict, whose long limbs were like steel and defied all fatigue, was ready to set out. Had he remarked Harris's disappearance? It would be imprudent to affirm it. Little disturbed him. Besides, he was under the effects of one of the most terrible catastrophes that could befall him.

In fact, a grave complication, Cousin Benedict had lost his magnifying-glass and his spectacles. Very happily, also, but without his suspecting it, Bat had found the two precious articles in the tall grass where they had slept, but, by Dick Sand's advice, he kept them safely. By this means they would be sure that the big child would keep quiet during the march, because he could see no farther, as they say, than the end of his nose.

Thus, placed between Acteon and Austin, with the formal injunction not to leave them, the woful Benedict uttered no complaint, but followed in his place, like a blind man led by a string.

The little party had not gone fifty steps when old Tom suddenly stopped it with one word.

"Dingo?" said he.

"In fact, Dingo is not here!" replied Hercules.

The black called the dog several times with his powerful voice.

No barking replied to him.

Dick Sand remained silent. The absence of the dog, was to be regretted, for he had preserved the little party from all surprise.

"Could Dingo have followed Harris?" asked Tom.

"Harris? No," replied Dick Sand; "but he may have put himself on

Negoro's scent. He felt him in our steps."

"This cook of misfortune would quickly end him with a ball!" cried

Hercules.

"Provided Dingo did not first strangle him," replied Bat.

"Perhaps so," replied the young novice. "But we cannot wait for Dingo's return. Besides, if he is living, the intelligent animal will know how to find us. Forward!"

The weather was very warm. Since daybreak large clouds obscured the horizon. Already a storm was threatened in the air. Probably the day would not end without some thunder-claps. Happily the forest, more or less dense, retained a little freshness of the surface of the soil. Here and there great forest trees inclosed prairies covered with a tall, thick grass. In certain spots enormous trunks, already petrified, lay on the ground, indicating the presence of coal mines, which are frequently met with on the African continent. Then, in the clearings, where the green carpet was mingled with some sprigs of roses, the flowers were various in color, yellow and blue ginger plants, pale lobelias, red orchids, incessantly visited by the insects which fertilized them.

The trees no longer formed impenetrable masses, but their nature was more varied. There were a kind of palm-tree, which gives an oil found only in Africa; cotton-trees forming thickets from eight to ten feet high, whose wood-stalks produce a cotton with long hairs, almost analogous to that of Fernambouc. From the copals there oozes, by the holes which certain insects make, an odorous gum, which runs along the ground and collects for the wants of the natives. Here spread the lemon-trees, the grenadiers of a savage condition of a country, and twenty other odorous plants, which prove the prodigious fertility of this plateau of Central Africa. In several places, also, the perfume was agreeably mingled with the tine odor of vanilla, although they could not discover what tree exhaled it.

This whole collection of trees and plants was perfectly green, although it was in the middle of the dry season, and only rare storms could water these luxuriant forests. It was then the time for fevers; but, as Livingstone has observed, they can be cured by leaving the place where they have been contracted. Dick Sand knew this remark of the great traveler, and he hoped that little Jack would not contradict it. He told it to Mrs. Weldon, after having observed that the periodical access had not returned as they feared, and that the child slept quietly in Hercules' arms.

Thus they went forward carefully and rapidly. Sometimes they discovered traces where men or animals had recently passed. The twisted and broken branches of the brushwood and the thickets afforded an opportunity to walk with a more equal step. But the greater part of the time numerous obstacles, which they had to overcome, retarded the little party, to Dick Sand's great disappointment.

There were twisted lianes that might justly be compared with the disordered rigging of a ship, certain vines similar to bent swords, whose blades were ornamented with long thorns, vegetable serpents, fifty or sixty feet long, which had the faculty of turning to prick the passer-by with their sharp spikes. The blacks, hatchet in hand, cut them down with vigorous blows, but the lianes reappeared constantly, reaching from the earth to the top of the highest trees which they encircled.

The animal kingdom was not less curious than the vegetable kingdom in this part of the province. Birds flew in vast numbers under these powerful branches; but it will be understood that they had no gunshot to fear from the men, who wished to pass as secretly as rapidly. There were Guinea fowls in large flocks, heath-cocks of various kinds, very difficult to approach, and some of those birds which the Americans of the North have, by onomatopoeia, called "whip-poor-wills," three syllables which exactly reproduce their cries. Dick Sand and Tom might truly have believed themselves in some province of the new continent. But, alas! they knew what to expect.

Until then the deer, so dangerous in Africa, had not approached the little troop. They again saw, in this first halt, some giraffes, which Harris had undoubtedly called ostriches. These swift animals passed rapidly, frightened by the apparition of a caravan in these little-frequented forests. In the distance, on the edge of the prairie, there arose at times a thick cloud of dust. It was a herd of buffaloes, which galloped with the noise of wagons heavily laden.

For two miles Dick Sand thus followed the course of the rivulet which must end in a more important river. He was in haste to confide his companions to the rapid current of one of the coast rivers. He felt sure that the dangers and the fatigue would be much less than on the shore.

Towards noon three miles had been cleared without any bad incident or meeting. There was no trace of either Harris or Negoro. Dingo had not reappeared. It was necessary to halt to take rest and nourishment.

The encampment was established in a bamboo thicket, which completely sheltered the little party.

They talked very little during this repast. Mrs. Weldon had taken her little boy in her arms; she could not take her eyes off of him; she could not eat.

"You must take some nourishment, Mrs. Weldon," Dick Sand repeated several times. "What will become of you if your strength gives out? Eat, eat! We will soon start again, and a good current will carry us without fatigue to the coast."

Mrs. Weldon looked in Dick Sand's face while he thus talked. The young novice's burning eyes spoke of the courage by which he felt animated. In seeing him thus, in observing these brave, devoted blacks, wife and mother, she could not yet despair; and, besides, why was she abandoned? Did she not think herself on hospitable ground? Harris's treason could not, in her eyes, have any very serious consequences. Dick Sand read her thought, and he kept his eyes on the ground.

## CHAPTER IV.

## THE BAD ROADS OF ANGOLA.

At this moment little Jack awoke, and put his arms around his mother's neck. His eyes looked better. The fever had not returned.

"You are better, my darling," said Mrs. Weldon, pressing the sick child to her heart.

"Yes, mama," replied Jack, "but I am a little thirsty."

They could only give the child some fresh water, of which he drank with pleasure.

"And my friend Dick?" he said.

"Here I am, Jack," replied Dick Sand, coming to take the young child's hand.

"And my friend Hercules?"

"Hercules is here, Mr. Jack," replied the giant, bringing nearer his good face.

"And the horse?" demanded little Jack.

"The horse? Gone, Mr. Jack," replied Hercules. "I will carry you. Will you find that I trot too hard?"

"No," replied little Jack; "but then I shall no longer have any bridle to hold."

"Oh! you will put a bit in my mouth, if you wish," said Hercules, opening his large mouth, "and you may pull back so long as that will give you pleasure."

"You know very well that I shall not pull back."

"Good! You would be wrong! I have a hard mouth."

"But Mr. Harris's farm?" the little boy asked again.

"We shall soon arrive there, my Jack," replied Mrs. Weldon. "Yes, soon!"

"Will we set out again?" then said Dick Sand, in order to cut short this conversation.

"Yes, Dick, let us go," replied Mrs. Weldon.

The camp was broken up, and the march continued again in the same order. It was necessary to pass through the underwood, so as not to leave the course of the rivulet. There had been some paths there, formerly, but those paths were dead, according to the native expression—that is, brambles and brushwood had usurped them. In these painful conditions they might spend three hours in making one mile. The blacks worked without relaxation. Hercules, after putting little Jack back in Nan's arms, took his part of the work; and what a part! He gave stout "heaves," making his ax turn round, and a hole was made before them, as if he had been a devouring fire.

Fortunately, this fatiguing work would not last. This first mile cleared, they saw a large hole, opened through the underwood, which ended obliquely at the rivulet and followed its bank. It was a passage made by elephants, and those animals, doubtless by hundreds, were in the habit of traversing this part of the forest. Great holes, made by the feet of the enormous pachyderms, riddled a soil softened during the rainy season. Its spongy nature also prepared it for those large imprints.

It soon appeared that this passage did not serve for those gigantic animals alone. Human beings had more than once taken this route, but as flocks, brutally led to the slaughter-house, would have followed it. Here and there bones of dead bodies strewed the ground; remains of skeletons, half gnawed by animals, some of which still bore the slave's fetters.

There are, in Central Africa, long roads thus marked out by human débris. Hundreds of miles are traversed by caravans, and how many unhappy wretches fall by the way, under the agents' whips, killed by fatigue or privations, decimated by sickness! How many more massacred by the traders themselves, when food fails! Yes, when they can no longer feed them, they kill them with the gun, with the sword, with the knife! These massacres are not rare.

So, then, caravans of slaves had followed this road. For a mile Dick Sand and his companions struck against these scattered bones at each step, putting to flight enormous fern-owls. Those owls rose at their approach, with a heavy flight, and turned round in the air.

Mrs. Weldon looked without seeing. Dick Sand trembled lest she should question him, for he hoped to lead her back to the coast without telling her that Harris's treachery had led them astray in an African province. Fortunately,

Mrs. Weldon did not explain to herself what she had under her eyes. She had desired to take her child again, and little Jack, asleep, absorbed all her care. Nan walked near her, and neither of them asked the young novice the terrible questions he dreaded.

Old Tom went along with his eyes down. He understood only too well why this opening was strewn with human bones.

His companions looked to the right, to the left, with an air of surprise, as if they were crossing an interminable cemetery, the tombs of which had been overthrown by a cataclysm; but they passed in silence.

Meanwhile, the bed of the rivulet became deeper and wider at the same time. Its current was less impetuous. Dick Sand hoped that it would soon become navigable, or that it would before long reach a more important river, tributary to the Atlantic.

Cost what it might, the young novice was determined to follow this stream of water. Neither did he hesitate to abandon this opening; because, as ending by an oblique line, it led away from the rivulet.

The little party a second time ventured through the dense underwood. They marched, ax in hand, through leaves and bushes inextricably interlaced.

But if this vegetation obstructed the ground, they were no longer in the thick forest that bordered the coast. Trees became rare. Large sheaves of bamboo alone rose above the grass, and so high that even Hercules was not a head over them. The passage of the little party was only revealed by the movement of these stalks.

Toward three o'clock in the afternoon of that day, the nature of the ground totally changed. Here were long plains, which must have been entirely inundated in the rainy season. The earth, now more swampy, was carpeted by thick mosses, beneath charming ferns. Should it be diversified by any steep ascents, they would see brown hematites appear, the last deposits of some rich vein of mineral.

Dick Sand then recalled—and very fortunately—what he had read in "Livingstone's Travels." More than once the daring doctor had nearly rested in these marshes, so treacherous under foot.

"Listen to me, my friends," said he, going ahead. "Try the ground before stepping on it."

"In fact," replied Tom, "they say that these grounds have been softened by the rain; but, however, it has not rained during these last days."

"No," replied Bat; "but the storm is not far off."

"The greater reason," replied Dick Sand, "why we should hurry and get clear of this swamp before it commences. Hercules, take little Jack in your arms. Bat, Austin, keep near Mrs. Weldon, so as to be able to help her if necessary. You, Mr. Benedict—Why, what are you doing, Mr. Benedict?"

"I am falling!" innocently replied Cousin Benedict, who had just disappeared as if a trap had been suddenly opened beneath his feet.

In fact, the poor man had ventured on a sort of quagmire, and had disappeared half-way in the sticky mud. They stretched out their hands, and he rose, covered with slime, but quite satisfied at not having injured his precious entomologist's box. Acteon went beside him, and made it his duty to preserve the unlucky, near-sighted man from any new disasters.

Besides, Cousin Benedict had made rather a bad choice of the quagmire for his plunge. When they drew him out of the sticky earth a large quantity of bubbles rose to the surface, and, in bursting, they emitted some gases of a suffocating odor. Livingstone, who had been sunk up to his chest in this slime, compared these grounds to a collection of enormous sponges, made of black, porous earth, from which numerous streams of water spouted when they were stepped upon. These places were always very dangerous.

For the space of half a mile Dick Sand and his companions must march over this spongy soil. It even became so bad that Mrs. Weldon was obliged to stop, for she sank deep in the mire. Hercules, Bat, and Austin, wishing to spare her the unpleasantness more than the fatigue of a passage across this marshy plain, made a litter of bamboos, on which she consented to sit. Her little Jack was placed in her arms, and they endeavored to cross that pestilential marsh in the quickest manner.

The difficulties were great. Acteon held Cousin Benedict firmly. Tom aided Nan, who, without him, would have disappeared several times in some crevice. The three other blacks carried the litter. At the head, Dick Sand sounded the earth. The choice of the place to step on was not made without trouble. They marched from preference on the edges, which were covered by a thick and tough grass. Often the support failed, and they sank to the knees in the slime.

At last, about five o'clock in the evening, the marsh being cleared, the soil regained sufficient firmness, thanks to its clayey nature; but they felt it damp underneath. Very evidently these lands lay below the neighboring rivers, and the water ran through their pores.

At that time the heat had become overwhelming. It would even have been unbearable, if thick storm clouds had not interposed between the burning rays and the ground. Distant lightnings began to rend the sky and low rollings of thunder grumbled in the depths of the heavens. A formidable storm was going to burst forth.

Now, these cataclysms are terrible in Africa: rain in torrents, squalls of wind which the strongest trees cannot resist, clap after clap of thunder, such is the contest of the elements in that latitude.

Dick Sand knew it well, and he became very uneasy. They could not pass the night without shelter. The plain was likely to be inundated, and it did not present a single elevation on which it was possible to seek refuge.

But refuge, where would they seek it in this low desert, without a tree, without a bush? The bowels of the earth even would not give it. Two feet below the surface they would find water.

However, toward the north a series of low hills seemed to limit the marshy plain. It was as the border of this depression of land. A few trees were profiled there on a more distant, clearer belt, left by the clouds on the line of the horizon.

There, if shelter were still lacking, the little band would at least no longer risk being caught in a possible inundation. There perhaps was salvation for all.

"Forward, my friends, forward!" repeated Dick Sand. "Three miles more and we shall be safer than in these bottom-lands."

"Hurry! hurry!" cried Hercules.

The brave black would have wished to take that whole world in big arms and carry it alone.

Those words inspired those courageous men, and in spite of the fatigue of a day's march, they advanced more quickly than they had done at the commencement from the halting-place.

When the storm burst forth the end to be attained was still more than two miles off. Now—a fact which was the more to be feared—the rain did not accompany the first lightnings exchanged between the ground and the electrical clouds. Darkness then became almost complete, though the sun had not disappeared below the horizon. But the dome of vapors gradually lowered, as if it threatened to fall in—a falling in which must result in a torrent of rain. Lightnings, red or blue, split it in a thousand places, and enveloped the plain in an inextricable network of fire.

Twenty times Dick and his companions ran the risk of being struck by lightning. On this plateau, deprived of trees, they formed the only projecting points which could attract the electrical discharges. Jack, awakened by the noise of the thunder, hid himself in Hercules' arms. He was very much afraid, poor little boy, but he did not wish to let his mother see it, for fear of afflicting her more. Hercules, while taking great steps, consoled him as well as he could.

"Do not be afraid, little Jack," he repeated. "If the thunder comes near us, I will break it in two with a single hand. I am stronger than it!"

And, truly, the giant's strength reassured Jack a little.

Meanwhile the rain must soon fall, and then it would in torrents, poured out by those clouds in condensing. What would become of Mrs. Weldon and her companions, if they did not find a shelter?

Dick Sand stopped a moment near old Tom.

"What must be done?" said he.

"Continue our march, Mr. Dick," replied Tom. "We cannot remain on this plain, that the rain is going to transform into a marsh!"

"No, Tom, no! But a shelter! Where? What? If it were only a hut—"

Dick Sand had suddenly broken off his sentence. A more vivid flash of lightning had just illuminated the whole plain.

"What have I seen there, a quarter of a mile off?" exclaimed Dick Sand.

"Yes, I also, I have seen—" replied old Tom, shaking his head.

"A camp, is it not?"

"Yes, Mr. Dick, it must be a camp, but a camp of natives!"

A new flash enabled them to observe this camp more closely. It occupied a part of the immense plain.

There, in fact, rose a hundred conical tents, symmetrically arranged, and measuring from twelve to fifteen feet in height. Not a soldier showed himself, however. Were they then shut up under their tents, so as to let the storm pass, or was the camp abandoned?

In the first case, whatever Heaven should threaten, Dick Sand must flee in the quickest manner. In the second, there was, perhaps, the shelter he asked.

"I shall find out," he said to himself; then, addressing old Tom: "Stay here. Let no one follow me. I shall go to reconnoiter that camp."

"Let one of us accompany you, Mr. Dick."

"No, Tom, I shall go alone. I can approach without being seen. Stay here."

The little troop, that followed Tom and Dick Sand, halted. The young novice left at once and disappeared in the darkness, which was profound when the lightning did not tear the sky.

Some large drops of rain already began to fall.

"What is the matter?" asked Mrs. Weldon, approaching the old black.

"We have perceived a camp, Mrs. Weldon," replied Tom; "a camp—or, perhaps, a village, and our captain wished to reconnoiter it before leading us to it."

Mrs. Weldon was satisfied with this reply. Three minutes after, Dick Sand was returning.

"Come! come!" he cried, in a voice which expressed his entire satisfaction.

"The camp is abandoned?" asked Tom.

"It is not a camp," replied the young novice; "it is not a village. They are ant-hills!"

"Ant-hills!" exclaimed Cousin Benedict, whom that word aroused.

"Yes, Mr. Benedict, but ant-hills twelve feet high, at least, and in which we shall endeavor to hide ourselves."

"But then," replied Cousin Benedict, "those would be ant-hills of the warlike termite or of the devouring termite. Only those ingenious insects raise such monuments, which the greatest architects would not disown."

"Whether they be termites or not, Mr. Benedict," replied Dick Sand, "we must dislodge them and take their place."

"They will devour us. They will be defending their rights."

"Forward! Forward!"

"But, wait now!" said Cousin Benedict again. "I thought those ant-hills only existed in Africa."

"Forward!" exclaimed Dick Sand, for the last time, with a sort of violence. He was so much afraid that Mrs. Weldon might hear the last word pronounced by the entomologist.

They followed Dick Sand with all haste. A furious wind had sprung up. Large drops crackled on the ground. In a few moments the squalls of wind would become unbearable. Soon one of those cones which stood on the plain was reached. No matter how threatening the termites might be, the human beings must not hesitate. If they could not drive the insects away, they must share their abode.

At the bottom of this cone, made with a kind of reddish clay, there was a very narrow hole. Hercules enlarged it with his cutlass in a few moments, so as to give a passage even to a man like himself.

To Cousin Benedict's extreme surprise, not one of the thousands of termites that ought to occupy the ant-hill showed itself. Was, then, the cone abandoned?

The hole enlarged, Dick and his companions glided into it. Hercules disappeared the last, just as the rain fell with such rage that it seemed to extinguish the lightnings.

But those wind squalls were no longer to be feared. A happy chance had furnished this little troop with a solid shelter, better than a tent, better than a native's hut.

It was one of those termite cones that, according to Lieutenant Cameron's comparison, are more astonishing than the pyramids of Egypt, raised by the hands of men, because they have been built by such small insects.

"It is," said he, "as if a nation had built Mount Everest, the highest mountain of the Himalaya chain."


## CHAPTER V.
## ANTS AND THEIR DWELLING.


At this moment the storm burst with a violence unknown in temperate latitudes.

It was providential that Dick Sand and his companions had found this refuge!

In fact, the rain did not fall in distinct drops, but in streams of various thickness. Sometimes it was a compact mass forming a sheet of water, like a cataract, a Niagara. Imagine an aerial basin, containing a whole sea, being upset. Under such showers the ground was hollowed out, the plains were changed to lakes, the streams to torrents, the rivers, overflowing, inundated vast territories. In temperate zones the violence of the storms decreases according to their duration; but in Africa, however heavy they are, they continue for several entire days. How can so much electricity be collected in the clouds? How can such quantities of vapor be accumulated? It is very difficult to comprehend this. However, such are the facts, and one might suppose himself transported to the extraordinary epochs of the diluvian period.

Fortunately, the ant-cone, with its thick walls, was perfectly impervious. A beaver's hut, of well-beaten earth, could not have been more water-tight. A torrent could have passed over it without a single drop of water filtering through its pores.

As soon as Dick Sand and his companions had taken possession of the cone they occupied themselves in examining its interior arrangement. The lantern was lighted, and the ant-hill was sufficiently illuminated. This cone, which measured twelve feet in height inside, was eleven feet wide, except in its upper part, which rounded in the form of a sugar loaf. Everywhere the walls were about one foot in thickness, and there was a distance between the stories of cells which adorned them.

We may be astonished at the construction of such monuments, due to these industrious swarms of insects, but it is true that they are frequently found in the interior of Africa. Smeathman, a Dutch traveler of the last century, with four of his companions, occupied the top of one of these cones. In the Lounde, Livingstone observed several of these ant-hills, built of reddish clay, and attaining a height of fifteen and twenty feet. Lieutenant Cameron has many a time mistaken for a camp these collections of cones which dotted the plain in N'yangwe. He has even stopped at the foot of great edifices, not more than twenty feet high, but composed of forty or fifty enormous rounded cones, flanked with bell-towers like the dome of a cathedral, such as Southern Africa possesses.

To what species of ant was due, then, the prodigious style of architecture of these cones?

"To the warlike termite," Cousin Benedict had replied, without hesitating, as soon as he had recognized the nature of the materials employed in their construction.

And, in fact, the walls, as has been said, were made of reddish clay. Had they been formed of a gray or black alluvian earth, they must have been attributed to the "termes mordax" or the "termes atrox." As we see, these insects have not very cheering names—a fact which cannot but please a strong entomologist, such as Cousin Benedict.

The central part of the cone, in which the little troop had first found shelter, and which formed the empty interior, would not have contained them; but large cavities, in close contact, made a number of divisions, in which a person of medium height could find refuge. Imagine a succession of open drawers, and at the bottom of those drawers millions of cells which the termites had occupied, and the interior disposition of the ant-hill is easily understood. To sum up, these drawers are in tiers, like the berths in a ship's cabin. In the upper ones Mrs. Weldon, little Jack, Nan, and Cousin Benedict took refuge. In the lower row Austin, Bat, and Acteon hid themselves. As for Dick Sand, Tom, and Hercules, they remained in the lower part of the cone.

"My friends," then said the young novice to the two blacks, "the ground is becoming damp. We must fill it up by crumbling the red clay from the base; but take care not to obstruct the hole by which the air enters. We cannot risk being smothered in this ant-hill."

"We have only one night to spend here," replied old Tom.

"Well, let us try and make it recover us from our fatigue. This is the first time in ten days that we have not to sleep in the open air."

"Ten days!" repeated Tom.

"Besides," added Dick Sand, "as this cone forms a solid shelter, perhaps we had better stay here twenty-four hours. During that time, I will go in search of the stream that we are in need of; it cannot be very distant. I think that until we have constructed our raft, it will be better not to quit this shelter. The storm cannot reach us here. Let us make the floor stronger and dryer."

Dick Sand's orders were executed at once. Hercules, with his ax, crumbled the first story of cells, which was composed of crisp red clay. He thus raised, more than a foot, the interior part of the swampy earth on which the ant-hill rested, and Dick Sand made sure that the air could freely penetrate to the interior of the cone through the orifice pierced at its base.

It was, certainly, a fortunate circumstance that the ant-hill had been abandoned by the termites. With a few thousands of these ants, it would have been uninhabitable. But, had it been evacuated for some time, or had the voracious newroptera but just quitted it? It was not superfluous to ponder this question.

Cousin Benedict was so much surprised at the abandonment, that he at once considered the reason for it, and he was soon convinced that the emigration had been recent.

In fact, he did not wait, but, descending to the lower part of the cone, and taking the lantern, he commenced to examine the most secret corners of the ant-hill. He thus discovered what is called the "general store-house" of the termites, that is to say, the place where these industrious insects lay up the provisions of the colony.

It was a cavity hollowed in the wall, not far from the royal cell, which Hercules's labor had destroyed, along with the cells destined for the young larvae.

In this store-room Cousin Benedict collected a certain quantity of particles of gum and the juices of plants, scarcely solidified, which proved that the termites had lately brought them from without.

"Well, no!" cried he. "No!" as if he were replying to some contradiction,

"No, this ant-hill has not been long abandoned."

"Who says to the contrary, Mr. Benedict?" said Dick Sand. "Recently or not, the important thing for us is that the termites have left it, because we have to take their place."

"The important thing," replied Cousin Benedict, "will be to know why they have left it. Yesterday—this morning, perhaps—these sagacious newroptera were still here, because, see these liquid juices; and this evening——"

"Well, what do you conclude, Mr. Benedict?" asked Dick Sand.

"That a secret presentiment has caused them to abandon the cone. Not only have all the termites left their cells, but they have taken care to carry away the young larvae, of which I cannot find one. Well, I repeat that all this was not done without a motive, and that these sagacious insects foresaw some near danger."

"They foresaw that we were going to invade their dwelling," replied

Hercules, laughing.

"Indeed!" replied Cousin Benedict, whom this answer sensibly shocked. "You think yourself so strong that you would be dangerous to these courageous insects? A few thousand of these newroptera would quickly reduce you to a skeleton if they found you dead on the road."

"Dead, certainly," replied Hercules, who would not give up; "but, living, I could crush masses of them."

"You might crush a hundred thousand, five hundred thousand, a million," replied Cousin Benedict, with animation, "but not a thousand millions; and a thousand millions would devour you, living or dead, to the last morsel."

During this discussion, which was less trifling than might be supposed, Dick Sand reflected on the observations made by Cousin Benedict. There was no doubt that the savant knew too much about the habits of the termites to be mistaken. If he declared that a secret instinct warned them to leave the ant-hill recently, it was because there was truly peril in remaining in it.

Meanwhile, as it was impossible to abandon this shelter at a moment when the storm was raging with unparalleled intensity, Dick Sand looked no farther for an explanation of what seemed to be inexplicable, and he contented himself with saying:

"Well, Mr. Benedict, if the termites have left their provisions in this ant-hill, we must not forget that we have brought ours, and let us have supper. Tomorrow, when the storm will be over, we will consult together on our future plans."

They then occupied themselves in preparing the evening meal, for, great as their fatigue was, it had not affected the appetite of these vigorous walkers. On the contrary, the food, which had to last for two more days, was very welcome. The damp had not reached the biscuits, and for several minutes it could be heard cracking under the solid teeth of Dick Sand and his companions. Between Hercules's jaws it was like grain under the miller's grindstone. It did not crackle, it powdered.

Mrs. Weldon alone scarcely eat, and even Dick Sand's entreaties were vain. It seemed to him that this brave woman was more preoccupied, more sad than she had been hitherto. Meanwhile her little Jack suffered less; the fever had not returned, and at this time he was sleeping, under his mother's eyes, in a cell well lined with garments. Dick Sand knew not what to think.

It is useless to say that Cousin Benedict did honor to the repast, not that he paid any attention either to the quality or to the quantity of the food that he devoured, but because he had found an opportunity to deliver a lecture in entomology on the termites. Ah! if he had been able to find a termite, a single one, in the deserted ant hill! But nothing.

"These admirable insects," said he, without taking the trouble to find out if any one were listening—"these admirable insects belong to the marvelous order of newroptera, whose horns are longer than the head, the jaws very distinct, and whose lower wings are generally equal to the upper ones. Five tribes constitute this order: the Panorpates (scorpion flies), the Myrmileoniens, the Hemerobins, the Termitines and the Perlides. It is useless to add that the insects which now interest us, and whose dwelling we occupy, perhaps unduly, are the Termitines."

At this moment Dick Sand listened very attentively to Cousin Benedict. Had the meeting with these termites excited in him the thought that he was perhaps on the African continent, without knowing by what chance he had arrived there? The young novice was very anxious to find out.

The savant, mounted on his favorite hobby, continued to ride it beautifully.

"Now these termitines," said he, "are characterized by four joints on the instep, horned jaws, and remarkable strength. We have the mantispe species, the raphidie, and the termite species. The last is often known under the term of white ants, in which we count the deadly termite, the yellow corslet termite, the termite that shuns the light, the biter, the destroyer—"

"And those that constructed this ant-hill?" asked Dick Sand.

"They are the martial ants," replied Cousin Benedict, who pronounced this word as if it had been the Macedonians, or some other ancient people brave in war. "Yes, the warlike ants, and of all sizes. Between Hercules and a dwarf the difference would be less than between the largest of these insects and the smallest. Among them are 'workers' of five millimeters in length 'soldiers' of ten, and males and females of twenty. We find also a kind otherwise very curious: the sirafous half an inch in length, which have pincers for jaws, and a head larger than the body, like the sharks. They are the sharks among insects, and in a fight between some sirafous and a shark, I would bet on the sirafous."

"And where are these sirafous commonly observed?" then asked Dick Sand.

"In Africa," replied Cousin Benedict; "in the central and southern provinces. Africa is, in fact, the country of ants. You should read what Livingstone says of them in the last notes reported by Stanley. More fortunate than myself, the doctor has witnessed a Homeric battle, joined between an army of black ants and an army of red ants. The latter, which are called 'drivers,' and which the natives name sirafous, were victorious.

"The others, the 'tchoungous,' took flight, carrying their eggs and their young, not without having bravely defended themselves. Never, according to Livingstone, never was the spirit of battle carried farther, either among men or beasts! With their tenacious jaws, which tear out the piece, these sirafous make the bravest man recoil. The largest animals—even lions and elephants—flee before them.

"Nothing stops them; neither trees, which they climb to the summit, nor streams, which they cross by making a suspension bridge of their own bodies, hooked together. And numerous! Another African traveler—Du Chaillu—has seen a column of these ants defile past him for twelve hours without stopping on the road. But why be astonished at the sight of such myriads? The fecundity of these insects is surprising; and, to return to our fighting termites, it has been proved that a female deposits as much as sixty thousand eggs in a day! Besides, these newroptera furnish the natives with a juicy food. Broiled ants, my friends; I know of nothing better in the world!"

"Have you then eaten them, Mr. Benedict?" asked Hercules.

"Never," replied the wise professor; "but I shall eat some."

"Where?"

"Here."

"Here; we are not in Africa!" said Tom, very quickly.

"No, no!" replied Cousin Benedict; "and, thus far, these warlike termites, and their villages of ant-hills, have only been observed on the African Continent. Ah! such travelers. They do not know how to see! Well! all the better, after all. I have discovered a tsetse in America. To the glory of this, I shall join that of having found the warlike termites on the same continent! What matter for an article that will make a sensation in educated Europe, and, perhaps, appear in folio form, with prints and engravings, besides the text!"

It was evident that the truth had not entered Cousin Benedict's brain. The poor man and all his companions, Dick Sand and Tom excepted, believed themselves, and must believe themselves, where they were not! It needed other incidents, facts still more grave than certain scientific curiosities, to undeceive them!

It was then nine o'clock in the morning. Cousin Benedict had talked for a long time. Did he perceive that his auditors, propped up in their cells, had gradually fallen asleep during his entomological lecture? No; certainly not. He lectured for himself. Dick Sand no longer questioned him, and remained motionless, although he did not sleep. As for Hercules, he had resisted longer than the others; but fatigue soon finished by shutting his eyes, and, with his eyes, his ears.

For some time longer Cousin Benedict continued to lecture. However, sleep finally got the best of him, and he mounted to the upper cavity of the cone, in which he had chosen his domicile.

Deep silence fell on the interior of the cone, while the storm filled space with noise and fire. Nothing seemed to indicate that the tempest was nearly over.

The lantern had been extinguished. The interior of the ant-hill was plunged in complete darkness.

No doubt all slept. However, Dick Sand, alone, did not seek in sleep the repose which was so necessary to him. Thought absorbed him. He dreamed of his companions, whom he would save at all hazards. The wrecking of the "Pilgrim" had not been the end of their cruel trials, and others, still more terrible, threatened them should they fall into the hands of these natives.

And how to avoid this danger, the worst of all, during their return to the coast. Harris and Negoro had not led them a hundred miles into the interior of Angola without a secret design to gain possession of them.

But what did this miserable Portuguese intend? Who had merited his hatred? The young novice repeated to himself, that he alone had incurred it. Then he passed in review all the incidents that had taken place during the "Pilgrim's" voyage; the meeting with the wreck and the blacks; the pursuit of the whale; the disappearance of Captain Hull and his crew.

Dick Sand had found himself, at the age of fifteen, intrusted with the command of a vessel, the compass and log of which were soon injured by

Negoro's criminal actions. He again saw himself using his authority in the presence of this insolent cook, threatening to put him in irons, or to blow out his brains with a pistol shot. Ah, why had he hesitated to do it? Negoro's corpse would have been thrown overboard, and none of these catastrophes would have happened.

Such were the young man's various thoughts. Then they dwelt a moment on the shipwreck which had ended the "Pilgrim's" voyage. The traitor Harris appeared then, and this province of South America gradually became transformed. Bolivia changed to the terrible Angola, with its feverish climate, its savage deer, its natives still more cruel. Could the little party escape during its return to the coast? This river which he was seeking, which he hoped to find, would it conduct them to the shore with more safety, and with less fatigue? He would not doubt it, for he knew well that a march of a hundred miles through this inhospitable country, in the midst of incessant dangers, was no longer possible.

"Happily," he said to himself, "Mrs. Weldon and all are ignorant of the danger of the situation. Old Tom and I, we alone are to know that Negoro has thrown us on the coast of Africa; and that Harris has led me into the wilds of Angola."

Dick Sand was thus sunk in overpowering thoughts, when he felt a breath on his forehead. A hand rested on his shoulder, and a trembling voice murmured these words in his ear:

"I know all, my poor Dick, but God can yet save us! His will be done!"

## CHAPTER VI.

## THE DIVING-BELL.

To this unexpected revelation Dick Sand could not reply. Besides, Mrs. Weldon had gone back at once to her place beside little Jack. She evidently did not wish to say any more about it, and the young novice had not the courage to detain her.

Thus Mrs. Weldon knew what to believe. The various incidents, of the way had enlightened her also, and perhaps, too, that word, "Africa!" so unluckily pronounced the night before by Cousin Benedict.

"Mrs. Weldon knows everything," repeated Dick Sand to himself. "Well, perhaps it is better so. The brave woman does not despair. I shall not despair either."

Dick Sand now longed for day to return, that he might explore the surroundings of this termite village. He must find a tributary of the Atlantic with a rapid course to transport all his little troop. He had a presentiment that this watercourse could not be far distant. Above all, they must avoid an encounter with the natives, perhaps already sent in pursuit of them under Harris's and Negoro's direction.

But it was not day yet. No light made its way into the cone through the lower orifice. Rumblings, rendered low by the thickness of the walls, indicated that the storm still raged. Listening, Dick Sand also heard the rain falling with violence at the base of the ant-hill. As the large drops no longer struck a hard soil, he must conclude that the whole plain was inundated.

It must have been about eleven o'clock. Dick Sand then felt that a kind of torpor, if not a true sleep, was going to overcome him. It would, however, be rest. But, just as he was yielding to it, the thought came to him that, by the settling of the clay, washed in, the lower orifice was likely to be obstructed. All passage for the outer air would be closed. Within, the respiration of ten persons would soon vitiate the air by loading it with carbonic acid.

Dick Sand then slipped to the ground, which had been raised by the clay from the first floor of cells.

That cushion was still perfectly dry, and the orifice entirely free. The air penetrated freely to the interior of the cone, and with it some flashes of lightning, and the loud noises of that storm, that a diluvian rain could not extinguish.

Dick Sand saw that all was well. No immediate danger seemed to menace these human termites, substituted for the colony of newroptera. The young novice then thought of refreshing himself by a few hours' sleep, as he already felt its influence. Only with supreme precaution Dick Sand lay on that bed of clay, at the bottom of the cone, near the narrow edifice.

By this means, if any accident happened outside, he would be the first to remark it. The rising day would also awaken him, and he would be ready to begin the exploration of the plain.

Dick Sand lay down then, his head against the wall, his gun under his hand, and almost immediately he was asleep.

How long this drowsiness lasted he could not tell, when he was awakened by a lively sensation of coolness.

He rose and recognized, not without great anxiety, that the water was invading the ant hill, and even so rapidly, that in a few seconds it would reach the story of cells occupied by Tom and Hercules.

The latter, awakened by Dick Sand, were told about this new complication.

The lighted lantern soon showed the interior of the cone.

The water had stopped at a height of about five feet, and remained stationary.

"What is the matter, Dick?" asked Mrs. Weldon.

"It is nothing," replied the young novice. "The lower part of the cone has been inundated. It is probably that during this storm a neighboring river has overflowed on this plain."

"Good!" said Hercules; "that proves the river is there!"

"Yes," replied Dick Sand, "and it will carry us to the coast. Be reassured, then, Mrs. Weldon; the water cannot reach you, nor little Jack, nor Nan, nor Mr. Benedict."

Mrs. Weldon did not reply. As to the cousin, he slept like a veritable termite.

Meanwhile the blacks, leaning over this sheet of water, which reflected the lantern's light, waited for Dick Sand to indicate to them what should be done. He was measuring the height of the inundation.

After having the provisions and arms put out of the reach of the inundation, Dick Sand was silent.

"The water has penetrated by the orifice," said Tom.

"Yes," replied Dick Sand, "and now it prevents the interior air from being renewed."

"Could we not make a hole in the wall above the level of the water?" asked the old black.

"Doubtless, Tom; but if we have five feet of water within, there are perhaps six or seven, even more, without."

"You think, Mr. Dick—?"

"I think, Tom, that the water, rising inside the ant-hill, has compressed the air in the upper part, and that this air now makes an obstacle to prevent the water from rising higher. But if we pierce a hole in the wall by which the air would escape, either the water would still rise till it reached the outside level, or if it passed the hole, it would rise to that point where the compressed air would again keep it back. We must be here like workmen in a diving-bell."

"What must be done?" asked Tom.

"Reflect well before acting," replied Dick Sand. "An imprudence might cost us our lives!"

The young novice's observation was very true.

In comparing the cone to a submerged bell, he was right. Only in that apparatus the air is constantly renewed by means of pumps. The divers breathe comfortably, and they suffer no other inconveniences than those resulting from a prolonged sojourn in a compressed atmosphere, no longer at a normal pressure.

But here, beside those inconveniences, space was already reduced a third by the invasion of the water. As to the air, it would only be renewed if they put it in communication with the outer atmosphere by means of a hole.

Could they, without running the danger spoken of by Dick Sand, pierce that hole? Would not the situation be aggravated by it?

What was certain was, that the water now rested at a level which only two causes could make it exceed, namely: if they pierced a hole, and the level of the rising waters was higher outside, or if the height of this rising water should still increase. In either of these cases, only a narrow space would remain inside the cone, where the air, not renewed, would be still more compressed.

But might not the ant-hill be torn from the ground and overthrown by the inundation, to the extreme danger of those within it? No, no more than a beaver's hut, so firmly did it adhere by its base.

Then, the event most to be feared was the persistence of the storm, and, consequently, the increase of the inundation. Thirty feet of water on the plain would cover the cone with eighteen feet of water, and bear on the air within with the pressure of an atmosphere.

Now, after reflecting well upon it, Dick Sand was led to fear that this inundation might increase considerably.

In fact, it could not be due solely to that deluge poured out by the clouds. It seemed more probable that a neighboring watercourse, swelled by the storm, had burst its banks, and was spreading over this plain lying below it. What proof had they that the ant-hill was not then entirely submerged, and that it was full time to leave it by the top part, which would not be difficult to demolish?

Dick Sand, now extremely anxious, asked himself what he ought to do. Must he wait or suddenly announce the probable result of the situation, after ascertaining the condition of things?

It was then three o'clock in the morning. All, motionless, silent, listened. The noise from outside came very feebly through the obstructed orifice. All the time a dull sound, strong and continued, well indicated that the contest of the elements had not ceased.

At that moment old Tom observed that the water level was gradually rising.

"Yes," replied Dick Sand, "and if it rises, as the air cannot escape from within, it is because the rising of the waters increases and presses it more and more."

"It is but slight so far," said Tom.

"Without doubt," replied Dick Sand; "but where will this level stop?"

"Mr. Dick," asked Bat, "would you like me to go out of the ant-hill?

By diving, I should try to slip out by the hole."

"It will be better for me to try it," replied Dick Sand.

"No, Mr. Dick, no," replied old Tom, quickly; "let my son do it, and trust to his skill. In case he could not return, your presence is necessary here."

Then, lower:

"Do not forget Mrs. Weldon and little Jack."

"Be it so," replied Dick Sand. "Go, then, Bat. If the ant-hill is submerged, do not seek to enter it again. We shall try to come out as you will have done. But if the cone still emerges, strike on its top with the ax that you will take with you. We will hear you, and it will be the signal for us to demolish the top from our side. You understand?"

"Yes, Mr. Dick," replied Bat.

"Go, then, boy," added old Tom, pressing his son's hand.

Bat, after laying in a good provision of air by a long aspiration, plunged under the liquid mass, whose depth then exceeded five feet. It was a rather difficult task, because he would have to seek the lower orifice, slip through it, and then rise to the outside surface of the waters.

That must be done quickly.

Nearly half a minute passed away. Dick Sand then thought that Bat had succeeded in passing outside when the black emerged.

"Well!" exclaimed Dick Sand.

"The hole is stopped up by rubbish!" replied Bat, as soon as he could take breath.

"Stopped up!" repeated Tom.

"Yes," replied Bat. "The water has probably diluted the clay. I have felt around the walls with my hand. There is no longer any hole."

Dick Sand shook his head. His companions and he were hermetically sequestered in this cone, perhaps submerged by the water.

"If there is no longer any hole," then said Hercules, "we must make one."

"Wait," replied the young novice, stopping Hercules, who, hatchet in hand, was preparing to dive.

Dick Sand reflected for a few moments, and then he said:

"We are going to proceed in another manner. The whole question is to know whether the water covers the ant-hill or not. If we make a small opening at the summit of the cone, we shall find out which it is. But in case the ant-hill should be submerged now, the water would fill it entirely, and we would be lost. Let us feel our way."

"But quickly," replied Tom.

In fact, the level continued to rise gradually. There were then six feet of water inside the cone. With the exception of Mrs. Weldon, her son, Cousin Benedict, and Nan, who had taken refuge in the upper cavities, all were immersed to the waist.

Then there was a necessity for quick action, as Dick Sand proposed.

It was one foot above the interior level, consequently seven feet from the ground, that Dick Sand resolved to pierce a hole in the clay wall.

If, by this hole, they were in communication with the outer air, the cone emerges. If, on the contrary, this hole was pierced below the water level outside, the air would be driven inward, and in that case they must stop it up at once, or the water would rise to its orifice. Then they would commence again a foot higher, and so on. If, at last, at the top, they did not yet find the outer air, it was because there was a depth of more than fifteen feet of water in the plain, and that the whole termite village had disappeared under the inundation. Then what chance had the prisoners in the ant-hill to escape the most terrible of deaths, death by slow asphyxia?

Dick Sand knew all that, but he did not lose his presence of mind for a moment. He had closely calculated the consequences of the experiment he wished to try. Besides, to wait longer was not possible. Asphyxia was threatening in this narrow space, reduced every moment, in a medium already saturated with carbonic acid.

The best tool Dick Sand could employ to pierce a hole through the wall was a ramrod furnished with a screw, intended to draw the wadding from a gun. By making it turn rapidly, this screw scooped out the clay like an auger, and the hole was made little by little. Then it would not have a larger diameter than that of the ramrod, but that would be sufficient. The air could come through very well.

Hercules holding up the lantern lighted Dick Sand. They had some wax candles to take its place, and they had not to fear lack of light from that source.

A minute after the beginning of the operation, the ramrod went freely through the wall. At once a rather dull noise was produced, resembling that made by globules of air escaping through a column of water. The air escaped, and, at the same moment, the level of the water rose in the cone, and stopped at the height of the hole. This proved that they had pierced too low—that is to say, below the liquid mass.

"Begin again," the young novice said, coolly, after rapidly stopping the hole with a handful of clay.

The water was again stationary in the cone, but the reserved space had diminished more than eight inches. Respiration became difficult, for the oxygen was beginning to fail. They saw it also by the lantern's light, which reddened and lost a part of its brightness.

One foot above the first hole, Dick Sand began at once to pierce a second by the same process. If the experiment failed, the water would rise still higher inside the cone—but that risk must be run.

While Dick Sand was working his auger, they heard Cousin Benedict cry out, suddenly:

"Mercy! look—look—look why!"

Hercules raised his lantern and threw its light on Cousin Benedict, whose face expressed the most perfect satisfaction.

"Yes," repeated he, "look why those intelligent termites have abandoned the ant-hill! They had felt the inundation beforehand. Ah! instinct, my friends, instinct. The termites are wiser than we are, much wiser."

And that was all the moral Cousin Benedict drew from the situation.

At that moment Dick Sand drew out the ramrod, which had penetrated the wall. A hissing was produced. The water rose another foot inside the cone—the hole had not reached the open air outside.

The situation was dreadful. Mrs. Weldon, then almost reached by the water, had raised little Jack in her arms. All were stifling in this narrow space. Their ears buzzed.

The lantern only threw a faint light.

"Is the cone, then, entirely under water?" murmured Dick Sand.

He must know; and, in order to know, he must pierce a third hole, at the very top.

But it was asphyxia, it was immediate death, if the result of this last attempt should prove fruitless. The air remaining inside would escape through the upper sheet of water, and the water would fill the whole cone.

"Mrs. Weldon," then said Dick Sand, "you know the situation. If we delay, respirable air will fail us. If the third attempt fails, water will fill all this space. Our only chance is that the summit of the cone is above the level of the inundation. We must try this last experiment. Are you willing?"

"Do it, Dick!" replied Mrs. Weldon.

At that moment the lantern went out in that medium already unfit for combustion. Mrs. Weldon and her companions were plunged in the most complete darkness.

Dick Sand was perched on Hercules's shoulders. The latter was hanging on to one of the lateral cavities. Only his head was above the bed of water.

Mrs. Weldon, Jack, and Cousin Benedict were in the last story of cells.

Dick Sand scratched the wall, and his ramrod pierced the clay rapidly. In this place the wall, being thicker and harder also, was more difficult to penetrate. Dick Sand hastened, not without terrible anxiety, for by this narrow opening either life was going to penetrate with the air, or with the water it was death.

Suddenly a sharp hissing was heard. The compressed air escaped—but a ray of daylight filtered through the wall. The water only rose eight inches, and stopped, without Dick Sand being obliged to close the hole. The equilibrium was established between the level within and that outside. The summit of the cone emerged. Mrs. Weldon and her companions were saved.

At once, after a frantic hurra, in which Hercules's thundering voice prevailed, the cutlasses were put to work. The summit, quickly attacked, gradually crumbled. The hole was enlarged, the pure air entered in waves, and with it the first rays of the rising sun. The top once taken off the cone, it would be easy to hoist themselves on to its wall, and they would devise means of reaching some neighboring height, above all inundations.

Dick Sand first mounted to the summit of the cone.

A cry escaped him.

That particular noise, too well known by African travelers, the whizzing of arrows, passed through the air.

Dick Sand had had time to perceive a camp a hundred feet from the ant-hill, and ten feet from the cone, on the inundated plain, long boats, filled with natives.

It was from one of those boats that the flight of arrows had come the moment the young novice's head appeared out of the hole.

Dick Sand, in a word, had told all to his companions. Seizing his gun, followed by Hercules, Acteon, and Bat, he reappeared at the summit of the cone, and all fired on one of the boats.

Several natives fell, and yells, accompanied by shots, replied to the detonation of the fire-arms.

But what could Dick Sand and his companions do against a hundred

Africans, who surrounded them on all sides?

The ant-hill was assailed. Mrs. Weldon, her child, and Cousin Benedict, all were brutally snatched from it, and without having had time to speak to each other or to shake hands for the last time, they saw themselves separated from each other, doubtless in virtue of orders previously given.

A last boat took away Mrs. Weldon, little Jack and Cousin Benedict.

Dick Sand saw them disappear in the middle of the camp.

As to him, accompanied by Nan, Old Tom, Hercules, Bat, Acteon and Austin, he was thrown into a second boat, which went toward another point of the hill.

Twenty natives entered this boat.

It was followed by five others.

Resistance was not possible, and nevertheless, Dick Sand and his companions attempted it. Some soldiers of the caravan were wounded by them, and certainly they would have paid for this resistance with their lives, if there had not been a formal order to spare them.

In a few minutes, the passage was made. But just as the boat landed, Hercules, with an irresistible bound, sprang on the ground. Two natives having sprung on him, the giant turned his gun like a club, and the natives fell, with their skulls broken.

A moment after, Hercules disappeared under the cover of the trees, in the midst of a shower of balls, as Dick Sand and his companions, having been put on land, were chained like slaves.

## CHAPTER VII.

## IN CAMP ON THE BANKS OF THE COANZA.

The aspect of the country was entirely changed since the inundation. It had made a lake of the plain where the termite village stood. The cones of twenty ant-hills emerged, and formed the only projecting points on this large basin.

The Coanza had overflowed during the night, with the waters of its tributaries swelled by the storm.

This Coanza, one of the rivers of Angola, flows into the Atlantic, a hundred miles from the cape where the "Pilgrim" was wrecked. It was this river that Lieutenant Cameron had to cross some years later, before reaching Benguela. The Coanza is intended to become the vehicle for the interior transit of this portion of the Portuguese colony. Already steamers ascend its lower course, and before ten years elapse, they will ply over its upper bed. Dick Sand had then acted wisely in seeking some navigable river toward the north. The rivulet he had followed had just been emptied into the Coanza. Only for this sudden attack, of which he had had no intimation to put him on his guard, he would have found the Coanza a mile farther on. His companions and he would have embarked on a raft, easily constructed, and they would have had a good chance to descend the stream to the Portuguese villages, where the steamers come into port. There, their safety would be secured.

It would not be so.

The camp, perceived by Dick Sand, was established on an elevation near the ant-hill, into which fate had thrown him, as in a trap. At the summit of that elevation rose an enormous sycamore fig-tree, which would easily shelter five hundred men under its immense branches. Those who have not seen those giant trees of Central Africa, can form no idea of them. Their branches form a forest, and one could be lost in it. Farther on, great banyans, of the kind whose seeds do not change into fruits, completed the outline of this vast landscape.

It was under the sycamore's shelter, hidden, as in a mysterious asylum, that a whole caravan—the one whose arrival Harris had announced to Negoro—had just halted. This numerous procession of natives, snatched from their villages by the trader Alvez's agents, were going to the Kazounde market. Thence the slaves, as needed, would be sent either to the barracks of the west coast, or to N'yangwe, toward the great lake region, to be distributed either in upper Egypt, or in the factories of Zanzibar.

As soon as they arrived at the camp, Dick Sand and his companions had been treated as slaves. Old Tom, his son Austin, Acteon, poor Nan, negroes by birth, though they did not belong to the African race, were treated like captive natives. After they were disarmed, in spite of the strongest resistance, they were held by the throat, two by two, by means of a pole six or seven feet long, forked at each end, and closed by an iron rod. By this means they were forced to march in line, one behind the other, unable to get away either to the right or to the left. As an over precaution, a heavy chain was attached to their waists. They had their arms free, to carry burdens, their feet free to march, but they could not use them to flee. Thus they were going to travel hundreds of miles under an overseer's lash. Placed apart, overcome by the reaction which followed the first moments of their struggle against the negroes, they no longer made a movement. Why had they not been able to follow Hercules in his flight? And, meanwhile, what could they hope for the fugitive? Strong as he was, what would become of him in that inhospitable country, where hunger, solitude, savage beasts, natives, all were against him? Would he not soon regret his companion's fate? They, however, had no pity to expect from the chiefs of the caravan, Arabs or Portuguese, speaking a language they could not understand. These chiefs only entered into communication with their prisoners by menacing looks and gestures.

Dick Sand himself was not coupled with any other slave. He was a white man, and probably they had not dared to inflict the common treatment on him. Unarmed, he had his feet and hands free, but a driver watched him especially. He observed the camp, expecting each moment to see Negoro or Harris appear. His expectation was in vain. He had no doubt, however, that those two miserable men had directed the attack against the ant-hill.

Thus the thought came to him that Mrs. Weldon, little Jack, and Cousin Benedict had been led away separately by orders from the American or from the Portuguese. Seeing neither one nor the other, he said to himself that perhaps the two accomplices even accompanied their victims. Where were they leading them? What would they do with them? It was his most cruel care. Dick Sand forgot his own situation to think only of Mrs. Weldon and hers.

The caravan, camped under the gigantic sycamore, did not count less than eight hundred persons, say five hundred slaves of both sexes, two hundred soldiers, porters, marauders, guards, drivers, agents, or chiefs.

These chiefs were of Arab and Portugese origin. It would be difficult to imagine the cruelties that these inhuman beings inflicted on their captives. They struck them without relaxation, and those who fell exhausted, not fit to be sold, were finished with gunshots or the knife. Thus they hold them by terror. But the result of this system is, that on the arrival of the caravan, fifty out of a hundred slaves are missing from the trader's list. A few may have escaped, but the bones of those who died from torture mark out the long routes from the interior to the coast.

It is supposed that the agents of European origin, Portuguese for the most part, are only rascals whom their country has rejected, convicts, escaped prisoners, old slave-drivers whom the authorities have been unable to hang— in a word, the refuse of humanity. Such was Negoro, such was Harris, now in the service of one of the greatest contractors of Central Africa, Jose-Antonio Alvez, well known by the traders of the province, about whom Lieutenant Cameron has given some curious information.

The soldiers who escort the captives are generally natives in the pay of the traders. But the latter have not the monopoly of those raids which procure the slaves for them. The negro kings also make atrocious wars with each other, and with the same object. Then the vanquished adults, the women and children, reduced to slavery, are sold by the vanquishers for a few yards of calico, some powder, a few firearms, pink or red pearls, and often even, as Livingstone says, in periods of famine, for a few grains of maize.

The soldiers who escorted old Alvez's caravan might give a true idea of what African armies are.

It was an assemblage of negro bandits, hardly clothed, who brandished long flint-lock guns, the gun-barrels garnished with a great number of copper rings. With such an escort, to which are joined marauders who are no better, the agents often have all they can do. They dispute orders, they insist on their own halting places and hours, they threaten to desert, and it is not rare for the agents to be forced to yield to the exactions of this soldiery.

Though the slaves, men or women, are generally subjected to carry burdens while the caravan is on the march, yet a certain number of porters accompany it. They are called more particularly "Pagazis," and they carry bundles of precious objects, principally ivory. Such is the size of these elephants' teeth sometimes, of which some weigh as much as one hundred and sixty pounds, that it takes two of these "Pagazis" to carry them to the factories. Thence this precious merchandise is exported to the markets of Khartoum, of Zanzibar and Natal.

On arriving, these "Pagazis" are paid the price agreed upon. It consists in twenty yards of cotton cloth, or of that stuff which bears the name of "Merikani," a little powder, a handful of cowry (shells very common in that country, which serve as money), a few pearls, or even those of the slaves who would be difficult to sell. The slaves are paid, when the trader has no other money.

Among the five hundred slaves that the caravan counted, there were few grown men. That is because, the "Razzia" being finished and the village set on fire, every native above forty is unmercifully massacred and hung to a neighboring tree. Only the young adults of both sexes and the children are intended to furnish the markets. After these men-hunts, hardly a tenth of the vanquished survive. This explains the frightful depopulation which changes vast territories of equatorial Africa into deserts.

Here, the children and the adults were hardly clothed with a rag of that bark stuff, produced by certain trees, and called "mbouzon" in the country. Thus the state of this troop of human beings, women covered with wounds from the "havildars'" whips, children ghastly and meager, with bleeding feet, whom their mothers tried to carry in addition to their burdens, young men closely riveted to the fork, more torturing than the convict's chain, is the most lamentable that can be imagined.

Yes, the sight of the miserable people, hardly living, whose voices have no sound, ebony skeletons according to Livingstone's expression, would touch the hearts of wild beasts. But so much misery did not touch those hardened Arabs nor those Portuguese, who, according to Lieutenant Cameron, are still more cruel. This is what Cameron says: "To obtain these fifty women, of whom Alvez called himself proprietor, ten villages had been destroyed, ten villages having each from one hundred to two hundred souls: a total of fifteen hundred inhabitants. Some had been able to escape, but the greater part—almost all—had perished in the flames, had been killed in defending their families, or had died of hunger in the jungle, unless the beasts of prey had terminated their sufferings more promptly.

"Those crimes, perpetrated in the center of Africa by men who boast of the name of Christians, and consider themselves Portuguese, would seem incredible to the inhabitants of civilized countries. It is impossible that the government of Lisbon knows the atrocities committed by people who boast of being her subjects." —Tour of the World.

In Portugal there have been very warm protestations against these assertions of Cameron's.

It need not be said that, during the marches, as during the halts, the prisoners were very carefully guarded. Thus, Dick Sand soon understood that he must not even attempt to get away. But then, how find Mrs. Weldon again? That she and her child had been carried away by Negoro was only too certain. The Portuguese had separated her from her companions for reasons unknown as yet to the young novice. But he could not doubt Negoro's intervention, and his heart was breaking at the thought of the dangers of all kinds which threatened Mrs. Weldon.

"Ah!" he said to himself, "when I think that I have held those two miserable men, both of them, at the end of my gun, and that I have not killed them!"

This thought was one of those which returned most persistently to Dick Sand's mind. What misfortunes the death, the just death of Harris and Negoro might have prevented! What misery, at least, for those whom these brokers in human flesh were now treating as slaves!

All the horror of Mrs. Weldon's and little Jack's situation now represented itself to Dick Sand. Neither the mother nor the child could count on Cousin Benedict. The poor man could hardly take care of himself.

Doubtless they were taking all three to some district remote from the province of Angola. But who was carrying the still sick child?

"His mother; yes, his mother," Dick Sand repeated to himself. "She will have recovered strength for him; she will have done what these unhappy female slaves do, and she will fall like them. Ah! may God put me again in front of her executioners, and I—"

But he was a prisoner! He counted one head in this live-stock that the overseers were driving to the interior of Africa. He did not even know whether Negoro and Harris themselves were directing the convoy of which their victims made a part. Dingo was no longer there to scent the Portuguese, to announce his approach. Hercules alone might come to the assistance of the unfortunate Mrs. Weldon. But was that miracle to be hoped for?

However, Dick Sand fell back again on that idea. He said to himself that the strong black man was free. Of his devotion there was no doubt. All that a human being could do, Hercules would do in Mrs. Weldon's interest. Yes, either Hercules would try to find them and put himself in communication with them; or if that failed him, he would endeavor to concert with him, Dick Sand, and perhaps carry him off, deliver him by force. During the night halts, mingling with these prisoners, black like them, could he not deceive the soldier's vigilance, reach him, break his bonds, and lead him away into the forest? And both of them, then free, what would they not do for Mrs. Weldon's safety. A water course would enable them to descend to the coast. Dick Sand would again take up that plan so unfortunately prevented by the natives' attack, with new chances of success and a greater knowledge of the difficulties.

The young novice thus alternated between fear and hope. In fact, he resisted despair, thanks to his energetic nature, and held himself in readiness to profit by the least chance that might offer itself to him.

What he most desired to know was to what market the agents were taking the convoy of slaves. Was it to one of the factories of Angola, and would it be an affair of a few halting-places only, or would this convoy travel for hundreds of miles still, across Central Africa? The principal market of the contractors is that of N'yangwe, in Manyema, on that meridian which divides the African continent into two almost equal parts, there where extends the country of the great lakes, that Livingstone was then traversing. But it was far from the camp on the Coanza to that village. Months of travel would not suffice to reach it.

That was one of Dick Sand's most serious thoughts; for, once at N'yangwe, in case even Mrs. Weldon, Hercules, the other blacks and he should succeed in escaping, how difficult it would be, not to say impossible, to return to the seacoast, in the midst of the dangers of such a long route.

But Dick Sand soon had reason to think that the convoy would soon reach its destination. Though he did not understand the language employed by the chiefs of the caravan, sometimes Arab, sometimes the African idiom, he remarked that the name of an important market of that region was often pronounced. It was the name Kazounde, and he knew that a very great trade in slaves was carried on there. He was then naturally led to believe that there the fate of the prisoners would be decided, whether for the profit of the king of that district or for the benefit of some rich trader of the country. We know that he was not mistaken.

Now, Dick Sand, being posted in the facts of modern geography, knew very exactly what is known of Kazounde. The distance from Saint Paul de Loanda to this city does not exceed four hundred miles, and consequently two hundred and fifty miles, at the most, separates it from the camp established on the Coanza. Dick Sand made his calculation approximately, taking the distance traveled by the little troop under Harris's lead as the base. Now, under ordinary circumstances, this journey would only require from ten to twelve days. Doubling that time for the needs of a caravan already exhausted by a long route, Dick Sand might estimate the length of the journey from the Coanza to Kazounde at three weeks.

Dick Sand wished very much to impart what he believed he knew to Tom and his companions. It would be a kind of consolation for them to be assured that they were not being led to the center of Africa, into those fatal countries which they could not hope to leave. Now, a few words uttered in passing would be sufficient to enlighten them. Would he succeed in saying those words?

Tom and Bat—chance had reunited the father and son—Acteon and Austin, forked two by two, were at the right extremity of the camp. An overseer and a dozen soldiers watched them.

Dick Sand, free in his movements, resolved to gradually diminish the distance that separated him from his companions to fifty steps. He then commenced to maneuver to that end.

Very likely old Tom divined Dick Sand's thought. A word, pronounced in a low voice, warned his companions to be attentive. They did not stir, but they kept themselves ready to see, as well as to hear.

Soon, with an indifferent air, Dick Sand had gained fifty steps more. From the place where he then was, he could have called out, in such a manner as to be heard, that name Kazounde, and tell them what the probable length of the journey would be. But to complete his instructions, and confer with them on their conduct during the journey, would be still better. He then continued to draw nearer to them. Already his heart was beating with hope; he was only a few steps from the desired end, when the overseer, as if he had suddenly penetrated his intention, rushed on him. At the cries of that enraged person, ten soldiers ran to the spot, and Dick Sand was brutally led back to the rear, while Tom and his companions were taken to the other extremity of the camp.

Exasperated, Dick Sand had thrown himself upon the overseer. He had ended by breaking his gun in his hands. He had almost succeeded in snatching it from him. But seven or eight soldiers assailed him at once, and force was used to secure him. Furious, they would have massacred him, if one of the chiefs of the caravan, an Arab of great height and ferocious physiognomy, had not intervened. This Arab was the chief Ibn Hamis, of whom Harris had spoken. He pronounced a few words which Dick Sand could not understand, and the soldiers, obliged to release their prey, went away.

It was, then, very evident, for one thing, that there had been a formal order not to allow the young novice to communicate with his companions; and for another, that his life should not be taken.

Who could have given such orders, if not Harris or Negoro?

At that moment—it was nine o'clock in the morning, April 19th—the harsh sounds from a "condou's" horn (a kind of ruminating animal among the African deer) burst forth, and the drum was heard. The halt was going to end.

All, chiefs, porters, soldiers, slaves, were immediately on foot. Laden with their packs, several groups of captives were formed under the leadership of an overseer, who unfurled a banner of bright colors.

The signal for departure was given. Songs then rose on the air; but they were the vanquished, not the vanquishers, who sang thus.

This is what they said in these songs—a threatening expression of a simple faith from the slaves against their oppressors—against their executioners:

"You have sent me to the coast, but I shall be dead; I shall have a yoke no longer, and I shall return to kill you."

## CHAPTER VIII.
## SOME OF DICK SAND'S NOTES.

Though the storm of the day before had ceased, the weather was still very unsettled. It was, besides, the period of the "masika," the second period of the rainy season, under this zone of the African heaven. The nights in particular would be rainy during one, two, or three weeks, which could only increase the misery of the caravan.

It set out that day in cloudy weather, and, after quitting the banks of the Coanza, made its way almost directly to the east. Fifty soldiers marched at the head, a hundred on each of the two sides of the convoy, the rest as a rear-guard. It would be difficult for the prisoners to flee, even if they had not been chained. Women, children, and men were going pell-mell, and the overseers urged them on with the whip. There were unfortunate mothers who, nursing one child, held a second by the hand that was free. Others dragged these little beings along, without clothing, without shoes, on the sharp grasses of the soil.

The chief of the caravan, that ferocious Ibn Hamis, who had interfered in the struggle between Dick Sand and his overseer, watched this whole troop, going backwards and forwards from the head to the foot of the long column. If his agents and he troubled themselves but little about the sufferings of their captives, they must reckon more seriously either with the soldiers who claimed some additional rations, or with the "pagazis" who wanted to halt. Thence discussions; often even an exchange of brutality. The slaves suffered more from the overseers' constant irritation. Nothing was heard but threats from one side, and cries of grief from the other. Those who marched in the last ranks treaded a soil that the first had stained with their blood.

Dick Sand's companions, always carefully kept in front of the convoy, could have no communication with him. They advanced in file, the neck held in the heavy fork, which did not permit a single head-movement. The whips did not spare them any more than their sad companions in misfortune.

Bat, coupled with his father, marched before him, taxing his ingenuity not to shake the fork, choosing the best places to step on, because old Tom must pass after him. From time to time, when the overseer was a little behind, he uttered various words of encouragement, some of which reached Tom. He even tried to retard his march, if he felt that Tom was getting tired. It was suffering, for this good son to be unable to turn his head towards his good father, whom he loved. Doubtless, Tom had the satisfaction of seeing his son; however, he paid dear for it. How many times great tears flowed from his eyes when the overseer's whip fell upon Bat! It was a worse punishment than if it had fallen on his own flesh.

Austin and Acteon marched a few steps behind, tied to each other, and brutally treated every moment. Ah, how they envied Hercules's fate! Whatever were the dangers that threatened the latter in that savage country, he could at least use his strength and defend his life.

During the first moments of their captivity, old Tom had finally made known the whole truth to his companions. They had learned from him, to their profound astonishment, that they were in Africa; that Negoro's and Harris's double treachery had first thrown them there, and then led them away, and that no pity was to be expected from their masters.

Nan was not better treated. She made part of a group of women who occupied the middle of the convoy. They had chained her with a young mother of two children, one at the breast, the other aged three years, who walked with difficulty. Nan, moved with pity, had burdened herself with the little creature, and the poor slave had thanked her by a tear. Nan then carried the infant, at the same time, sparing her the fatigue, to which she would have yielded, and the blows the overseer would have given her. But it was a heavy burden for old Nan. She felt that her strength would soon fail her, and then she thought of little Jack. She pictured him to herself in his mother's arms. Sickness had wasted him very much, but he must be still heavy for Mrs. Weldon's weakened arms. Where was she? What would become of her? Would her old servant ever see her again?

Dick Sand had been placed almost in the rear of the convoy. He could neither perceive Tom, nor his companions, nor Nan. The head of the long caravan was only visible to him when it was crossing some plain. He walked, a prey, to the saddest thoughts, from which the agents' cries hardly drew his attention. He neither thought of himself, nor the fatigues he must still support, nor of the tortures probably reserved for him by Negoro. He only thought of Mrs. Weldon. In rain he sought on the ground, on the brambles by the paths, on the lower branches of the trees, to find some trace of her passage. She could not have taken another road, if, as everything indicated, they were leading her to Kazounde. What would he not give to find some indication of her march to the destination where they themselves were being led!

Such was the situation of the young novice and his companions in body and mind. But whatever they might have to fear for themselves, great as was their own sufferings, pity took possession of them on seeing the frightful misery of that sad troop of captives, and the revolting brutality of their masters. Alas! they could do nothing to succor the afflicted, nothing to resist the others.

All the country situated east of the Coanza was only a forest for over an extent of twenty miles. The trees, however, whether they perish under the biting of the numerous insects of these countries, or whether troops of elephants beat them down while they are still young, are less crowded here than in the country next to the seacoast. The march, then, under the trees, would not present obstacles. The shrubs might be more troublesome than the trees. There was, in fact, an abundance of those cotton-trees, seven to eight feet high, the cotton of which serves to manufacture the black and white striped stuffs used in the interior of the province.

In certain places, the soil transformed itself into thick jungles, in which the convoy disappeared. Of all the animals of the country, the elephants and giraffes alone were taller than those reeds which resemble bamboos, those herbs, the stalks of which measure an inch in diameter. The agents must know the country marvelously well, not to be lost in these jungles.

Each day the caravan set out at daybreak, and only halted at midday for an hour. Some packs containing tapioca were then opened, and this food was parsimoniously distributed to the slaves. To this potatoes were added, or goat's meat and veal, when the soldiers had pillaged some village in passing. But the fatigue had been such, the repose so insufficient, so impossible even during these rainy nights, that when the hour for the distribution of food arrived the prisoners could hardly eat. So, eight days after the departure from the Coanza, twenty had fallen by the way, at the mercy of the beasts that prowled behind the convoy. Lions, panthers and leopards waited for the victims which could not fail them, and each evening after sunset their roaring sounded at such a short distance that one might fear a direct attack.

On hearing those roars, rendered more formidable by the darkness, Dick Sand thought with terror of the obstacles such encounters would present against Hercules's enterprise, of the perils that menaced each of his steps. And meanwhile if he himself should find an opportunity to flee, he would not hesitate.

Here are some notes taken by Dick Sand during this journey from the Coanza to Kazounde. Twenty-five "marches" were employed to make this distance of two hundred and fifty miles, the "march" in the traders' language being ten miles, halting by day and night.

From 25th to 27th April.—Saw a village surrounded by walls of reeds, eight or nine feet high. Fields cultivated with maize, beans, "sorghas" and various arachides. Two blacks seized and made prisoners. Fifteen killed. Population fled.

The next day crossed an impetuous river, one hundred and fifty yards wide. Floating bridge, formed of trunks of trees, fastened with lianes. Piles half broken. Two women, tied to the same fork, precipitated into the water. One was carrying her little child. The waters are disturbed and become stained with blood. Crocodiles glide between the parts of the bridge. There is danger of stepping into their open mouths.

April 28th.—Crossed a forest of bauhiniers. Trees of straight timber—those which furnish the iron wood for the Portuguese.

Heavy rain. Earth wet. March extremely painful.

Perceived, toward the center of the convoy, poor Nan, carrying a little negro child in her arms. She drags herself along with difficulty. The slave chained with her limps, and the blood flows from her shoulder, torn by lashes from the whip.

In the evening camped under an enormous baobab with white flowers and a light green foliage.

During the night roars of lions and leopards. Shots fired by one of the natives at a panther. What has become of Hercules?

April 29th and 30th.—First colds of what they call the African winter. Dew very abundant. End of the rainy season with the month of April; it commences with the month of November. Plains still largely inundated. East winds which check perspiration and renders one more liable to take the marsh fevers.

No trace of Mrs. Weldon, nor of Mr. Benedict. Where would they take them, if not to Kazounde? They must have followed the road of the caravan and preceded us. I am eaten up with anxiety. Little Jack must be seized again with the fever in this unhealthy region. But does he still live?

From May 1st to May 6th.—Crossed, with several halting-places, long plains, which evaporation has not been able to dry up. Water everywhere up to the waist. Myriads of leeches adhering to the skin. We must march for all that. On some elevations that emerge are lotus and papyrus. At the bottom, under the water, other plants, with large cabbage leaves, on which the feet slip, which occasions numerous falls.

In these waters, considerable quantities of little fish of the silurus species. The natives catch them by billions in wickers and sell them to the caravans.

Impossible to find a place to camp for the night. We see no limit to the inundated plain. We must march in the dark. To-morrow many slaves will be missing from the convoy. What misery! When one falls, why get up again? A few moments more under these waters, and all would be finished. The overseer's stick would not reach you in the darkness.

Yes, but Mrs. Weldon and her son! I have not the right to abandon them. I shall resist to the end. It is my duty.

Dreadful cries are heard in the night. Twenty soldiers have torn some branches from resinous trees whose branches were above water. Livid lights in the darkness.

This is the cause of the cries I heard. An attack of crocodiles; twelve or fifteen of those monsters have thrown themselves in the darkness on the flank of the caravan.

Women and children have been seized and carried away by the crocodiles to their "pasture lands"—so Livingstone calls those deep holes where this amphibious animal deposits its prey, after having drowned it, for it only eats it when it has reached a certain degree of decomposition.

I have been rudely grazed by the scales of one of these crocodiles. An adult slave has been seized near me and torn from the fork that held him by the neck. The fork was broken. What a cry of despair! What a howl of grief! I hear it still!

May 7th and 8th.—The next day they count the victims. Twenty slaves have disappeared.

At daybreak I look for Tom and his companions. God be praised! they are living. Alas! ought I to praise God? Is one not happier to be done with all this misery!

Tom is at the head of the convoy. At a moment when his son Bat made a turn, the fork was presented obliquely, and Tom was able to see me.

I search in vain for old Nan. Is she in the central group? or has she perished during that frightful night?

The next day, passed the limit of the inundated plain, after twenty-four hours in the water. We halt on a hill. The sun dries us a little. We eat, but what miserable food! A little tapioca, a few handfuls of maize. Nothing but the troubled water to drink. Prisoners extended on the ground—how many will not get up!

No! it is not possible that Mrs. Weldon and her son have passed through so much misery! God would be so gracious to them as to have them led to Kazounde by another road. The unhappy mother could not resist.

New case of small-pox in the caravan; the "ndoue," as they say. The sick could not be able to go far. Will they abandon them?

May 9th.—They have begun the march again at sunrise. No laggards. The overseer's whip has quickly raised those overcome by fatigue or sickness. Those slaves have a value; they are money. The agents will not leave them behind while they have strength enough to march.

I am surrounded by living skeletons. They have no longer voice enough to complain. I have seen old Nan at last. She is a sad sight. The child she was carrying is no longer in her arms. She is alone, too. That will be less painful for her; but the chain is still around her waist, and she has been obliged to throw the end over her shoulder.

By hastening, I have been able to draw near her. One would say that she did not recognize me. Am I, then, changed to that extent?

"Nan," I said.

The old servant looked at me a long time, and then she exclaimed:

"You, Mr. Dick! I—I—before long I shall be dead!"

"No, no! Courage!" I replied, while my eyes fell so as not to see what was only the unfortunate woman's bloodless specter.

"Dead!" she continued; "and I shall not see my dear mistress again, nor my little Jack. My God! my God! have pity on me!"

I wished to support old Nan, whose whole body trembled under her torn clothing. It would have been a mercy to see myself tied to her, and to carry my part of that chain, whose whole weight she bore since her companion's death.

A strong arm pushes me back, and the unhappy Nan is thrown back into the crowd of slaves, lashed by the whips. I wished to throw myself on that brutal——The Arab chief appears, seizes my arm, and holds me till I find myself again in the caravan's last rank.

Then, in his turn, he pronounces the name, "Negoro!"

Negoro! It is then by the Portuguese's orders that he acts and treats me differently from my companions in misfortune?

For what fate am I reserved?

May 10th.—To-day passed near two villages in flames. The stubble burns on all sides. Dead bodies are hung from the trees the fire has spared. Population fled.

Fields devastated. The razzie is exercised there. Two hundred murders, perhaps, to obtain a dozen slaves.

Evening has arrived. Halt for the night. Camp made under great trees.

High shrubs forming a thicket on the border of the forest.

Some prisoners fled the night before, after breaking their forks. They have been retaken, and treated with unprecedented cruelty. The soldiers' and overseers' watchfulness is redoubled.

Night has come. Roaring of lions and hyenas, distant snorting of hippopotami. Doubtless some lake or watercourse near.

In spite of my fatigue, I cannot sleep. I think of so many things.

Then, it seems to me that I hear prowling in the high grass. Some animal, perhaps. Would it dare force an entrance into the camp?

I listen. Nothing! Yes! An animal is passing through the reeds. I am unarmed! I shall defend myself, nevertheless. My life may be useful to Mrs. Weldon, to my companions.

I look through the profound darkness. There is no moon. The night is extremely dark.

Two eyes shine in the darkness, among the papyrus—two eyes of a hyena or a leopard. They disappear—reappear.

At last there is a rustling of the bushes. An animal springs upon me!

I am going to cry out, to give the alarm. Fortunately, I was able to restrain myself. I cannot believe my eyes! It is Dingo! Dingo, who is near me! Brave Dingo! How is it restored to me? How has it been able to find me again? Ah! instinct! Would instinct be sufficient to explain such miracles of fidelity? It licks my hands. Ah! good dog, now my only friend, they have not killed you, then!

It understands me.

I return its caresses.

It wants to bark.

I calm it. It must not be heard.

Let it follow the caravan in this way, without being seen, and perhaps—— But what! It rubs its neck obstinately against my hands. It seems to say to me: "Look for something." I look, and I feel something there, fastened to its neck. A piece of reed is slipped under the collar, on which are graven those two letters, S.V., the mystery of which is still inexplicable to us.

Yes. I have unfastened the reed. I have broken it! There is a letter inside. But this letter—I cannot read it. I must wait for daylight!—daylight! I should like to keep Dingo; but the good animal, even while licking my hands, seems in a hurry to leave me. It understands that its mission is finished. With one bound aside, it disappears among the bushes without noise. May God spare it from the lions' and hyenas' teeth!

Dingo has certainly returned to him who sent it to me.

This letter, that I cannot yet read, burns my hands! Who has written it?

Would it come from Mrs. Weldon? Does it come from Hercules? How has the faithful animal, that we believed dead, met either the one or the other? What is this letter going to tell me? Is it a plan of escape that it brings me? Or does it only give me news of those dear to me? Whatever it may be, this incident has greatly moved me, and has relaxed my misery.

Ah! the day comes so slowly. I watch for the least light on the horizon. I cannot close my eyes. I still hear the roaring of the animals. My poor Dingo, can you escape them? At last day is going to appear, and almost without dawn, under these tropical latitudes.

I settle myself so as not to be seen. I try to read—I cannot yet. At last I have read. The letter is from Hercules's hand. It is written on a bit of paper, in pencil. Here is what it says:

"Mrs. Weldon was taken away with little Jack in a kitanda. Harris and Negoro accompany it. They precede the caravan by three or four marches, with Cousin Benedict. I have not been able to communicate with her. I have found Dingo, who must have been wounded by a shot, but cured. Good hope, Mr. Dick. I only think of you all, and I fled to be more useful to you. HERCULES."

Ah! Mrs. Weldon and her son are living. God be praised! They have not to suffer the fatigues of these rude halting-places. A kitanda—it is a kind of litter of dry grass, suspended to a long bamboo, that two men carry on the shoulder. A stuff curtain covers it over. Mrs. Weldon and her little Jack are in that kitanda. What does Harris and Negoro want to do with them? Those wretches are evidently going to Kazounde. Yes, yes, I shall find them again. Ah! in all this misery it is good news, it is joy that Dingo has brought me!

From May 11th to 15th.—The caravan continues its march. The prisoners drag themselves along more and more painfully. The majority have marks of blood under their feet. I calculate that it will take ten days more to reach Kazounde. How many will have ceased to suffer before then? But I—I must arrive there, I shall arrive there.

It is atrocious! There are, in the convoy, unfortunate ones whose bodies are only wounds. The cords that bind them enter into the flesh.

Since yesterday a mother carries in her arms her little infant, dead from hunger. She will not separate from it.

Our route is strewn with dead bodies. The smallpox rages with new violence.

We have just passed near a tree. To this tree slaves were attached by the neck. They were left there to die of hunger.

From May 16th to 24th.—I am almost exhausted, but I have no right to give up. The rains have entirely ceased. We have days of "hard marching." That is what the traders call the "tirikesa," or afternoon march. We must go faster, and the ground rises in rather steep ascents.

We pass through high shrubs of a very tough kind. They are the "nyassi," the branches of which tear the skin off my face, whose sharp seeds penetrate to my skin, under my dilapidated clothes. My strong boots have fortunately kept good.

The agents have commenced to abandon the slaves too sick to keep up. Besides, food threatens to fail; soldiers and pagazis would revolt if their rations were diminished. They dare not retrench from them, and then so much worse for the captives.

"Let them eat one another!" said the chief.

Then it follows that young slaves, still strong, die without the appearance of sickness. I remember what Dr. Livingstone has said on that subject: "Those unfortunates complain of the heart; they put their hands there, and they fall. It is positively the heart that breaks! That is peculiar to free men, reduced to slavery unexpectedly!"

To-day, twenty captives who could no longer drag themselves along, have been massacred with axes, by the havildars! The Arab chief is not opposed to massacre. The scene has been frightful!

Poor old Nan has fallen under the knife, in this horrible butchery!

I strike against her corpse in passing! I cannot even give her a

Christian burial! She is first of the "Pilgrim's" survivors whom God

has called back to him. Poor good creature! Poor Nan!

I watch for Dingo every night. It returns no more! Has misfortune overtaken it or Hercules? No! no! I do not want to believe it! This silence, which appears so long to me, only proves one thing—it is that Hercules has nothing new to tell me yet. Besides, he must be prudent, and on his guard.

## CHAPTER IX.
## KAZOUNDE.

ON May 26th, the caravan of slaves arrived at Kazounde. Fifty per cent. of the prisoners taken in the last raid had fallen on the road. Meanwhile, the business was still good for the traders; demands were coming in, and the price of slaves was about to rise in the African markets.

Angola at this period did an immense trade in blacks. The Portuguese authorities of St. Paul de Loanda, or of Benguela, could not stop it without difficulty, for the convoys traveled towards the interior of the African continent. The pens near the coast overflowed with prisoners, the few slavers that succeeded in eluding the cruisers along the shore not being sufficient to carry all of them to the Spanish colonies of America.

Kazounde, situated three hundred miles from the mouth of the Coanza, is one of the principal "lakonis," one of the most important markets of the province. On its grand square the "tchitoka" business is transacted; there, the slaves are exposed and sold. It is from this point that the caravans radiate toward the region of the great lakes.

Kazounde, like all the large towns of Central Africa, is divided into two distinct parts. One is the quarter of the Arab, Portuguese or native traders, and it contains their pens; the other is the residence of the negro king, some ferocious crowned drunkard, who reigns through terror, and lives from supplies furnished by the contractors.

At Kazounde, the commercial quarter then belonged to that Jose-Antonio Alvez, of whom Harris and Negoro had spoken, they being simply agents in his pay. This contractor's principal establishment was there, he had a second at Bihe, and a third at Cassange, in Benguela, which Lieutenant Cameron visited some years later.

Imagine a large central street, on each side groups of houses, "tembes," with flat roofs, walls of baked earth, and a square court which served as an enclosure for cattle. At the end of the street was the vast "tchitoka" surrounded by slave-pens. Above this collection of buildings rose some enormous banyans, whose branches swayed with graceful movements. Here and there great palms, with their heads in the air, drove the dust on the streets like brooms. Twenty birds of prey watched over the public health. Such is the business quarter of Kazounde.

Near by ran the Louhi, a river whose course, still undetermined, is an affluent, or at least a sub-affluent, of the Coango, a tributary of the Zoire.

The residence of the King of Kazounde, which borders on the business quarter, is a confused collection of ill-built hovels, which spread over the space of a mile square. Of these hovels, some are open, others are inclosed by a palisade of reeds, or bordered with a hedge of fig-trees. In one particular enclosure, surrounded by a fence of papyrus, thirty of these huts served us dwellings for the chief's slaves, in another group lived his wives, and a "tembe," still larger and higher, was half hidden in a plantation of cassada. Such was the residence of the King of Kazounde, a man of fifty—named Moini Loungga; and already almost deprived of the power of his predecessors. He had not four thousand of soldiers there, where the principal Portuguese traders could count twenty thousand, and he could no longer, as in former times, decree the sacrifice of twenty-five or thirty slaves a day.

This king was, besides, a prematurely-aged man, exhausted by debauch, crazed by strong drink, a ferocious maniac, mutilating his subjects, his officers or his ministers, as the whim seized him, cutting the nose and ears off some, and the foot or the hand from others. His own death, not unlooked for, would be received without regret.

A single man in all Kazounde might, perhaps, lose by the death of Moini Loungga. This was the contractor, Jose-Antonio Alvez, who agreed very well with the drunkard, whose authority was recognized by the whole province. If the accession of his first wife, Queen Moini, should be contested, the States of Moini Loungga might be invaded by a neighboring competitor, one of the kings of Oukonson. The latter, being younger and more active, had already seized some villages belonging to the Kazounde government. He had in his services another trader, a rival of Alvez Tipo-Tipo, a black Arab of a pure race, whom Cameron met at N'yangwe.

What was this Alvez, the real sovereign under the reign of an imbruted negro, whose vices he had developed and served?

Jose-Antonio Alvez, already advanced in years, was not, as one might suppose, a "msoungou," that is to say, a man of the white race. There was nothing Portuguese about him but his name, borrowed, no doubt, for the needs of commerce. He was a real negro, well known among traders, and called Kenndele. He was born, in fact, at Donndo, or the borders of the Coanza. He had commenced by being simply the agent of the slave-brokers, and would have finished as a famous trader, that is to say, in the skin of an old knave, who called himself the most honest man in the world.

Cameron met this Alvez in the latter part of 1874, at Kilemmba, the capital of Kassonngo, chief of Ouroua. He guided Cameron with his caravan to his own establishment at Bihe, over a route of seven hundred miles. The convoy of slaves, on arriving at Kazounde, had been conducted to the large square.

It was the 26th of May. Dick Sand's calculations were then verified. The journey had lasted thirty-eight days from the departure of the army encamped on the banks of the Coanza. Five weeks of the most fearful miseries that human beings could support.

It was noon when the train entered Kazounde. The drums were beaten, horns were blown in the midst of the detonations of fire-arms. The soldiers guarding the caravan discharged their guns in the air, and the men employed by Jose-Antonio Alvez replied with interest. All these bandits were happy at meeting again, after an absence which had lasted for four months. They were now going to rest and make up for lost time in excesses and idleness.

The prisoners then formed a total of two hundred and fifty, the majority being completely exhausted. After having been driven like cattle, they were to be shut up in pens, which American farmers would not have used for pigs. Twelve or fifteen hundred other captives awaited them, all of whom would be exposed in the market at Kazounde on the next day but one. These pens were filled up with the slaves from the caravan. The heavy forks had been taken off them, but they were still in chains.

The "pagazis" had stopped on the square after having disposed of their loads of ivory, which the Kazounde dealers would deliver. Then, being paid with a few yards of calico or other stuff at the highest price, they would return and join some other caravan.

Old Tom and his companions had been freed from the iron collar which they had carried for five weeks. Bat and his father embraced each other, and all shook hands; but no one ventured to speak. What could they say that would not be an expression of despair. Bat, Acteon and Austin, all three vigorous, accustomed to hard work, had been able to resist fatigue; but old Tom, weakened by privations, was nearly exhausted. A few more days and his corpse would have been left, like poor Nan's, as food for the beasts of the province.

As soon as they arrived, the four men had been placed in a narrow pen, and the door had been at once shut upon them. There they had found some food, and they awaited the trader's visit, with whom, although quite in vain, they intended to urge the fact that they were Americans.

Dick Sand had remained alone on the square, under the special care of a keeper.

At length he was at Kazounde, where he did not doubt that Mrs. Weldon, little Jack, and Cousin Benedict had preceded him. He had looked for them in crossing the various quarters of the town, even in the depths of the "tembes" that lined the streets, on this "tchitoka" now almost deserted.

Mrs. Weldon was not there.

"Have they not brought her here?" he asked himself. "But where could she be? No; Hercules cannot be mistaken. Then, again, he must have learned the secret designs of Negoro and Harris; yet they, too—I do not see them."

Dick Sand felt the most painful anxiety. He could understand that Mrs. Weldon, retained a prisoner, would be concealed from him. But Harris and Negoro, particularly the latter, should hasten to see him, now in their power, if only to enjoy their triumph—to insult him, torture him, perhaps avenge themselves. From the fact that they were not there, must he conclude that they had taken another direction, and that Mrs. Weldon was to be conducted to some other point of Central Africa? Should the presence of the American and the Portuguese be the signal for his punishment, Dick Sand impatiently desired it. Harris and Negoro at Kazounde, was for him the certainty that Mrs. Weldon and her child were also there.

Dick Sand then told himself that, since the night when Dingo had brought him Hercules's note, the dog had not been seen. The young man had prepared an answer at great risks. In it he told Hercules to think only of Mrs. Weldon, not to lose sight of her, and to keep her informed as well as possible of what happened; but he had not been able to send it to its destination. If Dingo had been able to penetrate the ranks of the caravan once, why did not Hercules let him try it a second time? Had the faithful animal perished in some fruitless attempt? Perhaps Hercules was following Mrs. Weldon, as Dick Sand would have done in his place. Followed by Dingo, he might have plunged into the depths of the woody plateau of Africa, in the hope of reaching one of the interior establishments.

What could Dick Sand imagine if, in fact, neither Mrs. Weldon nor her enemies were there? He had been so sure, perhaps foolishly, of finding them at Kazounde, that not to see them there at once gave him a terrible shock. He felt a sensation of despair that he could not subdue. His life, if it were no longer useful to those whom he loved, was good for nothing, and he had only to die. But, in thinking in that manner, Dick Sand mistook his own character. Under the pressure of these trials, the child became a man, and with him discouragement could only be an accidental tribute paid to human nature.

A loud concert of trumpet-calls and cries suddenly commenced. Dick

Sand, who had just sunk down in the dust of the "tchitoka," stood up.

Every new incident might put him on the track of those whom he sought.

In despair a moment before, he now no longer despaired.

"Alvez! Alvez!" This name was repeated by a crowd of natives and soldiers who now invaded the grand square. The man on whom the fate of so many unfortunate people depended was about to appear. It was possible that his agents, Harris and Negoro, were with him. Dick Sand stood upright, his eyes open, his nostrils dilated. The two traitors would find this lad of fifteen years before them, upright, firm, looking them in the face. It would not be the captain of the "Pilgrim" who would tremble before the old ship's cook.

A hammock, a kind of "kitanda" covered by an old patched curtain, discolored, fringed with rags, appeared at the end of the principal street. An old negro descended. It was the trader, Jose-Antonio Alvez. Several attendants accompanied him, making strong demonstrations.

Along with Alvez appeared his friend Coimbra, the son of Major Coimbra of Bihe, and, according to Lieutenant Cameron, the greatest scamp in the province. He was a dirty creature, his breast was uncovered, his eyes were bloodshot, his hair was rough and curly, his face yellow; he was dressed in a ragged shirt and a straw petticoat. He would have been called a horrible old man in his tattered straw hat. This Coimbra was the confidant, the tool of Alvez, an organizer of raids, worthy of commanding the trader's bandits.

As for the trader, he might have looked a little less sordid than his attendant. He wore the dress of an old Turk the day after a carnival. He did not furnish a very high specimen of the factory chiefs who carry on the trade on a large scale.

To Dick Sand's great disappointment, neither Harris nor Negoro appeared in the crowd that followed Alvez. Must he, then, renounce all hope of finding them at Kazounde?

Meanwhile, the chief of the caravan, the Arab, Ibn Hamis, shook hands with Alvez and Coimbra. He received numerous congratulations. Alvez made a grimace at the fifty per cent. of slaves failing in the general count, but, on the whole, the affair was very satisfactory. With what the trader possessed of human merchandise in his pens, he could satisfy the demands from the interior, and barter slaves for ivory teeth and those "hannas" of copper, a kind of St. Andrew's cross, in which form this metal is carried into the center of Africa.

The overseers were also complimented. As for the porters, the trader gave orders that their salary should be immediately paid them.

Jose-Antonio Alvez and Coimbra spoke a kind of Portuguese mingled with a native idiom, which a native of Lisbon would scarcely have understood. Dick Sand could not hear what these merchants were saying. Were they talking of him and his companions, so treacherously joined to the persons in the convoy? The young man could not doubt it, when, at a gesture from the Arab, Ibn Hamis, an overseer, went toward the pen where Tom, Austin, Bat and Acteon had been shut up.

Almost immediately the four Americans were led before Alvez.

Dick Sand slowly approached. He wished to lose nothing of this scene.

Alvez's face lit up at the sight of these few well-made blacks, to whom rest and more abundant food had promptly restored their natural vigor. He looked with contempt at old Tom, whose age would affect his value, but the other three would sell high at the next Kazounde sale.

Alvez remembered a few English words which some agents, like the American, Harris, had taught him, and the old monkey thought he would ironically welcome his new slaves.

Tom understood the trader's words; he at once advanced, and, showing his companions, said:

"We are free men—citizens of the United States."

Alvez certainly understood him; he replied with a good-humored grimace, wagging his head:

"Yes, yes, Americans! Welcome, welcome!"

"Welcome," added Coimbra.

He advanced toward Austin, and like a merchant who examines a sample, after having felt his chest and his shoulders, he wanted to make him open his mouth, so as to see his teeth.

But at this moment Signor Coimbra received in his face the worst blow that a major's son had ever caught.

Alvez's confidant staggered under it.

Several soldiers threw themselves on Austin, who would perhaps pay dearly for this angry action.

Alvez stopped them by a look. He laughed, indeed, at the misfortune of his friend, Coimbra, who had lost two of the five or six teeth remaining to him.

Alvez did not intend to have his merchandise injured. Then, he was of a gay disposition, and it was a long time since he had laughed so much.

Meanwhile, he consoled the much discomfited Coimbra, and the latter, helped to his feet, again took his place near the trader, while throwing a menacing look at the audacious Austin.

At this moment Dick Sand, driven forward by an overseer, was led before Alvez.

The latter evidently knew all about the young man, whence he came, and how he had been taken to the camp on the Coanza.

So he said, after having given him an evil glance:

"The little Yankee!"

"Yes, Yankee!" replied Dick Sand. "What do they wish to do with my companions and me?"

"Yankee! Yankee! Yankee!" repeated Alvez.

Did he not or would he not understand the question put to him?

A second time Dick Sand asked the question regarding his companions and himself. He then turned to Coimbra, whose features, degraded as they were by the abuse of alcoholic liquors, he saw were not of native origin.

Coimbra repeated the menacing gesture already made at Austin, and did not answer.

During this time Alvez talked rapidly with the Arab, Ibn Hamis, and evidently of things that concerned Dick Sand and his friends.

No doubt they were to be again separated, and who could tell if another chance to exchange a few words would ever again be offered them.

"My friends," said Dick, in a low voice, and as if he were only speaking to himself, "just a few words! I have received, by Dingo, a letter from Hercules. He has followed the caravan. Harris and Negoro took away Mrs. Weldon, Jack, and Mr. Benedict. Where? I know not, if they are not here at Kazounde. Patience! courage! Be ready at any moment. God may yet have pity on us!"

"And Nan?" quickly asked old Tom.

"Nan is dead!"

"The first!"

"And the last!" replied Dick Sand, "for we know well——"

At this moment a hand was laid on his shoulder, and he heard these words, spoken in the amiable voice which he knew only too well:

"Ah, my young friend, if I am not mistaken! Enchanted to see you again!"

Dick Sand turned.

Harris was before him.

"Where is Mrs. Weldon?" cried Dick Sand, walking toward the American.

"Alas!" replied Harris, pretending a pity that he did not feel, "the poor mother! How could she survive!"

"Dead!" cried Dick Sand. "And her child?"

"The poor baby!" replied Harris, in the same tone, "how could he outlive such fatigue!"

So, all whom Dick Sand loved were dead!

What passed within him? An irresistible movement of anger, a desire for vengeance, which he must satisfy at any price!

Dick Sand jumped upon Harris, seized a dagger from the American's belt, and plunged it into his heart.

"Curse you!" cried Harris, falling.

Harris was dead.

## CHAPTER X.

## THE GREAT MARKET DAY.

Dick Sand's action had been so rapid that no one could stop him. A few natives threw themselves upon him, and he would have been murdered had not Negoro appeared.

At a sign from the Portuguese, the natives drew back, raised Harris's corpse and carried it away. Alvez and Coimbra demanded Dick Sand's immediate death, but Negoro said to them in a low voice that they would lose nothing by waiting. The order was given to take away the young novice, with a caution not to lose sight of him for a moment.

Dick Sand had seen Negoro for the first time since their departure from the coast. He knew that this wretch was alone responsible for the loss of the "Pilgrim." He ought to hate him still more than his accomplices. And yet, after having struck the American, he scorned to address a word to Negoro. Harris had said that Mrs. Weldon and her child had succumbed. Nothing interested him now, not even what they would do with him. They would send him away. Where? It did not matter.

Dick Sand, heavily chained, was left on the floor of a pen without a window, a kind of dungeon where the trader, Alvez, shut up the slaves condemned to death for rebellion or unlawful acts. There he could no longer have any communication with the exterior; he no longer dreamed of regretting it. He had avenged those whom he loved, who no longer lived. Whatever fate awaited him, he was ready for it.

It will be understood that if Negoro had stopped the natives who were about to punish Harris's murderer, it was only because he wished to reserve Dick Sand for one of those terrible torments of which the natives hold the secret. The ship's cook held in his power the captain of fifteen years. He only wanted Hercules to make his vengeance complete.

Two days afterward, May 28th, the sale began, the great "lakoni," during which the traders of the principal factories of the interior would meet the natives of the neighboring provinces. This market was not specially for the sale of slaves, but all the products of this fertile Africa would be gathered there with the producers.

From early morning all was intense animation on the vast "tchitoka" of Kazounde, and it is difficult to give a proper idea of the scene. It was a concourse of four or five thousand persons, including Alvez's slaves, among whom were Tom and his companions. These four men, for the reason that they belonged to a different race, are all the more valuable to the brokers in human flesh. Alvez was there, the first among all. Attended by Coimbra, he offered the slaves in lots. These the traders from the interior would form into caravans. Among these traders were certain half-breeds from Oujiji, the principal market of Lake Tanganyika, and some Arabs, who are far superior to the half-breeds in this kind of trade.

The natives flocked there in great numbers. There were children, men, and women, the latter being animated traders, who, as regards a genius for bargaining, could only be compared to their white sisters.

In the markets of large cities, even on a great day of sale, there is never much noise or confusion. Among the civilized the need of selling exceeds the desire to buy. Among these African savages offers are made with as much eagerness as demands.

The "lakoni" is a festival day for the natives of both sexes, and if for good reasons they do not put on their best clothes, they at least wear their handsomest ornaments.

Some wear the hair divided in four parts, covered with cushions, and in plaits tied like a chignon or arranged in pan-handles on the front of the head with bunches of red feathers. Others have the hair in bent horns sticky with red earth and oil, like the red lead used to close the joints of machines. In these masses of real or false hair is worn a bristling assemblage of skewers, iron and ivory pins, often even, among elegant people, a tattooing-knife is stuck in the crisp mass, each hair of which is put through a "sofi" or glass bead, thus forming a tapestry of different-colored grains. Such are the edifices most generally seen on the heads of the men.

The women prefer to divide their hair in little tufts of the size of a cherry, in wreaths, in twists the ends of which form designs in relief, and in corkscrews, worn the length of the face. A few, more simple and perhaps prettier, let their long hair hang down the back, in the English style, and others wear it cut over the forehead in a fringe, like the French. Generally they wear on these wigs a greasy putty, made of red clay or of glossy "ukola," a red substance extracted from sandal-wood, so that these elegant persons look as if their heads were dressed with tiles.

It must not be supposed that this luxury of ornamentation is confined to the hair of the natives. What are ears for if not to pass pins of precious wood through, also copper rings, charms of plaited maize, which draw them forward, or little gourds which do for snuff-boxes, and to such an extent that the distended lobes of these appendages fall sometimes to the shoulders of their owners?

After all, the African savages have no pockets, and how could they have any? This gives rise to the necessity of placing where they can their knives, pipes, and other customary objects. As for the neck, arms, wrists, legs, and ankles, these various parts of the body are undoubtedly destined to carry the copper and brass bracelets, the horns cut off and decorated with bright buttons, the rows of red pearls, called same-sames or "talakas," and which were very fashionable. Besides, with these jewels, worn in profusion, the wealthy people of the place looked like traveling shrines.

Again, if nature gave the natives teeth, was it not that they could pull out the upper and lower incisors, file them in points, and curve them in sharp fangs like the fangs of a rattlesnake? If she has placed nails at the end of the fingers, is it not that they may grow so immoderately that the use of the hand is rendered almost impossible? If the skin, black or brown, covers the human frame, is it not so as to zebra it by "temmbos" or tattooings representing trees, birds, crescents, full moons, or waving lines, in which Livingstone thought he could trace the designs of ancient Egypt? This tattooing, done by fathers, is practised by means of a blue matter introduced into the incisions, and is "stereotyped" point by point on the bodies of the children, thus establishing to what tribe or to what family they belong. The coat-of-arms must be engraved on the breast, when it cannot be painted on the panel of a carriage.

Such are the native fashions in ornament. In regard to garments properly so called, they are summed up very easily; for the men, an apron of antelope leather, reaching to the knees, or perhaps a petticoat of a straw material of brilliant colors; for the women, a belt of pearls, supporting at the hips a green petticoat, embroidered in silk, ornamented with glass beads or coury; sometimes they wear garments made of "lambba," a straw material, blue, black, and yellow, which is much prized by the natives of Zanzibar.

These, of course, are the negroes of the best families. The others, merchants, and slaves, are seldom clothed. The women generally act as porters, and reach the market with enormous baskets on their back, which they hold by means of a leathern strap passed over the forehead. Then, their places being taken, and the merchandise unpacked, they squat in their empty baskets.

The astonishing fertility of the country causes the choice alimentary produces to be brought to this "lakoni." There were quantities of the rice which returns a hundred per cent., of the maize, which, in three crops in eight months, produces two hundred per cent., the sesamum, the pepper of Ouroua, stronger than the Cayenne, allspice, tapioca, sorghum, nutmegs, salt, and palm-oil.

Hundreds of goats were gathered there, hogs, sheep without wool, evidently of Tartar origin, quantities of poultry and fish. Specimens of pottery, very gracefully turned, attracted the eyes by their violent colors.

Various drinks, which the little natives cried about in a squeaking voice, enticed the unwary, in the form of plantain wine, "pombe," a liquor in great demand, "malofou," sweet beer, made from the fruit of the banana-tree and mead, a limpid mixture of honey and water fermented with malt.

But what made the Kazounde market still more curious was the commerce in stuffs and ivory.

In the line of stuffs, one might count by thousands of "choukkas" or armfuls, the "Mericani" unbleached calico, come from Salem, in Massachusetts, the "kanaki," a blue gingham, thirty-four inches wide, the "sohari," a stuff in blue and white squares, with a red border, mixed with small blue stripes. It is cheaper than the "dioulis," a silk from Surat, with a green, red or yellow ground, which is worth from seventy to eighty dollars for a remnant of three yards when woven with gold.

As for ivory, it was brought from all parts of Central Africa, being destined for Khartoum, Zanzibar, or Natal. A large number of merchants are employed solely in this branch of African commerce.

Imagine how many elephants are killed to furnish the five hundred thousand kilograms of ivory, which are annually exported to European markets, and principally to the English! The western coast of Africa alone produces one hundred and forty tons of this precious substance. The average weight is twenty-eight pounds for a pair of elephant's tusks, which, in 1874, were valued as high as fifteen hundred francs; but there are some that weigh one hundred and seventy-five pounds, and at the Kazounde market, admirers would have found some admirable ones. They were of an opaque ivory, translucid, soft under the tool, and with a brown rind, preserving its whiteness and not growing yellow with time like the ivories of other provinces.

And, now, how are these various business affairs regulated between buyers and sellers? What is the current coin? As we have said, for the African traders this money is the slave.

The native pays in glass beads of Venetian manufacture, called "catchocolos," when they are of a lime white; "bouboulous," when they are black; "sikounderetches," when they are red. These beads or pearls, strung in ten rows or "khetes," going twice around the neck, make the "foundo," which is of great value. The usual measure of the beads is the "frasilah," which weighs seventy pounds. Livingstone, Cameron, and Stanley were always careful to be abundantly provided with this money.

In default of glass beads, the "pice," a Zanzibar piece, worth four centimes, and the "vroungouas," shells peculiar to the eastern coasts, are current in the markets of the African continent. As for the cannibal tribes, they attach a certain value to the teeth of the human jaw, and at the "lakoni," these chaplets were to be seen on the necks of natives, who had no doubt eaten their producers; but these teeth were ceasing to be used as money.

Such, then, was the appearance of the great market. Toward the middle of the day the gaiety reached a climax; the noise became deafening. The fury of the neglected venders, and the anger of the overcharged customers, were beyond description. Thence frequent quarrels, and, as we know, few guardians of the peace to quell the fray in this howling crowd.

Toward the middle of the day, Alvez gave orders to bring the slaves, whom he wished to sell, to the square. The crowd was thus increased by two thousand unfortunate beings of all ages, whom the trader had kept in pens for several months. This "stock" was not in a bad condition. Long rest and sufficient food had improved these slaves so as to look to advantage at the "lakoni." As for the last arrivals, they could not stand any comparison with them, and, after a month in the pens, Alvez could certainly have sold them with more profit. The demands, however, from the eastern coast, were so great that he decided to expose and sell them as they were.

This was a misfortune for Tom and his three companions. The drivers pushed them into the crowd that invaded the "tchitoka." They were strongly chained, and their glances told what horror, what fury and shame overwhelmed them.

"Mr. Dick is not there," Bat said, after some time, during which he had searched the vast plain with his eyes.

"No," replied Acteon, "they will not put him up for sale."

"He will be killed, if he is not already," added the old black. "As for us, we have but one hope left, which is, that the same trader will buy us all. It would be a great consolation not to be separated."

"Ah! to know that you are far away from me, working like a slave, my poor, old father!" cried Bat, sobbing aloud.

"No," said Tom. "No; they will not separate us, and perhaps we might ____"

"If Hercules were here!" cried Austin.

But the giant had not reappeared. Since the news sent to Dick Sand, they had heard no one mention either Hercules or Dingo. Should they envy him his fate? Why, yes; for if Hercules were dead, he was saved from the chains of slavery!

Meanwhile, the sale had commenced. Alvez's agents marched the various lots of men, women and children through the crowd, without caring if they separated mothers from their infants. May we not call these beings "unfortunates," who were treated only as domestic animals?

Tom and his companions were thus led from buyers to buyers. An agent walked before them naming the price adjudged to their lot. Arab or mongrel brokers, from the central provinces, came to examine them. They did not discover in them the traits peculiar to the African race, these traits being modified in America after the second generation. But these vigorous and intelligent negroes, so very different from the blacks brought from the banks of the Zambeze or the Loualaba, were all the more valuable. They felt them, turned them, and looked at their teeth. Horse-dealers thus examine the animals they wish to buy. Then they threw a stick to a distance, made them run and pick it up, and thus observed their gait.

This was the method employed for all, and all were submitted to these humiliating trials. Do not believe that these people are completely indifferent to this treatment! No, excepting the children, who cannot comprehend the state of degradation to which they are reduced, all, men or women, were ashamed.

Besides, they were not spared injuries and blows. Coimbra, half drunk, and Alvez's agents, treated them with extreme brutality, and from their new masters, who had just paid for them in ivory stuffs and beads, they would receive no better treatment. Violently separated, a mother from her child, a husband from his wife, a brother from a sister, they were not allowed a last caress nor a last kiss, and on the "lakoni" they saw each other for the last time.

In fact, the demands of the trade exacted that the slaves should be sent in different directions, according to their sex. The traders who buy the men do not buy women. The latter, in virtue of polygamy, which is legal among the Mussulmans, are sent to the Arabic countries, where they are exchanged for ivory. The men, being destined to the hardest labor, go to the factories of the two coasts, and are exported either to the Spanish colonies or to the markets of Muscat and Madagascar. This sorting leads to heart-breaking scenes between those whom the agents separate, and who will die without ever seeing each other again.

The four companions in turn submitted to the common fate. But, to tell the truth, they did not fear this event. It was better for them to be exported into a slave colony. There, at least, they might have a chance to protest. On the contrary, if sent to the interior, they might renounce all hope of ever regaining their liberty.

It happened as they wished. They even had the almost unhoped for consolation of not being separated. They were in brisk demand, being wanted by several traders. Alvez clapped his hands. The prices rose. It was strange to see these slaves of unknown value in the Kazounde market, and Alvez had taken good care to conceal where they came from. Tom and his friends, not speaking the language of the country, could not protest.

Their master was a rich Arab trader, who in a few days would send them to Lake Tanganyika, the great thoroughfare for slaves; then, from that point, toward the factories of Zanzibar.

Would they ever reach there, through the most unhealthy and the most dangerous countries of Central Africa? Fifteen hundred miles to march under these conditions, in the midst of frequent wars, raised and carried on between chiefs, in a murderous climate. Was old Tom strong enough to support such misery? Would he not fall on the road like old Nan? But the poor men were not separated. The chain that held them all was lighter to carry. The Arab trader would evidently take care of merchandise which promised him a large profit in the Zanzibar market.

Tom, Bat, Acteon, and Austin then left the place. They saw and heard nothing of the scene which was to end the great "lakoni" of Kazounde.

## CHAPTER XI

### THE KING OF KAZOUNDE IS OFFERED A PUNCH.

It was four o'clock in the afternoon when a loud noise of drums, cymbals, and other instruments of African origin resounded at the end of the principal street. In all corners of the market-place the animation was redoubled. Half a day of cries and wrestling had neither weakened the voices nor broken the limbs of these abominable traders. A large number of slaves still remained to be sold. The traders disputed over the lots with an ardor of which the London Exchange would give but an imperfect idea, even on a day when stocks were rising.

All business was stopped, and the criers took their breath as soon as the discordant concert commenced.

The King of Kazounde, Moini Loungga, had come to honor the great "lakoni" with a visit. A numerous train of women, officers, soldiers and slaves followed him. Alvez and some other traders went to meet him, and naturally exaggerated the attention which this crowned brute particularly enjoyed.

Moini Loungga was carried in an old palanquin, and descended, not without the aid of a dozen arms, in the center of the large square.

This king was fifty years old, but he looked eighty. Imagine a frightful monkey who had reached extreme old age; on his head a sort of crown, ornamented with leopard's claws, dyed red, and enlarged by tufts of whitish hair; this was the crown of the sovereigns of Kazounde. From his waist hung two petticoats made of leather, embroidered with pearls, and harder than a blacksmith's apron. He had on his breast a quantity of tattooing which bore witness to the ancient nobility of the king; and, to believe him, the genealogy of Moini Loungga was lost in the night of time. On the ankles, wrists and arms of his majesty, bracelets of leather were rolled, and he wore a pair of domestic shoes with yellow tops, which Alvez had presented him with about twenty years before.

His majesty carried in his left hand a large stick with a plated knob, and in his right a small broom to drive away flies, the handle of which was enriched with pearls.

Over his head was carried one of those old patched umbrellas, which seemed to have been cut out of a harlequin's dress.

On the monarch's neck and on his nose were the magnifying glass and the spectacles which had caused Cousin Benedict so much trouble. They had been hidden in Bat's pocket.

Such is the portrait of his negro majesty, who made the country tremble in a circumference of a hundred miles.

Moini Loungga, from the fact of occupying a throne, pretended to be of celestial origin, and had any of his subjects doubted the fact, he would have sent them into another world to discover it. He said that, being of a divine essence, he was not subject to terrestrial laws. If he ate, it was because he wished to do so; if he drank, it was because it gave him pleasure. It was impossible for him to drink any more. His ministers and his officers, all incurable drunkards, would have passed before him for sober men.

The court was alcoholized to the last chief, and incessantly imbibed strong beer, cider, and, above all, a certain drink which Alvez furnished in profusion.

Moini Loungga counted in his harem wives of all ages and of all kinds. The larger part of them accompanied him in this visit to the "lakoni."

Moini, the first, according to date, was a vixen of forty years, of royal blood, like her colleagues. She wore a bright tartan, a straw petticoat embroidered with pearls, and necklaces wherever she could put them. Her hair was dressed so as to make an enormous framework on her little head. She was, in fact, a monster.

The other wives, who were either the cousins or the sisters of the king, were less richly dressed, but much younger. They walked behind her, ready to fulfil, at a sign from their master, their duties as human furniture. These unfortunate beings were really nothing else. If the king wished to sit down, two of these women bent toward the earth and served him for a chair, while his feet rested on the bodies of some others, as if on an ebony carpet.

In Moini Loungga's suite came his officers, his captains, and his magicians.

A remarkable thing about these savages, who staggered like their master, was that each lacked a part of his body—one an ear, another an eye, this one the nose, that one the hand. Not one was whole. That is because they apply only two kinds of punishment in Kazounde—mutilation or death—all at the caprice of the king. For the least fault, some amputation, and the most cruelly punished are those whose ears are cut off, because they can no longer wear rings in their ears.

The captains of the kilolos, governors of districts, hereditary or named for four years, wore hats of zebra skin and red vests for their whole uniform. Their hands brandished long palm canes, steeped at one end with charmed drugs.

As to the soldiers, they had for offensive and defensive weapons, bows, of which the wood, twined with the cord, was ornamented with fringes; knives, whetted with a serpent's tongue; broad and long lances; shields of palm wood, decorated in arabesque style. For what there was of uniform, properly so called, it cost his majesty's treasury absolutely nothing.

Finally, the kind's cortege comprised, in the last place, the court magicians and the instrumentalists.

The sorcerers, the "mganngas," are the doctors of the country. These savages attach an absolute faith to divinatory services, to incantations, to the fetiches, clay figures stained with white and red, representing fantastic animals or figures of men and women cut out of whole wood. For the rest, those magicians were not less mutilated than the other courtiers, and doubtless the monarch paid them in this way for the cures that did not succeed.

The instrumentalists, men or women, made sharp rattles whizz, noisy drums sound or shudder under small sticks terminated by a caoutchouc ball, "marimehas," kinds of dulcimers formed of two rows of gourds of various dimensions—the whole very deafening for any one who does not possess a pair of African ears.

Above this crowd, which composed the royal cortege, waved some flags and standards, then at the ends of spears the bleached skulls of the rival chiefs whom Moini Loungga had vanquished.

When the king had quitted his palanquin, acclamations burst forth from all sides. The soldiers of the caravan discharged their old guns, the low detonations of which were but little louder than the vociferations of the crowd. The overseers, after rubbing their black noses with cinnabar powder, which they carried in a sack, bowed to the ground. Then Alvez, advancing in his turn, handed the king a supply of fresh tobacco—"soothing herb," as they call it in the country. Moini Loungga had great need of being soothed, for he was, they did not know why, in a very bad humor.

At the same time Alvez, Coimbra, Ibn Hamis, and the Arab traders, or mongrels, came to pay their court to the powerful sovereign of Kazounde. "Marhaba," said the Arabs, which is their word of welcome in the language of Central Africa. Others clapped their hands and bowed to the ground. Some daubed themselves with mud, and gave signs of the greatest servility to this hideous majesty.

Moini Loungga hardly looked at all these people, and walked, keeping his limbs apart, as if the ground were rolling and pitching. He walked in this manner, or rather he rolled in the midst of waves of slaves, and if the traders feared that he might take a notion to apportion some of the prisoners to himself, the latter would no less dread falling into the power of such a brute.

Negoro had not left Alvez for a moment, and in his company presented his homage to the king. Both conversed in the native language, if, however, that word "converse" can be used of a conversation in which Moini Loungga only took part by monosyllables that hardly found a passage through his drunken lips. And still, did he not ask his friend, Alvez, to renew his supply of brandy just exhausted by large libations?

"King Loungga is welcome to the market of Kazounde," said the trader.

"I am thirsty," replied the monarch.

"He will take his part in the business of the great 'lakoni,'" added

Alvez.

"Drink!" replied Moini Loungga.

"My friend Negoro is happy to see the King of Kazounde again, after such a long absence."

"Drink!" repeated the drunkard, whose whole person gave forth a disgusting odor of alcohol.

"Well, some 'pombe'! some mead!" exclaimed Jose-Antonio Alvez, like a man who well knew what Moini Loungga wanted.

"No, no!" replied the king; "my friend Alvez's brandy, and for each drop of his fire-water I shall give him——"

"A drop of blood from a white man!" exclaimed Negoro, after making a sign to Alvez, which the latter understood and approved.

"A white man! Put a white man to death!" repeated Moini Loungga, whose ferocious instincts were aroused by the Portuguese's proposition.

"One of Alvez's agents has been killed by this white man," returned

Negoro.

"Yes, my agent, Harris," replied the trader, "and his death must be avenged!"

"Send that white man to King Massongo, on the Upper Zaire, among the Assonas. They will cut him in pieces. They will eat him alive. They have not forgotten the taste of human flesh!" exclaimed Moini Loungga.

He was, in fact, the king of a tribe of man-eaters, that Massongo. It is only too true that in certain provinces of Central Africa cannibalism is still openly practised. Livingstone states it in his "Notes of Travel." On the borders of the Loualaba the Manyemas not only eat the men killed in the wars, but they buy slaves to devour them, saying that "human flesh is easily salted, and needs little seasoning." Those cannibals Cameron has found again among the Moene-Bongga, where they only feast on dead bodies after steeping them for several days in a running stream. Stanley has also encountered those customs of cannibalism among the inhabitants of the Oukonson. Cannibalism is evidently well spread among the tribes of the center.

But, cruel as was the kind of death proposed by the king for Dick

Sand, it did not suit Negoro, who did not care to give up his victim.

"It was here," said he, "that the white man killed our comrade

Harris."

"It is here that he ought to die!" added Alvez.

"Where you please, Alvez," replied Moini Loungga; "but a drop of fire-water for a drop of blood!"

"Yes," replied the trader, "fire-water, and you will see that it well merits that name! We shall make it blaze, this water! Jose-Antonio Alvez will offer a punch to the King Moini Loungga."

The drunkard shook his friend Alvez's hands. He could not contain his joy. His wives, his courtiers shared his ecstasy. They had never seen brandy blaze, and doubtless they counted on drinking it all blazing. Then, after the thirst for alcohol, the thirst for blood, so imperious among these savages, would be satisfied also.

Poor Dick Sand! What a horrible punishment awaited him. When we think of the terrible or grotesque effects of intoxication in civilized countries, we understand how far it can urge barbarous beings.

We will readily believe that the thought of torturing a white could displease none of the natives, neither Jose-Antonio Alvez, a negro like themselves, nor Coimbra, a mongrel of black blood, nor Negoro either, animated with a ferocious hatred against the whites.

The evening had come, an evening without twilight, that was going to make day change tonight almost at once, a propitious hour for the blazing of the brandy.

It was truly a triumphant idea of Alvez's, to offer a punch to this negro majesty, and to make him love brandy under a new form. Moini Loungga began to find that fire-water did not sufficiently justify its name. Perhaps, blazing and burning, it would tickle more agreeably the blunted papillas of his tongue.

The evening's program then comprised a punch first, a punishment afterwards.

Dick Sand, closely shut up in his dark prison, would only come out to go to his death. The other slaves, sold or not, had been put back in the barracks. There only remained at the "tchitoka," the traders, the overseers and the soldiers ready to take their part of the punch, if the king and his court allowed them.

Jose-Antonio Alvez, advised by Negoro, did the thing well. They brought a vast copper basin, capable of containing at least two hundred pints, which was placed in the middle of the great place. Barrels holding alcohol of inferior quality, but well refined, were emptied into the basin. They spared neither the cinnamon, nor the allspice, nor any of the ingredients that might improve this punch for savages.

All had made a circle around the king. Moini Loungga advanced staggering to the basin. One would say that this vat of brandy fascinated him, and that he was going to throw himself into it.

Alvez generously held him back and put a lighted match into his hand.

"Fire!" cried he with a cunning grimace of satisfaction.

"Fire!" replied Moini Loungga lashing the liquid with the end of the match.

What a flare and what an effect, when the bluish flames played on the surface of the basin. Alvez, doubtless to render that alcohol still sharper, had mingled with it a few handfuls of sea salt. The assistants' faces were then given that spectral lividness that the imagination ascribes to phantoms.

Those negroes, drunk in advance, began to cry out, to gesticulate, and, taking each other by the hand, formed an immense circle around the King of Kazounde.

Alvez, furnished with an enormous metal spoon, stirred the liquid, which threw a great white glare over those delirious monkeys.

Moini Loungga advanced. He seized the spoon from the trader's hands, plunged it into the basin, then, drawing it out full of punch in flames, he brought it to his lips.

What a cry the King of Kazounde then gave!

An act of spontaneous combustion had just taken place. The king had taken fire like a petroleum bonbon. This fire developed little heat, but it devoured none the less.

At this spectacle the natives' dance was suddenly stopped.

One of Moini Loungga's ministers threw himself on his sovereign to extinguish him; but, not less alcoholized than his master, he took fire in his turn.

In this way, Moini Loungga's whole court was in peril of burning up.

Alvez and Negoro did not know how to help his majesty. The women, frightened, had taken flight. As to Coimbra, he took his departure rapidly, well knowing his inflammable nature.

The king and the minister, who had fallen on the ground, were burning up, a prey to frightful sufferings.

In bodies so thoroughly alcoholized, combustion only produces a light and bluish flame, that water cannot extinguish. Even stifled outside, it would still continue to burn inwardly. When liquor has penetrated all the tissues, there exists no means of arresting the combustion.

A few minutes after, Moini Loungga and his minister had succumbed, but they still burned. Soon, in the place where they had fallen, there was nothing left but a few light coals, one or two pieces of the vertebral column, fingers, toes, that the fire does not consume, in cases of spontaneous combustion, but which it covers with an infectious and penetrating soot.

It was all that was left of the King of Kazounde and of his minister.

## CHAPTER XII.
## A ROYAL BURIAL.

The next day, May 29th, the city of Kazounde presented a strange aspect. The natives, terrified, kept themselves shut up in their huts. They had never seen a king, who said he was of divine essence, nor a simple minister, die of this horrible death. They had already burned some of their fellow-beings, and the oldest could not forget certain culinary preparations relating to cannibalism.

They knew then how the incineration of a human body takes place with difficulty, and behold their king and his minister had burnt all alone! That seemed to them, and indeed ought to seem to them, inexplicable.

Jose-Antonio Alvez kept still in his house. He might fear that he would be held responsible for the accident. Negoro had informed him of what had passed, warning him to take care of himself. To charge him with Moini Loungga's death might be a bad affair, from which he might not be able to extricate himself without damage.

But Negoro had a good idea. By his means Alvez spread the report that the death of Kazounde's sovereign was supernatural; that the great Manitou only reserved it for his elect. The natives, so inclined to superstition, accepted this lie. The fire that came out of the bodies of the king and his minister became a sacred fire. They had nothing to do but honor Moini Loungga by obsequies worthy of a man elevated to the rank of the gods.

These obsequies, with all the ceremonial connected with them among the African tribes, was an occasion offered to Negoro to make Dick Sand play a part. What this death of Moini Loungga was going to cost in blood, would be believed with difficulty, if the Central Africa travelers, Lieutenant Cameron among others, had not related facts that cannot be doubted.

The King of Kazounde's natural heir was the Queen Moini. In proceeding without delay with the funeral ceremonies she acted with sovereign authority, and could thus distance the competitors, among others that King of the Oukonson, who tended to encroach upon the rights of Kazounde's sovereigns. Besides, Moini, even by becoming queen, avoided the cruel fate reserved for the other wives of the deceased; at the same time she would get rid of the youngest ones, of whom she, first in date, had necessarily to complain. This result would particularly suit the ferocious temperament of that vixen. So she had it announced, with deer's horns and other instruments, that the obsequies of the defunct king would take place the next evening with all the usual ceremony.

No protestation was made, neither at court nor from the natives. Alvez and the other traders had nothing to fear from the accession of this Queen Moini. With a few presents, a few flattering remarks, they would easily subject her to their influence. Thus the royal heritage was transmitted without difficulty. There was terror only in the harem, and not without reason.

The preparatory labors for the funeral were commenced the same day. At the end of the principal street of Kazounde flowed a deep and rapid stream, an affluent of the Coango. The question was to turn this stream aside, so as to leave its bed dry. It was in that bed that the royal grave must be dug. After the burial the stream would be restored to its natural channel.

The natives were busily employed in constructing a dam, that forced the stream to make a provisional bed across the plain of Kazounde. At the last tableau of this funeral ceremony the barricade would be broken, and the torrent would take its old bed again.

Negoro intended Dick Sand to complete the number of victims sacrificed on the king's tomb. He had been a witness of the young novice's irresistible movement of anger, when Harris had acquainted him with the death of Mrs. Weldon and little Jack.

Negoro, cowardly rascal, had not exposed himself to the same fate as his accomplice. But now, before a prisoner firmly fastened by the feet and hands, he supposed he had nothing to fear, and resolved to pay him a visit. Negoro was one of those miserable wretches who are not satisfied with torturing their victims; they must also enjoy their sufferings.

Toward the middle of the day, then, he repaired to the barrack where Dick Sand was guarded, in sight of an overseer. There, closely bound, was lying the young novice, almost entirely deprived of food for twenty-four hours, weakened by past misery, tortured by those bands that entered into his flesh; hardly able to turn himself, he was waiting for death, no matter how cruel it might be, as a limit to so many evils.

However, at the sight of Negoro he shuddered from head to foot. He made an instinctive effort to break the bands that prevented him from throwing himself on that miserable man and having revenge.

But Hercules himself would not succeed in breaking them. He understood that it was another kind of contest that was going to take place between the two, and arming himself with calmness, Dick Sand compelled himself to look Negoro right in the face, and decided not to honor him with a reply, no matter what he might say.

"I believed it to be my duty," Negoro said to him it first, "to come to salute my young captain for the last time, and to let him know how I regret, for his sake, that he does not command here any longer, as he commanded on board the 'Pilgrim.'"

And, seeing that Dick Sand did not reply:

"What, captain, do you no longer recognize your old cook? He comes, however, to take your orders, and to ask you what he ought to serve for your breakfast."

At the same time Negoro brutally kicked the young novice, who was lying on the ground.

"Besides," added he, "I should have another question to address to you, my young captain. Could you yet explain to me, how, wishing to land on the American coast, you have ended by arriving in Angola, where you are?"

Certainly, Dick Sand had no more need of the Portuguese's words to understand what he had truly divined, when he knew at last that the "Pilgrim's" compass must have been made false by this traitor. But Negoro's question was an avowal. Still he only replied by a contemptuous silence.

"You will acknowledge, captain," continued Kegoro, "that it was fortunate for you that there was a seaman on board—a real one, at that. Great God, where would we be without him? Instead of perishing on some breaker, where the tempest would have thrown you, you have arrived, thanks to him, in a friendly port, and if it is to any one that you owe being at last in a safe place, it is to that seaman whom you have wronged in despising, my young master!"

Speaking thus, Negoro, whose apparent calmness was only the result of an immense effort, had brought his form near Dick Sand. His face, suddenly become ferocious, touched him so closely that one would believe that he was going to devour him. This rascal could no longer contain his fury.

"Every dog has his day!" he exclaimed, in the paroxysm of fury excited in him by his victim's calmness. "To-day I am captain, I am master! Your life is in my hands!"

"Take it," Sand replied, without emotion. "But, know there is in heaven a

God, avenger of all crimes, and your punishment is not distant!"

"If God occupies himself with human beings, there is only time for Him to take care of you!"

"I am ready to appear before the Supreme Judge," replied Dick Sand, coldly, "and death will not make me afraid."

"We shall see about that!" howled Negoro. "You count on help of some kind, perhaps—help at Kazounde, where Alvez and I are all-powerful! You are a fool! You say to yourself, perhaps, that your companions are still there, that old Tom and the others. Undeceive yourself. It is a long time since they were sold and sent to Zanzibar—too fortunate if they do not die of fatigue on the way!"

"God has a thousand ways of doing justice," replied Dick Sand. "The smallest instrument is sufficient for him. Hercules is free."

"Hercules!" exclaimed Negoro, striking the ground with his foot; "he perished long ago under the lions' and panthers' teeth. I regret only one thing, that is, that those ferocious beasts should have forestalled my vengeance!"

"If Hercules is dead," replied Dick Sand, "Dingo is alive. A dog like that, Negoro, is more than enough to take revenge on a man of your kind. I know you well, Negoro; you are not brave. Dingo will seek for you; it will know how to find you again. Some day you will die under his teeth!"

"Miserable boy!" exclaimed the Portuguese, exasperated. "Miserable boy! Dingo died from a ball that I fired at it. It is dead, like Mrs. Weldon and her son; dead, as all the survivors of the 'Pilgrim' shall die!"

"And as you yourself shall die before long," replied Dick Sand, whose tranquil look made the Portuguese grow pale.

Negoro, beside himself, was on the point of passing from words to deeds, and strangling his unarmed prisoner with his hands. Already he had sprung upon him, and was shaking him with fury, when a sudden reflection stopped him. He remembered that he was going to kill his victim, that all would be over, and that this would spare him the twenty-four hours of torture he intended for him. He then stood up, said a few words to the overseer, standing impassive, commanded him to watch closely over the prisoner, and went out of the barrack.

Instead of casting him down, this scene had restored all Dick Sand's moral force. His physical energy underwent a happy reaction, and at the same time regained the mastery. In bending over him in his rage, had Negoro slightly loosened the bands that till then had rendered all movement impossible? It was probable, for Dick Sand thought that his members had more play than before the arrival of his executioner. The young novice, feeling solaced, said to himself that perhaps it would be possible to get his arms free without too much effort. Guarded as he was, in a prison firmly shut, that would doubtless be only a torture—only a suffering less; but it was such a moment in life when the smallest good is invaluable.

Certainly, Dick Sand hoped for nothing. No human succor could come to him except from outside, and whence could it come to him? He was then resigned. To tell the truth, he no longer cared to live. He thought of all those who had met death before him, and he only aspired to join them. Negoro had just repeated what Harris had told him: "Mrs. Weldon and little Jack had succumbed." It was, indeed, only too probable that Hercules, exposed to so many dangers, must have perished also, and from a cruel death. Tom and his companions were at a distance, forever lost to him—Dick Sand ought to believe it. To hope for anything but the end of his troubles, by a death that could not be more terrible than his life, would be signal folly. He then prepared to die, above all throwing himself upon God, and asking courage from Him to go on to the end without giving way. But thoughts of God are good and noble thoughts! It is not in vain that one lifts his soul to Him who can do all, and, when Dick Sand had offered his whole sacrifice, he found that, if one could penetrate to the bottom of his heart, he might perhaps discover there a last ray of hope—that glimmer which a breath from on high can change, in spite of all probabilities, into dazzling light.

The hours passed away. Night came. The rays of light, that penetrated through the thatch of the barrack, gradually disappeared. The last noises of the "tchitoka," which, during that day had been very silent, after the frightful uproar of the night before—those last noises died out. Darkness became very profound in the interior of the narrow prison. Soon all reposed in the city of Kazounde.

Dick Sand fell into a restoring sleep, that lasted two hours. After that he awoke, still stronger. He succeeded in freeing one of his arms from their bands —it was already a little reduced—and it was a delight for him to be able to extend it and draw it back at will.

The night must be half over. The overseer slept with heavy sleep, due to a bottle of brandy, the neck of which was still held in his shut hand. The savage had emptied it to the last drop. Dick Sand's first idea was to take possession of his jailer's weapons, which might be of great use to him in case of escape; but at that moment he thought he heard a slight scratching at the lower part of the door of the barrack. Helping himself with his arms, he succeeded in crawling as far as the door-sill without wakening the overseer.

Dick Sand was not mistaken. The scratching continued, and in a more distinct manner. It seemed that from the outside some one was digging the earth under the door. Was it an animal? Was it a man?

"Hercules! If it were Hercules!" the young novice said to himself.

His eyes were fixed on his guard; he was motionless, and under the influence of a leaden sleep. Dick Sand, bringing his lips to the door-sill, thought he might risk murmuring Hercules's name. A moan, like a low and plaintive bark, replied to him.

"It is not Hercules," said Dick to himself, "but it is Dingo. He has scented me as far as this barrack. Should he bring me another word from Hercules? But if Dingo is not dead, Negoro has lied, and perhaps—"

At that moment a paw passed under the door. Dick Sand seized it, and recognized Dingo's paw. But, if it had a letter, that letter could only be attached to its neck. What to do? Was it possible to make that hole large enough for Dingo to put in its head? At all events, he must try it.

But hardly had Dick Sand begun to dig the soil with his nails, than barks that were not Dingo's sounded over the place. The faithful animal had just been scented by the native dogs, and doubtless could do nothing more than take to flight. Some detonations burst forth. The overseer half awoke. Dick Sand, no longer able to think of escaping, because the alarm was given, must then roll himself up again in his corner, and, after a lovely hope, he saw appear that day which would be without a to-morrow for him.

During all that day the grave-diggers' labors were pushed on with briskness. A large number of natives took part, under the direction of Queen Moini's first minister. All must be ready at the hour named, under penalty of mutilation, for the new sovereign promised to follow the defunct king's ways, point by point.

The waters of the brook having been turned aside, it was in the dry bed that the vast ditch was dug, to a depth of ten feet, over an extent of fifty feet long by ten wide.

Toward the end of the day they began to carpet it, at the bottom and along the walls, with living women, chosen among Moini Loungga's slaves. Generally those unfortunates are buried alive. But, on account of this strange and perhaps miraculous death of Moini Loungga, it had been decided that they should be drowned near the body of their master.

One cannot imagine what those horrible hecatombs are, when a powerful chief's memory must be fitly honored among these tribes of Central Africa. Cameron says that more than a hundred victims were thus sacrificed at the funeral ceremonies of the King of Kassongo's father.

It is also the custom for the defunct king to be dressed in his most costly clothes before being laid in his tomb. But this time, as there was nothing left of the royal person except a few burnt bones, it was necessary to proceed in another manner. A willow manikin was made, representing Moini Loungga sufficiently well, perhaps advantageously, and in it they shut up the remains the combustion had spared. The manikin was then clothed with the royal vestments—we know that those clothes are not worth much—and they did not forget to ornament it with Cousin Benedict's famous spectacles. There was something terribly comic in this masquerade.

The ceremony would take place with torches and with great pomp. The whole population of Kazounde, native or not, must assist at it.

When the evening had come, a long cortège descended the principal street, from the tchitoka as far as the burial place. Cries, funeral dances, magicians' incantations, noises from instruments and detonations from old muskets from the arsenals—nothing was lacking in it.

Jose-Antonio Alvez, Coimbra, Negoro, the Arab traders and their overseers had increased the ranks of Kazounde's people. No one had yet left the great lakoni. Queen Moini would not permit it, and it would not be prudent to disobey the orders of one who was trying the trade of sovereign.

The body of the king, laid in a palanquin, was carried in the last ranks of the cortège. It was surrounded by his wives of the second order, some of whom were going to accompany him beyond this life. Queen Moini, in great state, marched behind what might be called the catafalque. It was positively night when all the people arrived on the banks of the brook; but the resin torches, shaken by the porters, threw great bursts of light over the crowd.

The ditch was seen distinctly. It was carpeted with black, living bodies, for they moved under the chains that bound them to the ground. Fifty slaves were waiting there till the torrent should close over them. The majority were young natives, some resigned and mute, others giving a few groans. The wives all dressed as for a fête, and who must perish, had been chosen by the queen.

One of these victims, she who bore the title of second wife, was bent on her hands and knees, to serve as a royal footstool, as she had done in the king's lifetime. The third wife came to hold up the manikin, while the fourth lay at its feet, in the guise of a cushion.

Before the manikin, at the end of the ditch, a post, painted red, rose from the earth. To this post was fastened a white man, who was going to be counted also among the victims of these bloody obsequies.

That white man was Dick Sand. His body, half naked, bore the marks of the tortures he had already suffered by Negoro's orders. Tied to this post, he waited for death like a man who has no hope except in another life.

However, the moment had not yet arrived when the barricade would be broken.

On a signal from the queen, the fourth wife, she who was placed at the king's feet, was beheaded by Kazounde's executioner, and her blood flowed into the ditch. It was the beginning of a frightful scene of butchery. Fifty slaves fell under the executioner's knife. The bed of the river ran waves of blood.

During half an hour the victims' cries mingled with the assistants' vociferations, and one would seek in vain in that crowd for a sentiment of repugnance or of pity.

At last Queen Moini made a gesture, and the barricade that held back the upper waters gradually opened. By a refinement of cruelty, the current was allowed to filter down the river, instead of being precipitated by an instantaneous bursting open of the dam. Slow death instead of quick death!

The water first drowned the carpet of slaves which covered the bottom of the ditch. Horrible leaps were made by those living creatures, who struggled against asphyxia. They saw Dick Sand, submerged to the knees, make a last effort to break his bonds. But the water mounted. The last heads disappeared under the torrent, that took its course again, and nothing indicated that at the bottom of this river was dug a tomb, where one hundred victims had just perished in honor of Kazounde's king.

The pen would refuse to paint such pictures, if regard for the truth did not impose the duty of describing them in their abominable reality. Man is still there, in those sad countries. To be ignorant of it is not allowable.

## CHAPTER XIII.

### THE INTERIOR OF A FACTORY.

Harris and Negoro had told a lie in saying that Mrs. Weldon and little Jack were dead. She, her son, and Cousin Benedict were then in Kazounde.

After the assault on the ant-hill, they had been taken away beyond the camp on the Coanza by Harris and Negoro, accompanied by a dozen native soldiers.

A palanquin, the "kitanda" of the country, received Mrs. Weldon and little Jack. Why such care on the part of such a man as Negoro? Mrs. Weldon was afraid to explain it to herself.

The journey from the Counza to Kazounde was made rapidly and without fatigue. Cousin Benedict, on whom trouble seemed to have no effect, walked with a firm step. As he was allowed to search to the right and to the left, he did not think of complaining. The little troop, then, arrived at Kazounde eight days before Ibn Hamis's caravan. Mrs. Weldon was shut up, with her child and Cousin Benedict, in Alvez's establishment.

Little Jack was much better. On leaving the marshy country, where he had taken the fever, he gradually became better, and now he was doing well. No doubt neither he nor his mother could have borne the hardships of the caravan; but owing to the manner in which they had made this journey, during which they had been given a certain amount of care, they were in a satisfactory condition, physically at least.

As to her companions, Mrs. Weldon had heard nothing of them. After having seen Hercules flee into the forest, she did not know what had become of him. As to Dick Sand, as Harris and Negoro were no longer there to torture him, she hoped that his being a white man would perhaps spare him some bad treatment. As to Nan, Tom, Bat, Austin, and Acteon, they were blacks, and it was too certain that they would be treated as such. Poor people! who should never have trodden that land of Africa, and whom treachery had just cast there.

When Ibn Hamis's caravan had arrived at Kazounde, Mrs. Weldon, having no communication with the outer world, could not know of the fact: neither did the noises from the lakoni tell her anything. She did not know that Tom and his friends had been sold to a trader from Oujiji, and that they would soon set out. She neither knew of Harris's punishment, nor of King Moini Loungga's death, nor of the royal funeral ceremonies, that had added Dick Sand to so many other victims. So the unfortunate woman found herself alone at Kazounde, at the trader's mercy, in Negoro's power, and she could not even think of dying in order to escape him, because her child was with her.

Mrs. Weldon was absolutely ignorant of the fate that awaited her. Harris and Negoro had not addressed a word to her during the whole journey from the Coanza to Kazounde. Since her arrival, she had not seen either of them again, and she could not leave the enclosure around the rich trader's private establishment. Is it necessary to say now that Mrs. Weldon had found no help in her large child, Cousin Benedict? That is understood.

When the worthy savant learned that he was not on the American continent, as he believed, he was not at all anxious to know how that could have happened. No! His first movement was a gesture of anger. The insects that he imagined he had been the first to discover in America, those tsetses and others, were only mere African hexapodes, found by many naturalists before him, in their native places. Farewell, then, to the glory of attaching his name to those discoveries! In fact, as he was in Africa, what could there be astonishing in the circumstance that Cousin Benedict had collected African insects.

But the first anger over, Cousin Benedict said to himself that the "Land of the Pharaohs"—so he still called it—possessed incomparable entomological riches, and that so far as not being in the "Land of the Incas" was concerned, he would not lose by the change.

"Ah!" he repeated, to himself, and even repeated to Mrs. Weldon, who hardly listened to him, "this is the country of the manticores, those coleopteres with long hairy feet, with welded and sharp wing-shells, with enormous mandibles, of which the most remarkable is the tuberculous manticore. It is the country of the calosomes with golden ends; of the Goliaths of Guinea and of the Gabon, whose feet are furnished with thorns; of the sacred Egyptian ateuchus, that the Egyptians of Upper Egypt venerated as gods. It is here that those sphinxes with heads of death, now spread over all Europe, belong, and also those 'Idias Bigote,' whose sting is particularly dreaded by the Senegalians of the coast. Yes; there are superb things to be found here, and I shall find them, if these honest people will only let me."

We know who those "honest people" were, of whom Cousin Benedict did not dream of complaining. Besides, it has been stated, the entomologist had enjoyed a half liberty in Negoro's and Harris's company, a liberty of which Dick Sand had absolutely deprived him during the voyage from the coast to the Coanza. The simple-hearted savant had been very much touched by that condescension.

Finally, Cousin Benedict would be the happiest of entomologists if he had not suffered a loss to which he was extremely sensitive. He still possessed his tin box, but his glasses no longer rested on his nose, his magnifying glass no longer hung from his neck! Now, a naturalist without his magnifying glass and his spectacles, no longer exists. Cousin Benedict, however, was destined never to see those two optical attendants again, because they had been buried with the royal manikin. So, when he found some insect, he was reduced to thrusting it into his eyes to distinguish its most prominent peculiarities. Ah! it was a great loss to Cousin Benedict, and he would have paid a high price for a pair of spectacles, but that article was not current on the lakonis of Kazounde. At all events, Cousin Benedict could go and come in Jose-Antonio Alvez's establishment. They knew he was incapable of seeking to flee. Besides, a high palisade separated the factory from the other quarters of the city, and it would not be easy to get over it.

But, if it was well enclosed, this enclosure did not measure less than a mile in circumference. Trees, bushes of a kind peculiar to Africa, great herbs, a few rivulets, the thatch of the barracks and the huts, were more than necessary to conceal the continent's rarest insects, and to make Cousin Benedict's happiness, at least, if not his fortune. In fact, he discovered some hexapodes, and nearly lost his eyesight in trying to study them without spectacles. But, at least, he added to his precious collection, and laid the foundation of a great work on African entomology. If his lucky star would let him discover a new insect, to which he would attach his name, he would have nothing more to desire in this world!

If Alvez's establishment was sufficiently large for Cousin Benedict's scientific promenades, it seemed immense to little Jack, who could walk about there without restraint. But the child took little interest in the pleasures so natural to his age. He rarely quitted his mother, who did not like to leave him alone, and always dreaded some misfortune.

Little Jack often spoke of his father, whom he had not seen for so long. He asked to be taken back to him. He inquired after all, for old Nan, for his friend Hercules, for Bat, for Austin, for Acteon, and for Dingo, that appeared, indeed, to have deserted him. He wished to see his comrade, Dick Sand, again. His young imagination was very much affected, and only lived in those remembrances. To his questions Mrs. Weldon could only reply by pressing him to her heart, while covering him with kisses. All that she could do was not to cry before him.

Meanwhile, Mrs. Weldon had not failed to observe that, if bad treatment had been spared her during the journey from the Coanza, nothing in Alvez's establishment indicated that there would be any change of conduct in regard to her. There were in the factory only the slaves in the trader's service. All the others, which formed the object of his trade, had been penned up in the barracks of the tchitoka, then sold to the brokers from the interior.

Now, the storehouses of the establishment were overflowing with stuffs and ivory. The stuffs were intended to be exchanged in the provinces of the center, the ivory to be exported from the principal markets of the continent.

In fact, then, there were few people in the factory. Mrs. Weldon and Jack occupied a hut apart; Cousin Benedict another. They did not communicate with the trader's servants. They ate together. The food, consisting of goat's flesh or mutton, vegetables, tapioca, sorgho, and the fruits of the country, was sufficient.

Halima, a young slave, was especially devoted to Mrs. Weldon's service. In her way, and as she could, she even evinced for her a kind of savage, but certainty sincere, affection.

Mrs. Weldon hardly saw Jose-Antonio Alvez, who occupied the principal house of the factory. She did not see Negoro at all, as he lodged outside; but his absence was quite inexplicable. This absence continued to astonish her, and make her feel anxious at the same time.

"What does he want? What is he waiting for?" she asked herself. "Why has he brought us to Kazounde?"

So had passed the eight days that preceded and followed the arrival of Ibn Hamis's caravan—that is, the two days before the funeral ceremonies, and the six days that followed.

In the midst of so many anxieties, Mrs. Weldon could not forget that her husband must be a prey to the most frightful despair, on not seeing either his wife or his son return to San Francisco. Mr. Weldon could not know that his wife had adopted that fatal idea of taking passage on board the "Pilgrim," and he would believe that she had embarked on one of the steamers of the Trans-Pacific Company. Now, these steamers arrived regularly, and neither Mrs. Weldon, nor Jack, nor Cousin Benedict were on them. Besides, the "Pilgrim" itself was already overdue at Sun Francisco. As she did not reappear, James W. Weldon must now rank her in the category of ships supposed to be lost, because not heard of.

What a terrible blow for him, when news of the departure of the "Pilgrim" and the embarkation of Mrs. Weldon should reach him from his correspondents in Auckland! What had he done? Had he refused to believe that his son and she had perished at sea? But then, where would he search? Evidently on the isles of the Pacific, perhaps on the American coast. But never, no never, would the thought occur to him that she had been thrown on the coast of this fatal Africa!

So thought Mrs. Weldon. But what could she attempt? Flee! How? She was closely watched. And then to flee was to venture into those thick forests, in the midst of a thousand dangers, to attempt a journey of more than two hundred miles to reach the coast. And meanwhile Mrs. Weldon was decided to do it, if no other means offered themselves for her to recover her liberty. But, first, she wished to know exactly what Negoro's designs were.

At last she knew them.

On the 6th of June, three days after the burial of Kazounde's king, Negoro entered the factory, where he had not yet set foot since his return. He went right to the hut occupied by his prisoner.

Mrs. Weldon was alone. Cousin Benedict was taking one of his scientific walks. Little Jack, watched by the slave Halima, was walking in the enclosure of the establishment.

Negoro pushed open the door of the hut without knocking.

"Mrs. Weldon," said he, "Tom and his companions have been sold for the markets of Oujiji!"

"May God protect them!" said Mrs. "Weldon, shedding tears.

"Nan died on the way, Dick Sand has perished——"

"Nan dead! and Dick!" cried Mrs. Weldon.

"Yes, it is just for your captain of fifteen to pay for Harris's murder with his life," continued Negoro. "You are alone in Kazounde, mistress; alone, in the power of the 'Pilgrim's' old cook—absolutely alone, do you understand?"

What Negoro said was only too true, even concerning Tom and his friends. The old black man, his son Bat, Acteon and Austin had departed the day before with the trader of Oujiji's caravan, without the consolation of seeing Mrs. Weldon again, without even knowing that their companion in misery was in Kazounde, in Alvez's establishment. They had departed for the lake country, a journey figured by hundreds of miles, that very few accomplish, and from which very few return.

"Well?" murmured Mrs. Weldon, looking at Negoro without answering.

"Mrs. Weldon," returned the Portuguese, in an abrupt voice, "I could revenge myself on you for the bad treatment I suffered on board the 'Pilgrim.' But Dick Sand's death will satisfy my vengeance. Now, mistress, I become the merchant again, and behold my projects with regard to you."

Mrs. Weldon looked at him without saying a word.

"You," continued the Portuguese, "your child, and that imbecile who runs after the flies, you have a commercial value which I intend to utilize. So I am going to sell you."

"I am of a free race," replied Mrs. Weldon, in a firm tone.

"You are a slave, if I wish it."

"And who would buy a white woman?"

"A man who will pay for her whatever I shall ask him."

Mrs. Weldon bent her head for a moment, for she knew that anything was possible in that frightful country.

"You have heard?" continued Negoro.

"Who is this man to whom you will pretend to sell me?" replied Mrs. Weldon.

"To sell you or to re-sell you. At least, I suppose so!" added the Portuguese, sneering.

"The name of this man?" asked Mrs. Weldon.

"This man—he is James W. Weldon, your husband."

"My husband!" exclaimed Mrs. Weldon, who could not believe what she had just heard.

"Himself, Mrs. Weldon—your husband, to whom I do not wish simply to restore his wife, his child, and his cousin, but to sell them, and, at a high price."

Mrs. Weldon asked herself if Negoro was not setting a trap for her. However, she believed he was speaking seriously. To a wretch to whom money is everything, it seems that we can trust, when business is in question. Now, this was business.

"And when do you propose to make this business operation?" returned Mrs. Weldon.

"As soon as possible."

"Where?"

"Just here. Certainly James Weldon will not hesitate to come as far as Kazounde for his wife and son."

"No, he will not hesitate. But who will tell him?"

"I! I shall go to San Francisco to find James Weldon. I have money enough for this voyage."

"The money stolen from on board the 'Pilgrim?'"

"Yes, that, and more besides," replied Negoro, insolently. "But, if I wish to sell you soon, I also wish to sell you at a high price. I think that James Weldon will not regard a hundred thousand dollars——"

"He will not regard them, if he can give them," replied Mrs. Weldon, coldly. "Only my husband, to whom you will say, doubtless, that I am held a prisoner at Kazounde, in Central Africa——"

"Precisely!"

"My husband will not believe you without proofs, and he will not be so imprudent as to come to Kazounde on your word alone."

"He will come here," returned Negoro, "if I bring him a letter written by you, which will tell him your situation, which will describe me as a faithful servant, escaped from the hands of these savages."

"My hand shall never write that letter!" Mrs. Weldon replied, in a still colder manner.

"You refuse?" exclaimed Negoro.

"I refuse!"

The thought of the dangers her husband would pass through in coming as far as Kazounde, the little dependence that could be placed on the Portuguese's promises, the facility with which the latter could retain James Weldon, after taking the ransom agreed upon, all these reasons taken together made Mrs. Weldon refuse Negoro's proposition flatly and at once. Mrs. Weldon spoke, thinking only of herself, forgetting her child for the moment.

"You shall write that letter!" continued the Portuguese.

"No!" replied Mrs. Weldon again.

"Ah, take care!" exclaimed Negoro. "You are not alone here! Your child is, like you, in my power, and I well know how——"

Mrs. Weldon wished to reply that that would be impossible. Her heart was beating as if it would break; she was voiceless.

"Mrs. Weldon," said Negoro, "you will reflect on the offer I have made you. In eight days you will have handed me a letter to James Weldon's address, or you will repent of it."

That said, the Portuguese retired, without giving vent to his anger; but it was easy to see that nothing would stop him from constraining Mrs. Weldon to obey him.

## CHAPTER XIV.

### SOME NEWS OF DR. LIVINGSTONE.

Left alone, Mrs. Weldon at first only fixed her mind on this thought, that eight days would pass before Negoro would return for a definite answer. There was time to reflect and decide on a course of action. There could be no question of the Portuguese's probity except in his own interest. The "market value" that he attributed to his prisoner would evidently be a safeguard for her, and protect her for the time, at least, against any temptation that might put her in danger. Perhaps she would think of a compromise that would restore her to her husband without obliging Mr. Weldon to come to Kazounde. On receipt of a letter from his wife, she well knew that James Weldon would set out. He would brave the perils of this journey into the most dangerous countries of Africa. But, once at Kazounde, when Negoro should have that fortune of a hundred thousand dollars in his hands, what guaranty would James W. Weldon, his wife, his son and Cousin Benedict have, that they would be allowed to depart? Could not Queen Moini's caprice prevent them? Would not this "sale" of Mrs. Weldon and hers be better accomplished if it took place at the coast, at some point agreed upon, which would spare Mr. Weldon both the dangers of the journey to the interior, and the difficulties, not to say the impossibilities, of a return?

So reflected Mrs. Weldon. That was why she had refused at once to accede to Negoro's proposition and give him a letter for her husband. She also thought that, if Negoro had put off his second visit for eight days, it was because he needed that time to prepare for his journey. If not, he would return sooner to force her consent.

"Would he really separate me from my child?" murmured she.

At that moment Jack entered the hut, and, by an instinctive movement, his mother seized him, as if Negoro were there, ready to snatch him from her.

"You are in great grief, mother?" asked the little boy.

"No, dear Jack," replied Mrs. Weldon; "I was thinking of your papa!

You would be very glad to see him again?"

"Oh! yes, mother! Is he going to come?"

"No! no! He must not come!"

"Then we will go to see him again?"

"Yes, darling Jack!"

"With my friend Dick—and Hercules—and old Tom?"

"Yes! yes!" replied Mrs. Weldon, putting her head down to hide her tears.

"Has papa written to you?" asked little Jack.

"No, my love."

"Then you are going to write to him, mother?"

"Yes—yes—perhaps!" replied Mrs. Weldon.

And without knowing it, little Jack entered directly into his mother's thoughts. To avoid answering him further, she covered him with kisses.

It must be stated that another motive of some value was joined to the different reasons that had urged Mrs. Weldon to resist Negoro's injunctions. Perhaps Mrs. Weldon had a very unexpected chance of being restored to liberty without her husband's intervention, and even against Negoro's will. It was only a faint ray of hope, very vague as yet, but it was one.

In fact, a few words of conversation, overheard by her several days before, made her foresee a possible succor near at hand—one might say a providential succor.

Alvez and a mongrel from Oujiji were talking a few steps from the hut occupied by Mrs. Weldon. It is not astonishing that the slave-trade was the subject of conversation between those worthy merchants. The two brokers in human flesh were talking business. They were discussing the future of their commerce, and were worried about the efforts the English were making to destroy it—not only on the exterior, by cruisers, but in the interior, by their missionaries and their travelers.

Jose-Antonio Alvez found that the explorations of these hardy pioneers could only injure commercial operations. His interlocutor shared his views, and thought that all these visitors, civil or religious, should be received with gun-shots.

This had been done to some extent. But, to the great displeasure of the traders, if they killed some of these curious ones, others escaped them. Now, these latter, on returning to their country, recounted "with exaggerations," Alvez said, the horrors of the slave-trade, and that injured this commerce immensely—it being too much diminished already.

The mongrel agreed to that, and deplored it; above all, concerning the markets of N'yangwe, of Oujiji, of Zanzibar, and of all the great lake regions. There had come successively Speke, Grant, Livingstone, Stanley, and others. It was an invasion! Soon all England and all America would occupy the country!

Alvez sincerely pitied his comrade, and he declared that the provinces of Western Africa had been, till that time, less badly treated—that is to say, less visited; but the epidemic of travelers was beginning to spread. If Kazounde had been spared, it was not so with Cassange, and with Bihe, where Alvez owned factories. It may be remembered, also, that Harris had spoken to Negoro of a certain Lieutenant Cameron, who might, indeed, have the presumption to cross Africa from one side to the other, and after entering it by Zanzibar, leave it by Angola.

In fact, the trader had reason to fear, and we know that, some years after, Cameron to the south and Stanley to the north, were going to explore these little-known provinces of the west, describe the permanent monstrosities of the trade, unveil the guilty complicities of foreign agents, and make the responsibility fall on the right parties.

Neither Alvez nor the mongrel could know anything yet of this exploration of Cameron's and of Stanley's; but what they did know, what they said, what Mrs. Weldon heard, and what was of such great interest to her—in a word, what had sustained her in her refusal to subscribe at once to Negoro's demands, was this:

Before long, very probably, Dr. David Livingstone would arrive at

Kazounde.

Now, the arrival of Livingstone with his escort, the influence which the great traveler enjoyed in Africa, the concourse of Portuguese authorities from Angola that could not fail to meet him, all that might bring about the deliverance of Mrs. Weldon and hers, in spite of Negoro, in spite of Alvez. It was perhaps their restoration to their country within a short time, and without James W. Weldon risking his life in a journey, the result of which could only be deplorable.

But was there any probability that Dr. Livingstone would soon visit that part of the continent? Yes, for in following that missionary tour, he was going to complete the exploration of Central Africa.

We know the heroic life of this son of the tea merchant, who lived in Blantyre, a village in the county of Lanark. Born on the 13th of March, 1813, David Livingstone, the second of six children, became, by force of study, both a theologian and doctor. After making his novitiate in the "London Missionary Society," he embarked for the Cape in 1840, with the intention of joining the missionary Moffat in Southern Africa.

From the Cape, the future traveler repaired to the country of the Bechnanas, which he explored for the first time, returned to Kuruman and married Moffat's daughter, that brave companion who would be worthy of him. In 1843 he founded a mission in the valley of the Mabotsa.

Four years later, we find him established at Kolobeng, two hundred and twenty-five miles to the north of Kuruman, in the country of the Bechnanas.

Two years after, in 1849, Livingstone left Kolobeng with his wife, his three children and two friends, Messrs. Oswell and Murray. August 1st, of the same year, he discovered Lake N'gami, and returned to Kolobeng, by descending the Zouga.

In this journey Livingstone, stopped by the bad will of the natives, had not passed beyond the N'gami. A second attempt was not more fortunate. A third must succeed. Then, taking a northern route, again with his family and Mr. Oswell, after frightful sufferings (for lack of food, for lack of water) that almost cost him the lives of his children, he reached the country of the Makalolos beside the Chobe, a branch of the Zambezi. The chief, Sebituane, joined him at Linyanti. At the end of June, 1851, the Zambezi was discovered, and the doctor returned to the Cape to bring his family to England.

In fact, the intrepid Livingstone wished to be alone while risking his life in the daring journey he was going to undertake.

On leaving the Cape this time, the question was to cross Africa obliquely from the south to the west, so as to reach Saint Paul de Loanda.

On the third of June, 1852, the doctor set out with a few natives.

He arrived at Kuruman and skirted the Desert of Kalahari. The 31st

December he entered Litoubarouba and found the country of the

Bechnanas ravaged by the Boers, old Dutch colonists, who were masters

of the Cape before the English took possession of it.

Livingstone left Litoubarouba on the 15th of January, 1853, penetrated to the center of the country of the Bamangouatos, and, on May 23d, he arrived at Linyanti, where the young sovereign of the Makalolos, Sckeletou, received him with great honor.

There, the doctor held back by the intense fevers, devoted himself to studying the manners of the country, and, for the first time, he could ascertain the ravages made by the slave-trade in Africa.

One month after he descended the Chobe, reached the Zambezi, entered Naniele, visited Katonga and Libonta, arrived at the confluence of the Zambezi and the Leeba, formed the project of ascending by that watercourse as far as the Portuguese possessions of the west, and, after nine weeks' absence, returned to Linyanti to make preparations.

On the 11th of November, 1853, the doctor, accompanied by twenty-seven Makalolos, left Linyanti, and on the 27th of December he reached the mouth of the Leeba. This watercourse was ascended as far as the territory of the Balondas, there where it receives the Makonda, which comes from the east. It was the first time that a white man penetrated into this region.

January 14th, Livingstone entered Shinte's residence. He was the most powerful sovereign of the Balondas. He gave Livingstone a good reception, and, the 26th of the same month, after crossing the Leeba, he arrived at King Katema's. There, again, a good reception, and thence the departure of the little troop that on the 20th of February encamped on the borders of Lake Dilolo.

On setting out from this point, a difficult country, exigencies of the natives, attacks from the tribes, revolt of his companions, threats of death, everything conspired against Livingstone, and a less energetic man would have abandoned the party. The doctor persevered, and on the 4th of April, he reached the banks of the Coango, a large watercourse which forms the eastern boundary of the Portuguese possessions, and flows northward into the Zaire.

Six days after, Livingstone entered Cassange, where the trader Alvez had seen him passing through, and on the 31st of May he arrived at Saint Paul de Loanda. For the first time, and after a journey of two years, Africa had just been crossed obliquely from the south to the west.

David Livingstone left Loanda, September 24th of the same year. He skirted the right bank of that Coanza that had been so fatal to Dick Sand and his party, arrived at the confluence of the Lombe, crossing numerous caravans of slaves, passed by Cassange again, left it on the 20th of February, crossed the Coango, and reached the Zambezi at Kawawa. On the 8th of June he discovered Lake Dilolo again, saw Shinte again, descended the Zambezi, and reentered Linyanti, which he left on the 3d of November, 1855.

This second part of the journey, which would lead the doctor toward the eastern coast, would enable him to finish completely this crossing of Africa from the west to the east.

After having visited the famous Victoria Falls, the "thundering foam," David Livingstone abandoned the Zambezi to take a northeastern direction. The passage across the territory of the Batokas (natives who were besotted by the inhalation of hemp), the visit to Semalembone (the powerful chief of the region), the crossing of the Kafone, the finding of the Zambezi again, the visit to King Mbourouma, the sight of the ruins of Zambo (an ancient Portuguese city), the encounter with the Chief Mpende on the 17th of January, 1856 (then at war with the Portuguese), the final arrival at Tete, on the border of the Zambezi, on the 2d of March—such were the principal halting-places of this tour.

The 22d of April Livingstone left that station, formerly a rich one, descended as far as the delta of the river, and arrived at Quilimane, at its mouth, on the 20th of May, four years after leaving the Cape. On the 12th of July he embarked for Maurice, and on the 22d of December he was returning to England, after sixteen years' absence.

The prize of the Geographical Society of Paris, the grand medal of the London Geographical Society, and brilliant receptions greeted the illustrious traveler. Another would, perhaps, have thought that repose was well earned. The doctor did not think so, and departed on the 1st of March, 1858, accompanied by his brother Charles, Captain Bedinfield, the Drs. Kirk and

Meller, and by Messrs. Thornton and Baines. He arrived in May on the coast of Mozambique, having for an object the exploration of the basin of the Zambezi.

All would not return from this voyage. A little steamer, the "My Robert," enabled the explorers to ascend the great river by the Rongone. They arrived at Tete, September the 8th; thence reconnoissance of the lower course of the Zambezi and of the Chire, its left branch, in January, 1859; visit to Lake Chirona in April; exploration of the Manganjas' territory; discovery of Lake Nyassa on September 10th; return to the Victoria Falls, August 9th, 1860; arrival of Bishop Mackensie and his missionaries at the mouth of the Zambezi, January 31st, 1861; the exploration of the Rovouma, on the "Pioneer," in March; the return to Lake Nyassa in September, 1861, and residence there till the end of October; January 30th, 1862, arrival of Mrs. Livingstone and a second steamer, the "Lady Nyassa:" such were the events that marked the first years of this new expedition. At this time, Bishop Mackensie and one of his missionaries had already succumbed to the unhealthfulness of the climate, and on the 27th of April, Mrs. Livingstone died in her husband's arms.

In May, the doctor attempted a second reconnoissance of the Rovouma; then, at the end of November, he entered the Zambezi again, and sailed up the Chire again. In April, 1863, he lost his companion, Thornton, sent back to Europe his brother Charles and Dr. Kirk, who were both exhausted by sickness, and November 10th, for the third time, he saw Nyassa, of which he completed the hydrography. Three months after he was again at the mouth of the Zambezi, passed to Zanzibar, and July 20th, 1864, after five years' absence, he arrived in London, where he published his work entitled: "Exploration of the Zambezi and its Branches."

January 28th, 1866, Livingstone landed again at Zanzibar. He was beginning his fourth voyage.

August 8th, after having witnessed the horrible scenes provoked by the slave-trade in that country, the doctor, taking this time only a few cipayes and a few negroes, found himself again at Mokalaose, on the banks of the Nyassa. Six weeks later, the majority of the men forming the escort took flight, returned to Zanzibar, and there falsely spread the report of Livingstone's death.

He, however, did not draw back. He wished to visit the country comprised between the Nyassa and Lake Tanganyika. December 10th, guided by some natives, he traversed the Loangona River, and April 2d, 1867, he discovered Lake Liemmba. There he remained a month between life and death. Hardly well again August 30th he reached Lake Moero, of which he visited the northern shore, and November 21st he entered the town of Cayembe, where he lived forty days, during which he twice renewed his exploration of Lake

Moero.

From Cayembe Livingstone took a northern direction, with the design of reaching the important town of Oujiji, on the Tanganyika. Surprised by the rising of the waters, and abandoned by his guides, he was obliged to return to Cayembe. He redescended to the south June 6th, and six weeks after gained the great lake Bangoneolo. He remained there till August 9th, and then sought to reascend toward Lake Tanganyika.

What a journey! On setting out, January 7th, 1869, the heroic doctor's feebleness was such that be had to be carried. In February he at last reached the lake and arrived at Oujiji, where he found some articles sent to his address by the Oriental Company of Calcutta.

Livingstone then had but one idea, to gain the sources of the valley of the Nile by ascending the Tanganyika. September 21st he was at Bambarre, in the Manonyema, a cannibal country, and arrived at the Loualaba—that Loualaba that Cameron was going to suspect, and Stanley to discover, to be only the upper Zaire, or Congo. At Mamohela the doctor was sick for eighty days. He had only three servants. July 21st, 1871, he departed again for the Tanganyika, and only reentered Oujiji October 23d. He was then a mere skeleton.

Meanwhile, before this period, people had been a long time without news of the traveler. In Europe they believed him to be dead. He himself had almost lost hope of being ever relieved.

Eleven days after his entrance into Oujiji shots were heard a quarter of a mile from the lake. The doctor arrives. A man, a white man, is before him. "Doctor Livingstone, I presume?"

"Yes," replied the latter, raising his cap, with a friendly smile.

Their hands were warmly clasped.

"I thank God," continued the white man, "that He has permitted me to meet you."

"I am happy," said Livingstone, "to be here to receive you."

The white man was the American Stanley, a reporter of the New York Herald, whom Mr. Bennett, the proprietor of that journal, had just sent to find David Livingstone.

In the month of October, 1870, this American, without hesitation, without a word, simply as a hero, had embarked at Bombay for Zanzibar, and almost following Speke and Burton's route, after untold sufferings, his life being menaced several times, he arrived at Oujiji.

The two travelers, now become fast friends, then made an expedition to the north of Lake Tanganyika. They embarked, pushed as far as Cape Malaya, and after a minute exploration, were of the opinion that the great lake had for an outlet a branch of the Loualaba.

It was what Cameron and Stanley himself were going to determine positively some years after. December 12th, Livingstone and his companion were returning to Oujiji.

Stanley prepared to depart. December 27th, after a navigation of eight days, the doctor and he arrived at Ousimba; then, February 23d, they entered Kouihara.

March 12th was the day of parting.

"You have accomplished," said the doctor to his companion, "what few men would have done, and done it much better than certain great travelers. I am very grateful to you for it. May God lead you, my friend, and may He bless you!"

"May He," said Stanley, taking Livingstone's hand, "bring you back to us safe and sound, dear doctor!"

Stanley drew back quickly from this embrace, and turned so as to conceal his tears. "Good-by, doctor, dear friend," he said in a stifled voice.

"Good-by," replied Livingstone, feebly.

Stanley departed, and July 12th, 1872, he landed at Marseilles.

Livingstone was going to return to his discoveries. August 25th, after five months passed at Konihara, accompanied by his black servants, Souzi, Chouma, and Amoda, by two other servants, by Jacob Wainwright, and by fifty-six men sent by Stanley, he went toward the south of the Tanganyika.

A month after, the caravan arrived at M'oura, in the midst of storms, caused by an extreme drought. Then came the rains, the bad will of the natives, and the loss of the beasts of burden, from falling under the stings of the tsetse. January 24th, 1873, the little troop was at Tchitounkone. April 27th, after having left Lake Bangoneolo to the east, the troop was going toward the village of Tchitambo.

At that place some traders had left Livingstone. This is what Alvez and his colleague had learned from them. They had good reason to believe that the doctor, after exploring the south of the lake, would venture across the Loanda, and come to seek unknown countries in the west. Thence he was to ascend toward Angola, to visit those regions infested by the slave-trade, to push as far as Kazounde; the tour seemed to be all marked out, and it was very probable that Livingstone would follow it.

Mrs. Weldon then could count on the approaching arrival of the great traveler, because, in the beginning of June, it was already more than two months since he had reached the south of Lake Bangoneolo.

Now, June 13th, the day before that on which Negoro would come to claim from Mrs. Weldon the letter that would put one hundred thousand dollars in his hands, sad news was spread, at which Alvez and the traders only rejoiced.

May 1st, 1873, at dawn, Dr. David Livingstone died. In fact, on April 29th, the little caravan had reached the village of Tchitambo, to the south of the lake. The doctor was carried there on a litter. On the 30th, in the night, under the influence of excessive grief, he moaned out this complaint, that was hardly heard: "Oh, dear! dear!" and he fell back from drowsiness.

At the end of an hour he called his servant, Souzi, asking for some medicine, then murmuring in a feeble voice: "It is well. Now you can go."

Toward four o'clock in the morning, Souzi and five men of the escort entered the doctor's hut. David Livingstone, kneeling near his bed, his head resting on his hands, seemed to be engaged in prayer. Souzi gently touched his cheek; it was cold. David Livingstone was no more.

Nine months after, his body, carried by faithful servants at the price of unheard-of fatigues, arrived at Zanzibar. On April 12th, 1874, it was buried in Westminster Abbey, among those of her great men, whom England honors equally with her kings.

## CHAPTER XV.

### WHERE A MANTICORE MAY LEAD.

To what plank of safety will not an unfortunate being cling? Will not the eyes of the condemned seek to seize any ray of hope, no matter how vague?

So it had been with Mrs. Weldon. One can understand what she must have felt when she learned, from Alvez himself, that Dr. Livingstone had just died in a little Bangoneolo village.

It seemed to her that she was more isolated than ever; that a sort of bond that attached her to the traveler, and with him to the civilized world, had just been broken.

The plank of safety sank under her hand, the ray of hope went out before her eyes. Tom and his companions had left Kazounde for the lake region. Not the least news of Hercules. Mrs. Weldon was not sure of any one. She must then fall back on Negoro's proposition, while trying to amend it and secure a definite result from it.

June 14th, the day fixed by him, Negoro presented himself at Mrs. Weldon's hut.

The Portuguese was, as always, so he said, perfectly practical. However, he abated nothing from the amount of the ransom, which his prisoner did not even discuss. But Mrs. Weldon also showed herself very practical in saying to him:

"If you wish to make an agreement, do not render it impossible by unacceptable conditions. The exchange of our liberty for the sum you exact may take place, without my husband coming into a country where you see what can be done with a white man! Now, I do not wish him to come here at any price!"

After some hesitation Negoro yielded, and Mrs. Weldon finished with the concession that James Weldon should not venture as far as Kazounde. A ship would land him at Mossamedes, a little port to the south of Angola, ordinarily frequented by slave-ships, and well-known by Negoro. It was there that the Portuguese would conduct James W. Weldon; and at a certain time Alvez's agent would bring thither Mrs. Weldon, Jack, and Cousin Benedict. The ransom would be given to those agents on the giving up of the prisoners, and Negoro, who would play the part of a perfectly honest man with James Weldon, would disappear on the ship's arrival.

Mrs. Weldon had gained a very important point. She spared her husband the dangers of a voyage to Kazounde, the risk of being kept there, after paying the exacted ransom, and the perils of the return. As to the six hundred miles that separated Kazounde from Mossamedes, by going over them as she had traveled on leaving the Coanza, Mrs. Weldon would only have a little fatigue to fear. Besides, it would be to Alvez's interest—for he was in the affair—for the prisoners to arrive safe and sound.

The conditions being thus settled, Mrs. Weldon wrote to her husband, leaving to Negoro the care of passing himself off as a devoted servant, who had escaped from the natives. Negoro took the letter, which did not allow James Weldon to hesitate about following him as far as Mossamedes, and, the next day, escorted by twenty blacks, he traveled toward the north.

Why did he take that direction? Was it, then, Negoro's intention to embark on one of the vessels which frequent the mouths of the Congo, and thus avoid the Portuguese stations, as well as the penitentiaries in which he had been an involuntary guest? It was probable. At least, that was the reason he gave Alvez.

After his departure, Mrs. Weldon must try to arrange her existence in such a manner as to pass the time of her sojourn at Kazounde as happily as possible. Under the most favorable circumstances, it would last three or four months. Negoro's going and returning would require at least that time.

Mrs. Weldon's intention was, not to leave the factory. Her child, Cousin Benedict, and she, were comparatively safe there. Halima's good care softened the severity of this sequestration a little. Besides, it was probable that the trader would not permit her to leave the establishment. The great premium that the prisoner's ransom would procure him, made it well worth while to guard her carefully.

It was even fortunate that Alvez was not obliged to leave Kazounde to visit his two other factories of Bihe and Cassange. Coimbra was going to take his place in the expedition on new razzias or raids. There was no motive for regretting the presence of that drunkard. Above all, Negoro, before setting out, had given Alvez the most urgent commands in regard to Mrs. Weldon. It was necessary to watch her closely. They did not know what had become of Hercules. If he had not perished in that dreadful province of Kazounde, perhaps he would attempt to get near the prisoner and snatch her from Alvez's hands. The trader perfectly understood a situation which ciphered itself out by a good number of dollars. He would answer for Mrs. Weldon as for his own body.

So the monotonous life of the prisoner during the first days after her arrival at the factory, was continued. What passed in this enclosure reproduced very exactly the various acts of native existence outside. Alvez lived like the other natives of Kazounde. The women of the establishment worked as they would have done in the town, for the greater comfort of their husbands or their masters. Their occupations included preparing rice with heavy blows of the pestle in wooden mortars, to perfect decortication; cleansing and winnowing maize, and all the manipulations necessary to draw from it a granulous substance which serves to compose that potage called "mtyelle" in the country; the harvesting of the sorgho, a kind of large millet, the ripening of which had just been solemnly celebrated at this time; the extraction of that fragrant oil from the "mpafon" drupes, kinds of olives, the essence of which forms a perfume sought for by the natives; spinning of the cotton, the fibers of which are twisted by means of a spindle a foot and a half long, to which the spinners impart a rapid rotation; the fabrication of bark stuffs with the mallet; the extraction from the tapioca roots, and the preparation of the earth for the different products of the country, cassava, flour that they make from the manioc beans, of which the pods, fifteen inches long, named "mositsanes," grow on trees twenty feet high; arachides intended to make oil, perennial peas of a bright blue, known under the name of "tchilobes," the flowers of which relieve the slightly insipid taste of the milk of sorgho; native coffee, sugar canes, the juice of which is reduced to a syrup; onions, Indian pears, sesamum, cucumbers, the seeds of which are roasted like chestnuts; the preparation of fermented drinks, the "malofori," made with bananas, the "pombe" and other liquors; the care of the domestic animals, of those cows that only allow themselves to be milked in the presence of their little one or of a stuffed calf; of those heifers of small race, with short horns, some of which have a hump; of those goats which, in the country where their flesh serves for food, are an important object of exchange, one might say current money like the slave; finally, the feeding of the birds, swine, sheep, oxen, and so forth.

This long enumeration shows what rude labors fall on the feeble sex in those savage regions of the African continent.

During this time the men smoke tobacco or hemp, chase the elephant or the buffalo, and hire themselves to the traders for the raids. The harvest of maize or of slaves is always a harvest that takes place in fixed seasons.

Of those various occupations, Mrs. Weldon only saw in Alvez's factory the part laid on the women. Sometimes she stopped, looking at them, while the slaves, it must be said, only replied to her by ugly grimaces. A race instinct led these unfortunates to hate a white woman, and they had no commiseration for her in their hearts. Halima alone was an exception, and Mrs. Weldon, having learned certain words of the native language, was soon able to exchange a few sentences with the young slave.

Little Jack often accompanied his mother when she walked in the inclosure; but he wished very much to go outside. There was, however, in an enormous baobab, marabout nests, formed of a few sticks, and "souimangas" nests, birds with scarlet breasts and throats, which resemble those of the tissirms; then "widows," that strip the thatch for the benefit of their family; "calaos," whose song was agreeable, bright gray parrots with red tails, which, in the Manyema, are called "rouss," and give their name to the chiefs of the tribes; insectivorous "drougos," similar to gray linnets, with large, red beaks. Here and there also fluttered hundreds of butterflies of different species, especially in the neighborhood of the brooks that crossed the factory; but that was rather Cousin Benedict's affair than little Jack's, and the latter regretted greatly not being taller, so as to look over the walls. Alas! where was his poor friend, Dick Sand—he who had brought him so high up in the "Pilgrim's" masts? How he would have followed him on the branches of those trees, whose tops rose to more than a hundred feet! What good times they would have had together!

Cousin Benedict always found himself very well where he was, provided insects were not lacking. Happily, he had discovered in the factory—and he studied as much as he could without magnifying glass or spectacles—a small bee which forms its cells among the worm-holes of the wood, and a "sphex" that lays its eggs in cells that are not its own, as the cuckoo in the nests of other birds. Mosquitoes were not lacking either, on the banks of the rivulets, and they tattooed him with bites to the extent of making him unrecognizable. And when Mrs. Weldon reproached him with letting himself be thus devoured by those venomous insects: "It is their instinct, Cousin Weldon," he replied to her, scratching himself till the blood came; "it is their instinct, and we must not have a grudge against them!"

At last, one day—it was the 17th of June—Cousin Benedict was on the point of being the happiest of entomologists. But this adventure, which had unexpected consequences, needs to be related with some minuteness.

It was about eleven o'clock in the morning. An overpowering heat had obliged the inhabitants of the factory to keep in their huts, and one would not even meet a single native in the streets of Kazounde.

Mrs. Weldon was dozing near little Jack, who was sleeping soundly. Cousin Benedict, himself, suffering from the influence of this tropical temperature, had given up his favorite hunts, which was a great sacrifice for him, for, in those rays of the midday sun, he heard the rustle of a whole world of insects. He was sheltered, then, at the end of his hut, and there, sleep began to take possession of him in this involuntary siesta.

Suddenly, as his eyes half closed, he heard a humming; this is one of those insupportable buzzings of insects, some of which can give fifteen or sixteen thousand beats of their wings in a second.

"A hexapode!" exclaimed Cousin Benedict, awakened at once, and passing from the horizontal to the vertical position.

There was no doubt that it was a hexapode that was buzzing in his hut. But, if Cousin Benedict was very near-sighted, he had at least very acute hearing, so acute even that he could recognize one insect from another by the intensity of its buzz, and it seemed to him that this one was unknown, though it could only be produced by a giant of the species.

"What is this hexapode?" Cousin Benedict asked himself.

Behold him, seeking to perceive the insect, which was very difficult to his eyes without glasses, but trying above all to recognize it by the buzzing of its wings.

His instinct as an entomologist warned him that he had something to accomplish, and that the insect, so providentially entered into his hut, ought not to be the first comer.

Cousin Benedict no longer moved. He listened. A few rays of light reached him. His eyes then discovered a large black point that flew about, but did not pass near enough for him to recognize it. He held his breath, and if he felt himself stung in some part of the face or hands, he was determined not to make a single movement that might put his hexapode to flight. At last the buzzing insect, after turning around him for a long time, came to rest on his head. Cousin Benedict's mouth widened for an instant, as if to give a smile— and what a smile! He felt the light animal running on his hair. An irresistible desire to put his hand there seized him for a moment; but he resisted it, and did well.

"No, no!" thought he, "I would miss it, or what would be worse, I would injure it. Let it come more within my reach. See it walking! It descends. I feel its dear little feet running on my skull! This must be a hexapode of great height. My God! only grant that it may descend on the end of my nose, and there, by squinting a little, I might perhaps see it, and determine to what order, genus, species, or variety it belongs."

So thought Cousin Benedict. But it was a long distance from his skull, which was rather pointed, to the end of his nose, which was very long. How many other roads the capricious insect might take, beside his ears, beside his forehead—roads that would take it to a distance from the savant's eyes— without counting that at any moment it might retake its flight, leave the hut, and lose itself in those solar rays where, doubtless, its life was passed, and in the midst of the buzzing of its congeners that would attract it outside!

Cousin Benedict said all that to himself. Never, in all his life as an entomologist, had he passed more touching minutes. An African hexapode, of a new species, or, at least, of a new variety, or even of a new sub-variety, was there on his head, and he could not recognize it except it deigned to walk at least an inch from his eyes.

However, Cousin Benedict's prayer must be heard. The insect, after having traveled over the half-bald head, as on the summit of some wild bush, began to descend Cousin Benedict's forehead, and the latter might at last conceive the hope that it would venture to the top of his nose. Once arrived at that top, why would it not descend to the base?

"In its place, I—I would descend," thought the worthy savant.

What is truer than that, in Cousin Benedict's place, any other would have struck his forehead violently, so as to crush the enticing insect, or at least to put it to flight. To feel six feet moving on his skin, without speaking of the fear of being bitten, and not make a gesture, one will agree that it was the height of heroism. The Spartan allowing his breast to be devoured by a fox; the Roman holding burning coals between his fingers, were not more masters of themselves than Cousin Benedict, who was undoubtedly descended from those two heroes.

After twenty little circuits, the insect arrived at the top of the nose. Then there was a moment's hesitation that made all Cousin Benedict's blood rush to his heart. Would the hexapode ascend again beyond the line of the eyes, or would it descend below?

It descended. Cousin Benedict felt its caterpillar feet coming toward the base of his nose. The insect turned neither to the right nor to the left. It rested between its two buzzing wings, on the slightly hooked edge of that learned nose, so well formed to carry spectacles. It cleared the little furrow produced by the incessant use of that optical instrument, so much missed by the poor cousin, and it stopped just at the extremity of his nasal appendage.

It was the best place this haxapode could choose. At that distance, Cousin Benedict's two eyes, by making their visual rays converge, could, like two lens, dart their double look on the insect.

"Almighty God!" exclaimed Cousin Benedict, who could not repress a cry, "the tuberculous manticore."

Now, he must not cry it out, he must only think it. But was it not too much to ask from the most enthusiastic of entomologists?

To have on the end of his nose a tuberculous manticore, with large elytrums—an insect of the cicendeletes tribe—a very rare specimen in collections—one that seems peculiar to those southern parts of Africa, and yet not utter a cry of admiration; that is beyond human strength.

Unfortunately the manticore heard this cry, which was almost immediately followed by a sneeze, that shook the appendage on which it rested. Cousin Benedict wished to take possession of it, extended his hand, shut it violently, and only succeeded in seizing the end of his own nose.

"Malediction!" exclaimed he. But then he showed a remarkable coolness.

He knew that the tuberculous manticore only flutters about, so to say, that it walks rather than flies. He then knelt, and succeeded in perceiving, at less than ten inches from his eyes, the black point that was gliding rapidly in a ray of light.

Evidently it was better to study it in this independent attitude. Only he must not lose sight of it.

"To seize the manticore would be to risk crushing it," Cousin Benedict said to himself. "No; I shall follow it! I shall admire it! I have time enough to take it!"

Was Cousin Benedict wrong? However that may be, see him now on all fours, his nose to the ground like a dog that smells a scent, and following seven or eight inches behind the superb hexapode. One moment after he was outside his hut, under the midday sun, and a few minutes later at the foot of the palisade that shut in Alvez's establishment.

At this place was the manticore going to clear the enclosure with a bound, and put a wall between its adorer and itself? No, that was not in its nature, and Cousin Benedict knew it well. So he was always there, crawling like a snake, too far off to recognize the insect entomologically—besides, that was done— but near enough to perceive that large, moving point traveling over the ground.

The manticore, arrived near the palisade, had met the large entrance of a mole-hill that opened at the foot of the enclosure. There, without hesitating, it entered this subterranean gallery, for it is in the habit of seeking those obscure passages. Cousin Benedict believed that he was going to lose sight of it. But, to his great surprise, the passage was at least two feet high, and the mole-hill formed a gallery where his long, thin body could enter. Besides, he put the ardor of a ferret into his pursuit, and did not even perceive that in "earthing" himself thus, he was passing outside the palisade.

In fact, the mole-hill established a natural communication between the inside and the outside. In half a minute Cousin Benedict was outside of the factory. That did not trouble him. He was absorbed in admiration of the elegant insect that was leading him on. But the latter, doubtless, had enough of this long walk. Its elytrums turned aside, its wings spread out. Cousin Benedict felt the danger, and, with his curved hand, he was going to make a provisional prison for the manticore, when—f-r-r-r-r!—it flew away!

What despair! But the manticore could not go far. Cousin Benedict rose; he looked, he darted forward, his two hands stretched out and open. The insect flew above his head, and he only perceived a large black point, without appreciable form to him.

Would the manticore come to the ground again to rest, after having traced a few capricious circles around Cousin Benedict's bald head? All the probabilities were in favor of its doing so.

Unfortunately for the unhappy savant, this part of Alvez's establishment, which was situated at the northern extremity of the town, bordered on a vast forest, which covered the territory of Kazounde for a space of several square miles. If the manticore gained the cover of the trees, and if there, it should flutter from branch to branch, he must renounce all hope of making it figure in that famous tin box, in which it would be the most precious jewel.

Alas! that was what happened. The manticore had rested again on the ground. Cousin Benedict, having the unexpected hope of seeing it again, threw himself on the ground at once. But the manticore no longer walked: it proceeded by little jumps.

Cousin Benedict, exhausted, his knees and hands bleeding, jumped also. His two arms, his hands open, were extended to the right, to the left, according as the black point bounded here or there. It might be said that he was drawing his body over that burning soil, as a swimmer does on the surface of the water.

Useless trouble! His two hands always closed on nothing. The insect escaped him while playing with him, and soon, arrived under the fresh branches, it arose, after throwing into Cousin Benedict's ear, which it touched lightly, the most intense but also the most ironical buzzing of its coleopter wings.

"Malediction!" exclaimed Cousin Benedict, a second time. "It escapes me. Ungrateful hexapode! Thou to whom I reserved a place of honor in my collection! Well, no, I shall not give thee up! I shall follow thee till I reach thee!"

He forgot, this discomfited cousin, that his nearsighted eyes would not enable him to perceive the manticore among the foliage. But he was no longer master of himself. Vexation, anger, made him a fool. It was himself, and only himself, that he must blame for his loss. If he had taken possession of the insect at first, instead of following it "in its independent ways," nothing of all that would have happened, and he would possess that admirable specimen of African manticores, the name of which is that of a fabulous animal, having a man's head and a lion's body.

Cousin Benedict had lost his head. He little thought that the most unforeseen of circumstances had just restored him to liberty. He did not dream that the ant-hill, into which he had just entered, had opened to him an escape, and that he had just left Alvez's establishment. The forest was there, and under the trees was his manticore, flying away! At any price, he wanted to see it again.

See him, then, running across the thick forest, no longer conscious even of what he was doing, always imagining he saw the precious insect, beating the air with his long arms like a gigantic field-spider. Where he was going, how he would return, and if he should return, he did not even ask himself, and for a good mile he made his way thus, at the risk of being met by some native, or attacked by some beast.

Suddenly, as he passed near a thicket, a gigantic being sprang out and threw himself on him. Then, as Cousin Benedict would have done with the manticore, that being seized him with one hand by the nape of the neck, with the other by the lower part of the back, and before he had time to know what was happening, he was carried across the forest.

Truly, Cousin Benedict had that day lost a fine occasion of being able to proclaim himself the happiest entomologist of the five parts of the world.

## CHAPTER XVI.
## A MAGICIAN.

When Mrs. Weldon, on the 17th of the month, did not see Cousin Benedict reappear at the accustomed hour, she was seized with the greatest uneasiness. She could not imagine what had become of her big baby. That he had succeeded in escaping from the factory, the enclosure of which was absolutely impassable, was not admissible. Besides, Mrs. Weldon knew her cousin. Had one proposed to this original to flee, abandoning his tin box and his collection of African insects, he would have refused without the shadow of hesitation. Now, the box was there in the hut, intact, containing all that the savant had been able to collect since his arrival on the continent. To suppose that he was voluntarily separated from his entomological treasures, was inadmissible.

Nevertheless, Cousin Benedict was no longer in Jose-Antonio Alvez's establishment.

During all that day Mrs. Weldon looked for him persistently. Little

Jack and the slave Halima joined her. It was useless.

Mrs. Weldon was then forced to adopt this sad hypothesis: the prisoner had been carried away by the trader's orders, for motives that she could not fathom. But then, what had Alvez done with him? Had he incarcerated him in one of the barracks of the large square? Why this carrying away, coming after the agreement made between Mrs. Weldon and Negoro, an agreement which included Cousin Benedict in the number of the prisoners whom the trader would conduct to Mossamedes, to be placed in James W. Weldon's hands for a ransom?

If Mrs. Weldon had been a witness of Alvez's anger, when the latter learned of the prisoner's disappearance, she would have understood that this disappearance was indeed made against his will. But then, if Cousin Benedict had escaped voluntarily, why had he not let her into the secret of his escape?

However, the search of Alvez and his servants, which was made with the greatest care, led to the discovery of that mole-hill, which put the factory in direct communication with the neighboring forest. The trader no longer doubted that the "fly-hunter" had fled by that narrow opening. One may then judge of his fury, when he said to himself that this flight would doubtless be put to account, and would diminish the prize that the affair would bring him.

"That imbecile is not worth much," thought he, "nevertheless, I shall be compelled to pay dear for him. Ah! if I take him again!"

But notwithstanding the searchings that were made inside, and though the woods were beaten over a large radius, it was impossible to find any trace of the fugitive.

Mrs. Weldon must resign herself to the loss of her cousin, and Alvez mourn over his prisoner. As it could not be admitted that the latter had established communications with the outside, it appeared evident that chance alone had made him discover the existence of the mole-hill, and that he had taken flight without thinking any more of those he left behind than if they had never existed.

Mrs. Weldon was forced to allow that it must be so, but she did not dream of blaming the poor man, so perfectly unconscious of his actions.

"The unfortunate! what will become of him?" she asked herself.

It is needless to say that the mole-hill had been closed up the same day, and with the greatest care, and that the watch was doubled inside as well as outside the factory.

The monotonous life of the prisoners then continued for Mrs. Weldon and her child.

Meanwhile, a climatic fact, very rare at that period of the year, was produced in the province. Persistent rains began about the 19th of June, though the masika period, that finishes in April, was passed. In fact, the sky was covered, and continual showers inundated the territory of Kazounde.

What was only a vexation for Mrs. Weldon, because she must renounce her walks inside the factory, became a public misfortune for the natives. The low lands, covered with harvests already ripe, were entirely submerged. The inhabitants of the province, to whom the crop suddenly failed, soon found themselves in distress. All the labors of the season were compromised, and Queen Moini, any more than her ministers, did not know how to face the catastrophe.

They then had recourse to the magicians, but not to those whose profession is to heal the sick by their incantations and sorceries, or who predict success to the natives. There was a public misfortune on hand, and the best "mganngas," who have the privilege of provoking or stopping the rains, were prayed to, to conjure away the peril.

Their labor was in vain. It was in vain that they intoned their monotonous chant, rang their little bells and hand-bells, employed their most precious amulets, and more particularly, a horn full of mud and bark, the point of which was terminated by three little horns. The spirits were exorcised by throwing little balls of dung, or in spitting in the faces of the most august personages of the court; but they did not succeed in chasing away the bad spirits that presided over the formation of the clouds.

Now, things were going from bad to worse, when Queen Moini thought of inviting a celebrated magician, then in the north of Angola. He was a magician of the first order, whose power was the more marvelous because they had never tested it in this country where he had never come. But there was no question of its success among the Masikas.

It was on the 25th of June, in the morning, that the new magician suddenly announced his arrival at Kazounde with great ringing of bells.

This sorcerer came straight to the "tchitoka," and immediately the crowd of natives rushed toward him. The sky was a little less rainy, the wind indicated a tendency to change, and those signs of calm, coinciding with the arrival of the magician, predisposed the minds of the natives in his favor.

Besides, he was a superb man—a black of the finest water. He was at least six feet high, and must be extraordinarily strong. This prestige already influenced the crowd.

Generally, the sorcerers were in bands of three, four, or five when they went through the villages, and a certain number of acolytes, or companions, made their cortege. This magician was alone. His whole breast was zebraed with white marks, done with pipe clay. The lower part of his body disappeared under an ample skirt of grass stuff, the "train" of which would not have disgraced a modern elegant. A collar of birds' skulls was round his neck; on his head was a sort of leathern helmet, with plumes ornamented with pearls; around his loins a copper belt, to which hung several hundred bells, noisier than the sonorous harness of a Spanish mule: thus this magnificent specimen of the corporation of native wizards was dressed.

All the material of his art was comprised in a kind of basket, of which a calebash formed the bottom, and which was filled with shells, amulets, little wooden idols, and other fetiches, plus a notable quantity of dung balls, important accessories to the incantations and divinatory practises of the center of Africa.

One peculiarity was soon discovered by the crowd. This magician was dumb. But this infirmity could only increase the consideration with which they were disposed to surround him. He only made a guttural sound, low and languid, which had no signification. The more reason for being well skilled in the mysteries of witchcraft.

The magician first made the tour of the great place, executing a kind of dance which put in motion all his chime of bells. The crowd followed, imitating his movements—it might be said, as a troop of monkeys following a gigantic, four-handed animal. Then, suddenly, the sorcerer, treading the principal street of Kazounde, went toward the royal residence.

As soon as Queen Moini had been informed of the arrival of the new wizard, she appeared, followed by her courtiers.

The magician bowed to the ground, and lifted up his head again, showing his superb height. His arms were then extended toward the sky, which was rapidly furrowed by masses of clouds. The sorcerer pointed to those clouds with his hand; he imitated their movements in an animated pantomime. He showed them fleeing to the west, but returning to the east by a rotary movement that no power could stop.

Then, suddenly, to the great surprise of the town and the court, this sorcerer took the redoubtable sovereign of Kazounde by the hand. A few courtiers wished to oppose this act, which was contrary to all etiquette; but the strong magician, seizing the nearest by the nape of the neck, sent him staggering fifteen paces off.

The queen did not appear to disapprove of this proud manner of acting. A sort of grimace, which ought to be a smile, was addressed to the wizard, who drew the queen on with rapid steps, while the crowd rushed after him.

This time it was toward Alvez's establishment that the sorcerer directed his steps. He soon reached the door, which was shut. A simple blow from his shoulder threw it to the ground, and he led the conquered queen into the interior of the factory.

The trader, his soldiers and his slaves, ran to punish the daring being who took it upon himself to throw down doors without waiting for them to be opened to him. Suddenly, seeing that their sovereign did not protest, they stood still, in a respectful attitude.

No doubt Alvez was about to ask the queen why he was honored by her visit, but the magician did not give him time. Making the crowd recede so as to leave a large space free around him, he recommenced his pantomime with still greater animation. He pointed to the clouds, he threatened them, he exorcised them; he made a sign as if he could first stop them, and then scatter them. His enormous cheeks were puffed out, and he blew on this mass of heavy vapors as if he had the strength to disperse them. Then, standing upright, he seemed to intend stopping them in their course, and one would have said that, owing to his gigantic height, he could have seized them.

The superstitious Moini, "overcome" by the acting of this tall comedian, could no longer control herself. Cries escaped her. She raved in her turn, and instinctively repeated the magician's gestures. The courtiers and the crowd followed her example, and the mute's guttural sounds were lost amid those songs; cries, and yells which the native language furnishes with so much prodigality.

Did the clouds cease to rise on the eastern horizon and veil the tropical sun? Did they vanish before the exorcisms of this new wizard? No. And just at this moment, when the queen and her people imagined that they had appeased the evil spirits that had watered them with so many showers, the sky, somewhat clear since daybreak, became darker than ever. Large drops of rain fell pattering on the ground.

Then a sudden change took place in the crowd. They then saw that this sorcerer was worth no more than the others. The queen's brows were frowning. They understood that he at least was in danger of losing his ears. The natives had contracted the circle around him; fists threatened him, and they were about to punish him, when an unforeseen incident changed the object of their evil intentions.

The magician, who overlooked the whole yelling crowd, stretched his arms toward one spot in the enclosure. The gesture was so imperious that all turned to look at it.

Mrs. Weldon and little Jack, attracted by the noise and the clamor, had just left their hut. The magician, with an angry gesture, had pointed to them with his left hand, while his right was raised toward the sky.

They! it was they'! It was this white woman—it was her child—they were causing all this evil. They had brought these clouds from their rainy country, to inundate the territories of Kazounde.

It was at once understood. Queen Moini, pointing to Mrs. Weldon, made a threatening gesture. The natives, uttering still more terrible cries, rushed toward her.

Mrs. Weldon thought herself lost, and clasping her son in her arms, she stood motionless as a statue before this over-excited crowd.

The magician went toward her. The natives stood aside in the presence of this wizard, who, with the cause of the evil, seemed to have found the remedy.

The trader, Alvez, knowing that the life of the prisoner was precious, now approached, not being sure of what he ought to do.

The magician had seized little Jack, and snatching him from his mother's arms, he held him toward the sky. It seemed as if he were about to dash the child to the earth, so as to appease the gods.

With a terrible cry, Mrs. Weldon fell to the ground insensible.

But the magician, after having made a sign to the queen, which no doubt reassured her as to his intentions, raised the unhappy mother, and while the crowd, completely subdued, parted to give him space, he carried her away with her child.

Alvez was furious, not expecting this result. After having lost one of the three prisoners, to see the prize confided to his care thus escape, and, with the prize, the large bribe promised him by Negoro! Never! not if the whole territory of Kazounde were submerged by a new deluge! He tried to oppose this abduction.

The natives now began to mutter against him. The queen had him seized by her guards, and, knowing what it might cost him, the trader was forced to keep quiet, while cursing the stupid credulity of Queen Moini's subjects.

The savages, in fact, expected to see the clouds disappear with those who had brought them, and they did not doubt that the magician would destroy the scourge, from which they suffered so much, in the blood of the strangers.

Meanwhile, the magician carried off his victims as a lion would a couple of kids which did not satisfy his powerful appetite. Little Jack was terrified, his mother was unconscious. The crowd, roused to the highest degree of fury, escorted the magician with yells; but he left the enclosure, crossed Kazounde, and reentered the forest, walking nearly three miles, without resting for a moment. Finally he was alone, the natives having understood that he did not wish to be followed. He arrived at the bank of a river, whose rapid current flowed toward the north.

There, at the end of a large opening, behind the long, drooping branches of a thicket which hid the steep bank, was moored a canoe, covered by a sort of thatch.

The magician lowered his double burden into the boat, and following himself, shoved out from the bank, and the current rapidly carried them down the stream. The next minute he said, in a very distinct voice:

"Captain, here are Mrs. Weldon and little Jack; I present them to you.

Forward. And may all the clouds in heaven fall on those idiots of

Kazounde!"

## CHAPTER XVII.

## DRIFTING.

It was Hercules, not easily recognized in his magician's attire, who was speaking thus, and it was Dick Sand whom he was addressing—Dick Sand, still feeble enough, to lean on Cousin Benedict, near whom Dingo was lying.

Mrs. Weldon, who had regained consciousness, could only pronounce these words:

"You! Dick! You!"

The young novice rose, but already Mrs. Weldon was pressing him in her arms, and Jack was lavishing caresses on him.

"My friend Dick! my friend Dick!" repeated the little boy. Then, turning to Hercules: "And I," he added, "I did not know you!"

"Hey! what a disguise!" replied Hercules, rubbing his breast to efface the variety of colors that striped it.

"You were too ugly!" said little Jack.

"Bless me! I was the devil, and the devil is not handsome."

"Hercules!" said Mrs. Weldon, holding out her hand to the brave black.

"He has delivered you," added Dick Sand, "as he has saved me, though he will not allow it."

"Saved! saved! We are not saved yet!" replied Hercules. "And besides, without Mr. Benedict, who came to tell us where you were, Mrs. Weldon, we could not have done anything."

In fact, it was Hercules who, five days before, had jumped upon the savant at the moment when, having been led two miles from the factory, the latter was running in pursuit of his precious manticore. Without this incident, neither Dick Sand nor the black would have known Mrs. Weldon's retreat, and Hercules would not have ventured to Kazounde in a magician's dress.

While the boat drifted with rapidity in this narrow part of the river, Hercules related what had passed since his flight from the camp on the Coanza; how, without being seen, he had followed the kitanda in which Mrs. Weldon and her son were; how he had found Dingo wounded; how the two had arrived in the neighborhood of Kazounde; how a note from Hercules, carried by the dog, told Dick Sand what had become of Mrs. Weldon; how, after the unexpected arrival of Cousin Benedict, he had vainly tried to make his way into the factory, more carefully guarded than ever; how, at last, he had found this opportunity of snatching the prisoner from that horrible Jose-Antonio Alvez. Now, this opportunity had offered itself that same day. A mgannga, or magician, on his witchcraft circuit, that celebrated magician so impatiently expected, was passing through the forest in which Hercules roamed every night, watching, waiting, ready for anything.

To spring upon the magician, despoil him of his baggage, and of his magician's vestments, to fasten him to the foot of a tree with liane knots that the Davenports themselves could not have untied, to paint his body, taking the sorcerer's for a model, and to act out his character in charming and controlling the rains, had been the work of several hours. Still, the incredible credulity of the natives was necessary for his success.

During this recital, given rapidly by Hercules, nothing concerning

Dick Sand had been mentioned.

"And you, Dick!" asked Mrs. Weldon.

"I, Mrs. Weldon!" replied the young man. "I can tell you nothing. My last thought was for you, for Jack! I tried in vain to break the cords that fastened me to the stake. The water rose over my head. I lost consciousness. When I came to myself, I was sheltered in a hole, concealed by the papyrus of this bank, and Hercules was on his knees beside me, lavishing his care upon me."

"Well! that is because I am a physician," replied Hercules; "a diviner, a sorcerer, a magician, a fortuneteller!"

"Hercules," said Mrs. Weldon, "tell me, how did you save Dick Sand?"

"Did I do it, Mrs. Weldon?" replied Hercules; "Might not the current have broken the stake to which our captain was tied, and in the middle of the night, carried him half-dead on this beam, to the place where I received him? Besides, in the darkness, there was no difficulty in gliding among the victims that carpeted the ditch, waiting for the bursting of the dam, diving under water, and, with a little strength, pulling up our captain and the stake to which these scoundrels had bound him! There was nothing very extraordinary in all that! The first-comer could have done as much. Mr. Benedict himself, or even Dingo! In fact, might it not have been Dingo?"

A yelping was heard; and Jack, taking hold of the dog's large head, gave him several little friendly taps.

"Dingo," he asked, "did you save our friend Dick?"

At the same time he turned the dog's head from right to left.

"He says, no, Hercules!" said Jack. "You see that it was not he.

Dingo, did Hercules save our captain?"

The little boy forced Dingo's good head to move up and down, five or six times.

"He says, yes, Hercules! he says, yes!" cried little Jack. "You see then that it was you!"

"Friend Dingo," replied Hercules, caressing the dog, "that is wrong.

You promised me not to betray me."

Yes, it was indeed Hercules, who had risked his life to save Dick Sand. But he had done it, and his modesty would not allow him to agree to the fact. Besides, he thought it a very simple thing, and he repeated that any one of his companions would have done the same under the circumstances.

This led Mrs. Weldon to speak of old Tom, of his son, of Acteon and

Bat, his unfortunate companions.

They had started for the lake region. Hercules had seen them pass with the caravan of slaves. He had followed them, but no opportunity to communicate with them had presented itself. They were gone! they were lost!

Hercules had been laughing heartily, but now he shed tears which he did not try to restrain.

"Do not cry, my friend," Mrs. Weldon said to him. "God may be merciful, and allow us to meet them again."

In a few words she informed Dick Sand of all that had happened during her stay in Alvez's factory.

"Perhaps," she added, "it would have been better to have remained at

Kazounde."

"What a fool I was!" cried Hercules.

"No, Hercules, no!" said Dick Sand. "These wretches would have found means to draw Mr. Weldon into some new trap. Let us flee together, and without delay. We shall reach the coast before Negoro can return to Mossamedes. There, the Portuguese authorities will give us aid and protection; and when Alvez comes to take his one hundred thousand dollars—"

"A hundred thousand blows on the old scoundrel's skull!" cried

Hercules; "and I will undertake to keep the count."

However, here was a new complication, although it was very evident that Mrs. Weldon would not dream of returning to Kazounde. The point now was to anticipate Negoro. All Dick Sand's projects must tend toward that end.

Dick Sand was now putting in practise the plan which he had long contemplated, of gaining the coast by utilizing the current of a river or a stream. Now, the watercourse was there; its direction was northward, and it was possible that it emptied into the Zaire. In that case, instead of reaching St. Paul de Loanda, it would be at the mouth of the great river that Mrs. Weldon and her companions would arrive. This was not important, because help would not fail them in the colonies of Lower Guinea.

Having decided to descend the current of this river, Dick Sand's first idea was to embark on one of the herbaceous rafts, a kind of floating isle (of which Cameron has often spoken), which drifts in large numbers on the surface of African rivers.

But Hercules, while roaming at night on the bank, had been fortunate enough to find a drifting boat. Dick Sand could not hope for anything better, and chance had served him kindly. In fact, it was not one of those narrow boats which the natives generally use.

The perogue found by Hercules was one of those whose length exceeds thirty feet, and the width four—and they are carried rapidly on the waters of the great lakes by the aid of numerous paddles. Mrs. Weldon and her companions could install themselves comfortably in it, and it was sufficient to keep it in the stream by means of an oar to descend the current of the river.

At first, Dick Sand, wishing to pass unseen, had formed a project to travel only at night. But to drift twelve hours out of the twenty-four, was to double the length of a journey which might be quite long. Happily, Dick Sand had taken a fancy to cover the perogue with a roof of long grasses, sustained on a rod, which projected fore and aft. This, when on the water, concealed even the long oar. One would have said that it was a pile of herbs which drifted down stream, in the midst of floating islets. Such was the ingenious arrangement of the thatch, that the birds were deceived, and, seeing there some grains to pilfer, red-beaked gulls, "arrhinisgas" of black plumage, and gray and white halcyons frequently came to rest upon it.

Besides, this green roof formed a shelter from the heat of the sun. A voyage made under these conditions might then be accomplished almost without fatigue, but not without danger.

In fact, the journey would be a long one, and it would be necessary to procure food each day. Hence the risk of hunting on the banks if fishing would not suffice, and Dick Sand had no firearms but the gun carried off by Hercules after the attack on the ant-hill; but he counted on every shot. Perhaps even by passing his gun through the thatch of the boat he might fire with surety, like a butter through the holes in his hut.

Meanwhile, the perogue drifted with the force of the current a distance not less than two miles an hour, as near as Dick Sand could estimate it.

He hoped to make, thus, fifty miles a day. But, on account of this very rapidity of the current, continual care was necessary to avoid obstacles—rocks, trunks of trees, and the high bottoms of the river. Besides, it was to be feared that this current would change to rapids, or to cataracts, a frequent occurrence on the rivers of Africa.

The joy of seeing Mrs. Weldon and her child had restored all Dick Sand's strength, and he had posted himself in the fore-part of the boat. Across the long grasses, his glance observed the downward course, and, either by voice or gesture, he indicated to Hercules, whose vigorous hands held the oar, what was necessary so as to keep in the right direction.

Mrs. Weldon reclined on a bed of dry leaves in the center of the boat, and grew absorbed in her own thoughts. Cousin Benedict was taciturn, frowning at the sight of Hercules, whom he had not forgiven for his intervention in the affair of the manticore. He dreamed of his lost collection, of his entomological notes, the value of which would not be appreciated by the natives of Kazounde. So he sat, his limbs stretched out, and his arms crossed on his breast, and at times he instinctively made a gesture of raising to his forehead the glasses which his nose did not support. As for little Jack, he understood that he must not make a noise; but, as motion was not forbidden, he imitated his friend Dingo, and ran on his hands and feet from one end of the boat to the other.

During the first two days Mrs. Weldon and her companions used the food that Hercules had been able to obtain before they started. Dick Sand only stopped for a few hours in the night, so as to gain rest. But he did not leave the boat, not wishing to do it except when obliged by the necessity of renewing their provisions.

No incident marked the beginning of the voyage on this unknown river, which measured, at least, more than a hundred and fifty feet in width. Several islets drifted on the surface, and moved with the same rapidity as the boat. So there was no danger of running upon them, unless some obstacle stopped them.

The banks, besides, seemed to be deserted. Evidently these portions of the territory of Kazounde were little frequented by the natives.

Numerous wild plants covered the banks, and relieved them with a profusion of the most brilliant colors. Swallow-wort, iris, lilies, clematis, balsams, umbrella-shaped flowers, aloes, tree-ferns, and spicy shrubs formed a border of incomparable brilliancy. Several forests came to bathe their borders in these rapid waters. Copal-trees, acacias, "bauhinias" of iron-wood, the trunks covered with a dross of lichens on the side exposed to the coldest winds, fig-trees which rose above roots arranged in rows like mangroves, and other trees of magnificent growth, overhung the river. Their high tops, joining a hundred feet above, formed a bower which the solar rays could not penetrate. Often, also, a bridge of lianes was thrown from one bank to the other, and during the 27th little Jack, to his intense admiration, saw a band of monkeys cross one of these vegetable passes, holding each other's tail, lest the bridge should break under their weight.

These monkeys are a kind of small chimpanzee, which in Central Africa has received the name of "sokos." They have low foreheads, clear yellow faces, and high-set ears, and are very ugly examples of the simiesque race. They live in bands of a dozen, bark like dogs, and are feared by the natives, whose children they often carry off to scratch or bite.

In passing the liane bridge they never suspected that, beneath that mass of herbs which the current bore onward, there was a little boy who would have exactly served to amuse them. The preparations, designed by Dick Sand, were very well conceived, because these clear-sighted beasts were deceived by them.

Twenty miles farther on, that same day, the boat was suddenly stopped in its progress.

"What is the matter?" asked Hercules, always posted at his oar.

"A barrier," replied Dick Sand; "but a natural barrier."

"It must be broken, Mr. Dick."

"Yes, Hercules, and with a hatchet. Several islets have drifted upon it, and it is quite strong."

"To work, captain! to work!" replied Hercules, who came and stood in the fore-part of the perogue.

This barricade was formed by the interlacing of a sticky plant with glossy leaves, which twists as it is pressed together, and becomes very resisting. They call it "tikatika," and it will allow people to cross watercourses dry-shod, if they are not afraid to plunge twelve inches into its green apron. Magnificent ramifications of the lotus covered the surface of this barrier.

It was already dark. Hercules could, without imprudence, quit the boat, and he managed his hatchet so skilfully that two hours afterward the barrier had given way, the current turned up the broken pieces on the banks, and the boat again took the channel.

Must it be confessed! That great child of a Cousin Benedict had hoped for a moment that they would not be able to pass. Such a voyage seemed to him unnecessary. He regretted Alvez's factory and the hut that contained his precious entomologist's box. His chagrin was real, and indeed it was pitiful to see the poor man. Not an insect; no, not one to preserve!

What, then, was his joy when Hercules, "his pupil" after all, brought him a horrible little beast which he had found on a sprig of the tikatika. Singularly enough the brave black seemed a little confused in presenting it to him.

But what exclamations Cousin Benedict uttered when he had brought this insect, which he held between his index finger and his thumb, as near as possible to his short-sighted eyes, which neither glasses nor microscope could now assist.

"Hercules!" he cried, "Hercules! Ah! see what will gain your pardon! Cousin Weldon! Dick! a hexapode, unique in its species, and of African origin! This, at least, they will not dispute with me, and it shall quit me only with my life!"

"It is, then, very precious?" asked Mrs. Weldon.

"Precious!" cried Cousin Benedict. "An insect which is neither a coleopter, nor a neuropteran, nor a hymenopter; which does not belong to any of the ten orders recognized by savants, and which they will be rather tempted to rank in the second section of the arachnides. A sort of spider, which would be a spider if it had eight legs, and is, however, a hexapode, because it has but six. Ah! my friends, Heaven owed me this joy; and at length I shall give my name to a scientific discovery! That insect shall be the 'Hexapodes Benedictus.'"

The enthusiastic savant was so happy—he forgot so many miseries past and to come in riding his favorite hobby—that neither Mrs. Weldon nor Dick Sand grudged him his felicitations.

All this time the perogue moved on the dark waters of the river. The silence of night was only disturbed by the clattering scales of the crocodiles, or the snorting of the hippopotami that sported on the banks.

Then, through the sprigs of the thatch, the moon appeared behind the tops of the trees, throwing its soft light to the interior of the boat.

Suddenly, on the right bank, was heard a distant hubbub, then a dull noise as if giant pumps were working in the dark.

It was several hundred elephants, that, satiated by the woody roots which they had devoured during the day, came to quench their thirst before the hour of repose. One would really have supposed that all these trunks, lowered and raised by the same automatic movement, would have drained the river dry.

## CHAPTER XVIII.

## VARIOUS INCIDENTS.

For eight days the boat drifted, carried by the current under the conditions already described. No incident of any importance occurred. For a space of many miles the river bathed the borders of superb forests; then the country, shorn of these fine trees, spread in jungles to the limits of the horizon.

If there were no natives in this country—a fact which Dick Sand did not dream of regretting—the animals at least abounded there. Zebras sported on the banks, elks, and "caamas," a species of antelope which were extremely graceful, and they disappeared at night to give place to the leopards, whose growls could be heard, and even to the lions which bounded in the tall grasses. Thus far the fugitives had not suffered from these ferocious creatures, whether in the forests or in the river.

Meanwhile, each day, generally in the afternoon, Dick Sand neared one bank or the other, moored the boat, disembarked, and explored the shore for a short distance.

In fact, it was necessary to renew their daily food. Now, in this country, barren of all cultivation, they could not depend upon the tapioca, the sorgho, the maize, and the fruits, which formed the vegetable food of the native tribes. These plants only grew in a wild state, and were not eatable. Dick Sand was thus forced to hunt, although the firing of his gun might bring about an unpleasant meeting.

They made a fire by rubbing a little stick against a piece of the wild fig-tree, native fashion, or even simiesque style, for it is affirmed that certain of the gorillas procure a fire by this means. Then, for several days, they cooked a little elk or antelope flesh. During the 4th of July Dick Sand succeeded in killing, with a single ball, a "pokou," which gave them a good supply of venison. This animal, was five feet long; it had long horns provided with rings, a yellowish red skin, dotted with brilliant spots, and white on the stomach; and the flesh was found to be excellent.

It followed then, taking into account these almost daily landings and the hours of repose that were necessary at night, that the distance on the 8th of July could hot be estimated as more than one hundred miles. This was considerable, however, and already Dick Sand asked himself where this interminable river ended. Its course absorbed some small tributaries and did not sensibly enlarge. As for the general direction, after having been north for a long time, it took a bend toward the northwest.

However, this river furnished its share of food. Long lianes, armed with thorns, which served as fishhooks, caught several of those delicately-flavored "sandjikas", which, once smoked, are easily carried in this region; black "usakas" were also caught, and some "mormdes," with large heads, the genciva of which have teeth like the hairs of a brush, and some little "dagalas," the friends of running waters, belonging to the clupe species, and resembling the whitebait of the Thames.

During the 9th of July, Dick Sand had to give proof of extreme coolness. He was alone on the shore, carrying off a "caama," the horns of which showed above the thicket. He had just shot it, and now there bounded, thirty feet off, a formidable hunter, that no doubt came to claim its prey, and was not in a humor to give it up. It was a lion of great height, one of those which the natives call "karamos," and not one of the kind without a mane, named "lion of the Nyassi." This one measured five feet in height—a formidable beast. With one bound the lion had fallen on the "caama," which Dick Sand's ball had just thrown to the ground, and, still full of life, it shook and cried under the paw of the powerful animal.

Dick Sand was disarmed, not having had time to slide a second cartridge into his gun.

Dick Sand, in front, lowering his voice, gave directions to avoid striking against these rotten constructions. The night was clear. They saw well to direct the boat, but they could also be seen.

Then came a terrible moment. Two natives, who talked in loud tones, were squatting close to the water on the piles, between which the current carried the boat, and the direction could not be changed for a narrower pass. Now, would they not see it, and at their cries might not the whole village be alarmed?

A space of a hundred feet at most remained to be passed, when Dick Sand heard the two natives call more quickly to each other. One showed the other the mass of drifting herbs, which threatened to break the long liane ropes which they were occupied in stretching at that moment.

Rising hastily, they called out for help. Five or six other blacks ran at once along the piles and posted themselves on the cross-beams which supported them, uttering loud exclamations which the listeners could not understand.

In the boat, on the contrary, was absolute silence, except for the few orders given by Dick Sand in a low voice, and complete repose, except the movement of Hercules's right arm moving the oar; at times a low growl from Dingo, whose jaws Jack held together with his little hands; outside, the murmur of the water which broke against the piles, then above, the cries of the ferocious cannibals.

The natives, meanwhile, rapidly drew up their ropes. If they were raised in time the boat would pass, otherwise it would be caught, and all would be over with those who drifted in it! As for slackening or stopping its progress, Dick Sand could do neither, for the current, stronger under this narrow construction, carried it forward more rapidly.

In half a minute the boat was caught between the piles. By an unheard-of piece of fortune, the last effort made by the natives had raised the ropes.

But in passing, as Dick Sand had feared, the boat was deprived of a part of the grasses which now floated at its right.

One of the natives uttered a cry. Had he had time to recognize what the roof covered, and was he going to alarm his comrades? It was more than probable.

Dick Sand and his friends were already out of reach, and in a few moments, under the impetus of this current, now changed into a kind of rapid, they had lost sight of the lacustrine village.

"To the left bank!" Dick Sand ordered, as being more prudent. "The stream is again navigable."

"To the left bank!" replied Hercules, giving the oar a vigorous stroke.

Dick Sand stood beside him and looked at the surface of the water, which the moon lit up. He saw nothing suspicious. Not a boat had started in pursuit. Perhaps these savages had none; and at daybreak not a native appeared, either on the bank or on the water. After that, increasing their precautions, the boat kept close to the left bank.

During the four following days, from the 11th to the 14th of July, Mrs. Weldon and her companions remarked that this portion of the territory had decidedly changed. It was no longer a deserted country; it was also a desert, and they might have compared it to that Kalahari explored by Livingstone on his first voyage.

The arid soil recalled nothing of the fertile fields of the upper country.

And always this interminable stream, to which might be given the name of river, as it seemed that it could only end at the Atlantic Ocean.

The question of food, in this desert country, became a problem. Nothing remained of their former stock. Fishing gave little; hunting was no longer of any use. Elks, antelopes, pokous, and other animals, could find nothing to live on in this desert, and with them had also disappeared the carnivorous animals.

The nights no longer echoed the accustomed roarings. Nothing broke the silence but the concert of frogs, which Cameron compares with the noise of calkers calking a ship; with riveters who rivet, and the drillers who drill, in a shipbuilder's yard.

The country on the two banks was flat and destitute of trees as far as the most distant hills that bounded it on the east and west. The spurges grew alone and in profusion—not the euphosbium which produces cassava or tapioca flour, but those from which they draw an oil which does not serve as food.

Meantime it is necessary to provide some nourishment.

Dick Sand knew not what to do, and Hercules reminded him that the natives often eat the young shoots of the ferns and the pith which the papyrus leaf contains. He himself, while following the caravan of Ibn Ilamis across the desert, had been more than once reduced to this expedient to satisfy his hunger. Happily, the ferns and the papyrus grew in profusion along the banks, and the marrow or pith, which has a sweet flavor, was appreciated by all, particularly by little Jack.

This was not a very cheering prospect; the food was not strengthening, but the next day, thanks to Cousin Benedict, they were better served. Since the discovery of the "Hexapodus Benedictus," which was to immortalize his name, Cousin Benedict had recovered his usual manners. The insect was put in a safe place, that is to say, stuck in the crown of his hat, and the savant had recommenced his search whenever they were on shore. During that day, while hunting in the high grass, he started a bird whose warbling attracted him.

Dick Sand was going to shoot it, when Cousin Benedict cried out:

"Don't fire, Dick! Don't fire! A bird among five persons would not be enough."

"It will be enough for Jack," replied Dick Sand, taking aim at the bird, which was in no hurry to fly away.

"No, no!" said Cousin Benedict, "do not fire! It is an indicator, and it will bring us honey in abundance."

Dick Sand lowered his gun, realizing that a few pounds of honey were worth more than one bird; and Cousin Benedict and he followed the bird, which rose and flew away, inviting them to go with it.

They had not far to go, and a few minutes after, some old trunks, hidden in between the spurges, appeared in the midst of an intense buzzing of bees.

Cousin Benedict would have preferred not to have robbed these industrious hymenopters of the "fruit of their labors," as he expressed it. But Dick Sand did not understand it in that way. He smoked out the bees with some dry herbs and obtained a considerable quantity of honey. Then leaving to the indicator the cakes of wax, which made its share of the profit, Cousin Benedict and he returned to the boat.

The honey was well received, but it was but little, and, in fact, all would have suffered cruelly from hunger, if, during the day of the 12th, the boat had not stopped near a creek where some locusts swarmed. They covered the ground and the shrubs in myriads, two or three deep. Now, Cousin Benedict not failing to say that the natives frequently eat these orthopters—which was perfectly true—they took possession of this manna. There was enough to fill the boat ten times, and broiled over a mild fire, these edible locusts would have seemed excellent even to less famished people. Cousin Benedict, for his part, eat a notable quantity of them, sighing, it is true—still, he eat them.

Nevertheless, it was time for this long series of moral and physical trials to come to an end. Although drifting on this rapid river was not so fatiguing as had been the walking through the first forests near the coast, still, the excessive heat of the day, the damp mists at night, and the incessant attacks of the mosquitoes, made this descent of the watercourse very painful. It was time to arrive somewhere, and yet Dick Sand could see no limit to the journey. Would it last eight days or a month? Nothing indicated an answer. Had the river flowed directly to the west, they would have already reached the northern coast of Angola; but the general direction had been rather to the north, and they could travel thus a long time before reaching the coast.

Dick Sand was, therefore, extremely anxious, when a sudden change of direction took place on the morning of the 14th of July.

Little Jack was in the front of the boat, and he was gazing through the thatch, when a large expanse of water appeared on the horizon.

"The sea!" he shouted.

At this word Dick Sand trembled, and came close to little Jack.

"The sea?" he replied. "No, not yet; but at least a river which flows toward the west, and of which this stream is only a tributary. Perhaps it is the Zaire itself."

"May God grant that is!" replied Mrs. Weldon.

Yes; for if this were the Zaire or Congo, which Stanley was to discover a few years later, they had only to descend its course so as to reach the Portuguese settlements at its mouth. Dick Sand hoped that it might be so, and he was inclined to believe it.

During the 15th, 16th, 17th and 18th of July, in the midst of a more fertile country, the boat drifted on the silvery waters of the river. They still took the same precautions, and it was always a mass of herbs that the current seemed to carry on its surface.

A few days more, and no doubt the survivors of the "Pilgrim" would see the termination of their miseries. Self-sacrifice had been shared in by all, and if the young novice would not claim the greater part of it, Mrs. Weldon would demand its recognition for him.

But on the 18th of July, during the night, an incident took place which compromised the safety of the party. Toward three o'clock in the morning a distant noise, still very low, was heard in the west. Dick Sand, very anxious, wished to know what caused it. While Mrs. Weldon, Jack, and Cousin Benedict slept in the bottom of the boat, he called Hercules to the front, and told him to listen with the greatest attention. The night was calm. Not a breeze stirred the atmosphere.

"It is the noise of the sea," said Hercules, whose eyes shone with joy.

"No," replied Dick Sand, holding down his head.

"What is it then?" asked Hercules.

"Wait until day; but we must watch with the greatest care."

At this answer, Hercules returned to his post.

Dick Sand stood in front, listening all the time. The noise increased.

It was soon like distant roaring.

Day broke almost without dawn. About half a mile down the river, just above the water, a sort of cloud floated in the atmosphere. But it was not a mass of vapor, and this became only too evident, when, under the first solar rays, which broke in piercing it, a beautiful rainbow spread from one bank to the other.

"To the shore!" cried Dick Sand, whose voice awoke Mrs. Weldon. "It is a cataract! Those clouds are spray! To the shore, Hercules!"

Dick Sand was not mistaken. Before them, the bed of the river broke in a descent of more than a hundred feet, and the waters rushed down with superb but irresistible impetuosity. Another half mile, and the boat would have been engulfed in the abyss.

## CHAPTER XIX.

## S. V.

With a vigorous plow of the oar, Hercules had pushed toward the left bank. Besides, the current was not more rapid in that place, and the bed of the river kept its normal declivity to the falls. As has been said, it was the sudden sinking of the ground, and the attraction was only felt three or four hundred feet above the cataract.

On the left bank were large and very thick trees. No light penetrated their impenetrable curtain. It was not without terror that Dick Sand looked at this territory, inhabited by the cannibals of the Lower Congo, which he must now cross, because the boat could no longer follow the stream. He could not dream of carrying it below the falls. It was a terrible blow for these poor people, on the eve perhaps of reaching the Portuguese villages at its mouth. They were well aided, however. Would not Heaven come to their assistance?

The boat soon reached the left bank of the river. As it drew near,

Dingo gave strange marks of impatience and grief at the same time.

Dick Sand, who was watching the animal—for all was danger—asked himself if some beast or some native was not concealed in the high papyrus of the bank. But he soon saw that the animal was not agitated by a sentiment of anger.

"One would say that Dingo was crying!" exclaimed little Jack, clasping

Dingo in his two arms.

Dingo escaped from him, and, springing into the water, when the boat was only twenty feet from the bank, reached the shore and disappeared among the bushes.

Neither Mrs. Weldon, nor Dick Sand, nor Hercules, knew what to think.

They landed a few moments after in the middle of a foam green with hairweed and other aquatic plants. Some kingfishers, giving a sharp whistle, and some little herons, white as snow, immediately flew away. Hercules fastened the boat firmly to a mangrove stump, and all climbed up the steep bank overhung by large trees.

There was no path in this forest. However, faint traces on the ground indicated that this place had been recently visited by natives or animals.

Dick Sand, with loaded gun, and Hercules, with his hatchet in his hand, had not gone ten steps before they found Dingo again. The dog, nose to the ground, was following a scent, barking all the time. A first inexplicable presentiment had drawn the animal to this part of the shore, a second led it into the depths of the wood. That was clearly visible to all.

"Attention!" said Dick Sand. "Mrs. Weldon, Mr. Benedict, Jack, do not leave us! Attention, Hercules!"

At this moment Dingo raised its head, and, by little bounds, invited them to follow.

A moment after Mrs. Weldon and her companions rejoined it at the foot of an old sycamore, lost in the thickest part of the wood.

There was a dilapidated hut, with disjoined boards, before which Dingo was barking lamentably.

"Who can be there?" exclaimed Dick Sand.

He entered the hut.

Mrs. Weldon and the others followed him.

The ground was scattered with bones, already bleached under the discoloring action of the atmosphere.

"A man died in that hut!" said Mrs. Weldon.

"And Dingo knew that man!" replied Dick Sand. "It was, it must have been, his master! Ah, see!"

Dick Sand pointed to the naked trunk of the sycamore at the end of the hut.

There appeared two large red letters, already almost effaced, but which could be still distinguished.

Dingo had rested its right paw on the tree, and it seemed to indicate them.

"S. V.!" exclaimed Dick Sand. "Those letters which Dingo knew among all others! Those initials that it carries on its collar!"

He did not finish, and stooping, he picked up a little copper box, all oxydized, which lay in a corner of the hut.

That box was opened, and a morsel of paper fell from it, on which Dick

Sand read these few words:

"Assassinated—robbed by my guide, Negoro—3d December,

1871—here—120 miles from the coast—Dingo!—with me!

"S. VERNON."

The note told everything. Samuel Vernon set out with his dog, Dingo, to explore the center of Africa, guided by Negoro. The money which he carried had excited the wretch's cupidity, and he resolved to take possession of it. The French traveler, arrived at this point of the Congo's banks, had established his camp in this hut. There he was mortally wounded, robbed, abandoned. The murder accomplished, no doubt Negoro took to flight, and it was then that he fell into the hands of the Portuguese. Recognized as one of the trader Alvez's agents, conducted to Saint Paul de Loanda, he was condemned to finish his days in one of the penitentiaries of the colony. We know that he succeeded in escaping, in reaching New Zealand, and how he embarked on the "Pilgrim" to the misfortune of those who had taken passage on it. But what happened after the crime? Nothing but what was easy to understand! The unfortunate Vernon, before dying, had evidently had time to write the note which, with the date and the motive of the assassination, gave the name of the assassin. This note he had shut up in that box where, doubtless, the stolen money was, and, in a last effort, his bloody finger had traced like an epitaph the initials of his name. Before those two red letters, Dingo must have remained for many days! He had learned to know them! He could no longer forget them! Then, returned to the coast, the dog had been picked up by the captain of the "Waldeck," and finally, on board the "Pilgrim," found itself again with Negoro. During this time, the bones of the traveler were whitening in the depths of this lost forest of Central Africa, and he no longer lived except in the remembrance of his dog.

Yes, such must have been the way the events had happened. As Dick Sand and Hercules prepared to give a Christian burial to the remains of Samuel Vernon, Dingo, this time giving a howl of rage, dashed out of the hut.

Almost at once horrible cries were heard at a short distance.

Evidently a man was struggling with the powerful animal.

Hercules did what Dingo had done. In his turn he sprang out of the hut, and Dick Sand, Mrs. Weldon, Jack, Benedict, following his steps, saw him throw himself on a man, who fell to the ground, held at the neck by the dog's formidable teeth.

It was Negoro.

In going to the mouth of the Zaire, so as to embark for America, this rascal, leaving his escort behind, had come to the very place where he had assassinated the traveler who had trusted himself to him.

But there was a reason for it, and all understood it when they perceived some handfuls of French gold which glittered in a recently-dug hole at the foot of a tree. So it was evident that after the murder, and before falling into the hands of the Portuguese, Negoro had hidden the product of his crime, with the intention of returning some day to get it. He was going to take possession of this gold when Dingo scented him and sprang at his throat. The wretch, surprised, had drawn his cutlass and struck the dog at the moment when Hercules threw himself on him, crying:

"Ah, villain! I am going to strangle you at last!"

There was nothing more to do. The Portuguese gave no sign of life, struck, it maybe said, by divine justice, and on the very spot where the crime had been committed. But the faithful dog had received a mortal blow, and dragging itself to the hut, it came to die there—where Samuel Vernon had died.

Hercules buried deep the traveler's remains, and Dingo, lamented by all, was put in the same grave as its master.

Negoro was no more, but the natives who accompanied him from Kazounde could not be far away. On not seeing him return, they would certainly seek him along the river. This was a very serious danger.

Dick Sand and Mrs. Weldon took counsel as to what they should do, and do without losing an instant.

One fact acquired was that this stream was the Congo, which the natives call Kwango, or Ikoutouya Kongo, and which is the Zaire under one longitude, the Loualaba under another. It was indeed that great artery of Central Africa, to which the heroic Stanley has given the glorious name of "Livingstone," but which the geographers should perhaps replace by his own.

But, if there was no longer any doubt that this was the Congo, the French traveler's note indicated that its mouth was still one hundred and twenty miles from this point, and, unfortunately, at this place it was no longer navigable. High falls—very likely the falls of Ntamo—forbid the descent of any boat. Thus it was necessary to follow one or the other bank, at least to a point below the cataracts, either one or two miles, when they could make a raft, and trust themselves again to the current.

"It remains, then," said Dick Sand, in conclusion, "to decide if we shall descend the left bank, where we are, or the right bank of the river. Both, Mrs. Weldon, appear dangerous to me, and the natives are formidable. However, it seems as if we risk more on this bank, because we have the fear of meeting Negoro's escort."

"Let us pass over to the other bank," replied Mrs. Weldon.

"Is it practicable?" observed Dick Sand. "The road to the Congo's mouths is rather on the left bank, as Negoro was following it. Never mind. We must not hesitate. But before crossing the river with you, Mrs. Weldon, I must know if we can descend it below the falls."

That was prudent, and Dick Sand wished to put his project into execution on the instant.

The river at this place was not more than three or four hundred feet wide, and to cross it was easy for the young novice, accustomed to handling the oar. Mrs. Weldon, Jack, and Cousin Benedict would remain under Hercules's care till his return.

These arrangements made, Dick Sand was going to set out, when Mrs. Weldon said to him:

"You do not fear being carried away by the falls, Dick?"

"No, Mrs. Weldon. I shall cross four hundred feet above."

"But on the other bank—"

"I shall not land if I see the least danger."

"Take your gun."

"Yes, but do not be uneasy about me."

"Perhaps it would be better for us not to separate, Dick," added Mrs. Weldon, as if urged by some presentiment.

"No—let me go alone," replied Dick Sand. "I must act for the security of all. Before one hour I shall be back. Watch well, Hercules."

On this reply the boat, unfastened, carried Dick Sand to the other side of the Zaire.

Mrs. Weldon and Hercules, lying in the papyrus thickets, followed him with their eyes.

Dick Sand soon reached the middle of the stream. The current, without being very strong, was a little accentuated there by the attraction of the falls. Four hundred feet below, the imposing roaring of the waters filled the space, and some spray, carried by the western wind, reached the young novice. He shuddered at the thought that the boat, if it had been less carefully watched during the last night, would have been lost over those cataracts, that would only have restored dead bodies. But that was no longer to be feared, and, at that moment, the oar skilfully handled sufficed to maintain it in a direction a little oblique to the current.

A quarter of an hour after, Dick Sand had reached the opposite shore, and was preparing to spring on the bank.

At that moment cries were heard, and ten natives rushed on the mass of plants that still hid the boat.

They were the cannibals from the lake village. For eight days they had followed the right bank of the river. Under that thatch, which was torn by the stakes of their village, they had discovered the fugitives, that is to say, a sure prey for them, because the barrier of the falls would sooner or later oblige those unfortunate ones to land on one or the other side of the river.

Dick Sand saw that he was lost, but he asked himself if the sacrifice of his life might not save his companions. Master of himself, standing in the front of the boat, his gun pointed, he held the cannibals in check.

Meanwhile, they snatched away the thatch, under which they expected to find other victims. When they saw that the young novice alone had fallen into their hands, they betrayed their disappointment by frightful cries. A boy of fifteen among ten!

But, then, one of those natives stood up, his arm stretched toward the left bank, and pointed to Mrs. Weldon and her companions, who, having seen all and not knowing what to do, had just climbed up the bank!

Dick Sand, not even dreaming of himself, waited for an inspiration from Heaven that might save them.

The boat was going to be pushed out into the stream. The cannibals were going to cross the river. They did not budge before the gun aimed at them, knowing the effect of fire-arms. But one of them had seized the oar; he managed it like a man who knew how to use it, and the boat crossed the river obliquely. Soon it was not more than a hundred feet from the left bank.

"Flee!" cried Dick Sand to Mrs. Weldon. "Flee!"

Neither Mrs. Weldon nor Hercules stirred. One would say that their feet were fastened to the ground.

Flee! Besides, what good would it do? In less than an hour they would fall into the hands of the cannibals!

Dick Sand understood it. But, then, that supreme inspiration which he asked from Heaven was sent him. He saw the possibility of saving all those whom he loved by making the sacrifice of his own life! He did not hesitate to do it.

"May God protect them!" murmured he, "and in His infinite goodness may

He have pity on me!"

At the same instant Dick Sand pointed his gun at the native who was steering the boat, and the oar, broken by a ball, flew into fragments.

The cannibals gave a cry of terror.

In fact, the boat, no longer directed by the oar, went with the stream. The current bore it along with increasing swiftness, and, in a few moments, it was only a hundred feet from the falls.

Mrs. Weldon and Hercules understood all. Dick Sand attempted to save them by precipitating the cannibals, with himself, into the abyss. Little Jack and his mother, kneeling on the bank, sent him a last farewell. Hercules's powerless hand was stretched out to him.

At that moment the natives, wishing to gain the left bank by swimming, threw themselves out of the boat, which they capsized.

Dick Sand had lost none of his coolness in the presence of the death which menaced him. A last thought then came to him. It was that this boat, even because it was floating keel upward, might serve to save him.

In fact, two dangers were to be feared when Dick Sand should be going over the cataract: asphyxia by the water, and asphyxia by the air. Now, this overturned hull was like a box, in which he might, perhaps, keep his head out of the water, at the same time that he would be sheltered from the exterior air, which would certainly have stifled him in the rapidity of his fall. In these conditions, it seems that a man would have some chance of escaping the double asphyxia, even in descending the cataracts of a Niagara.

Dick Sand saw all that like lightning. By a last instinct he clung to the seat which united the two sides of the boat, and, his head out of the water, under the capsized hull, he felt the irresistible current carrying him away, and the almost perpendicular fall taking place.

The boat sank into the abyss hollowed out by the waters at the foot of the cataract, and, after plunging deep, returned to the surface of the river.

Dick Sand, a good swimmer, understood that his safety now depended on the vigor of his arms.

A quarter of an hour after he reached the left bank, and there found Mrs. Weldon, little Jack, and Cousin Benedict, whom Hercules had led there in all haste.

But already the cannibals had disappeared in the tumult of the waters. They, whom the capsized boat had not protected, had ceased to live even before reaching the last depths of the abyss, and their bodies were going to be torn to pieces on those sharp rocks on which the under-current of the stream dashed itself.

## CHAPTER XX.
## CONCLUSION.

Two days after, the 20th of July, Mrs. Weldon and her companions met a caravan going toward Emboma, at the mouth of the Congo. These were not slave merchants, but honest Portuguese traders, who dealt in ivory. They made the fugitives welcome, and the latter part of the journey was accomplished under more agreeable conditions.

The meeting with this caravan was really a blessing from Heaven. Dick Sand would never have been able to descend the Zaire on a raft. From the Falls of Ntamo, as far as Yellala, the stream was a succession of rapids and cataracts. Stanley counted seventy-two, and no boat could undertake to pass them. It was at the mouth of the Congo that the intrepid traveler, four years later, fought the last of the thirty-two combats which he waged with the natives. Lower down, in the cataracts of Mbelo, he escaped death by a miracle.

On the 11th of August, Mrs. Weldon, Dick Sand, Jack, Hercules, and Cousin Benedict arrived at Emboma. Messrs. Motta Viega and Harrison received them with generous hospitality. A steamer was about sailing for the Isthmus of Panama. Mrs. Weldon and her companions took passage in it, and happily reached the American coast.

A despatch sent to San Francisco informed Mr. Weldon of the unlooked-for return of his wife and his child. He had vainly searched for tidings of them at every place where he thought the "Pilgrim" might have been wrecked.

Finally, on the 25th of August, the survivors of the shipwreck reached the capital of California. Ah! if old Tom and his companions had only been with them!

What shall we say of Dick Sand and of Hercules? One became the son, the other the friend, of the family. James Weldon knew how much he owed to the young novice, how much to the brave black. He was happy; and it was fortunate for him that Negoro had not reached him, for he would have paid the ransom of his wife and child with his whole fortune. He would have started for the African coast, and, once there, who can tell to what dangers, to what treachery, he would have been exposed?

A single word about Cousin Benedict. The very day of his arrival the worthy savant, after having shaken hands with Mr. Weldon, shut himself up in his study and set to work, as if finishing a sentence interrupted the day before. He meditated an enormous work on the "Hexapodes Benedictus," one of the desiderata of entomological science.

There, in his study, lined with insects, Cousin Benedict's first action was to find a microscope and a pair of glasses. Great heaven! What a cry of despair he uttered the first time he used them to study the single specimen furnished by the African entomology!

The "Hexapodes Benedictus" was not a hexapode! It was a common spider! And if it had but six legs, instead of eight, it was simply because the two front legs were missing! And if they were missing, these two legs, it was because, in taking it, Hercules had, unfortunately, broken them off! Now, this mutilation reduced the pretended "Hexapodes Benedictus" to the condition of an invalid, and placed it in the most ordinary class of spiders—a fact which Cousin Benedict's near-sightedness had prevented him from discovering sooner. It gave him a fit of sickness, from which, however, he happily recovered.

Three years after, little Jack was eight years old, and Dick Sand made him repeat his lessons, while working faithfully at his own studies. In fact, hardly was he at home when, realizing how ignorant he was, he had commenced to study with a kind of remorse—like a man who, for want of knowledge, finds himself unequal to his task.

"Yes," he often repeated; "if, on board of the 'Pilgrim,' I had known all that a sailor should know, what misfortunes we would have escaped!"

Thus spoke Dick Sand. At the age of eighteen he finished with distinction his hydrographical studies, and, honored with a brevet by special favor, he took command of one of Mr. Weldon's vessels.

See what the little orphan, rescued on the beach at Sandy Hook, had obtained by his work and conduct. He was, in spite of his youth, surrounded by the esteem, one might say the respect, of all who knew him; but his simplicity and modesty were so natural to him, that he was not aware of it. He did not even suspect—although no one could attribute to him what are called brilliant exploits—that the firmness, courage, and fidelity displayed in so many trials had made of him a sort of hero.

Meanwhile, one thought oppressed him. In his rare leisure hours he always dreamed of old Tom, of Bat, of Austin, and of Acteon, and of the misfortune for which he held himself responsible. It was also a subject of real grief to Mrs. Weldon, the actual situation of her former companions in misery. Mr. Weldon, Dick Sand, and Hercules moved heaven and earth to find traces of them. Finally they succeeded—thanks to the correspondents which the rich shipowner had in different parts of the world. It was at Madagascar—where, however, slavery was soon to be abolished—that Tom and his companions had been sold. Dick Sand wished to consecrate his little savings to ransom them, but Mr. Weldon would not hear of it. One of his correspondents arranged the affair, and one day, the 15th of November, 1877, four blacks rang the bell of his house.

They were old Tom, Bat, Acteon, and Austin. The brave men, after escaping so many dangers, came near being stifled, on that day, by their delighted friends.

Only poor Nan was missing from those whom the "Pilgrim" had thrown on the fatal coast of Africa. But the old servant could not be recalled to life, and neither could Dingo be restored to them. Certainly it was miraculous that these two alone had succumbed amid such adventures.

It is unnecessary to say that on that occasion they had a festival at the house of the California merchant. The best toast, which all applauded, was that given by Mrs. Weldon to Dick Sand, "To the Captain at Fifteen!"

THE END.

www.ingramcontent.com/pod-product-compliance
Lightning Source LLC
LaVergne TN
LVHW040042080526
838202LV00045B/3451